The stomach for fighting

MANCHESTER
1824
Manchester University Press

Cultural History of Modern War

Series editors   Ana Carden-Coyne, Peter Gatrell, Max Jones, Penny
Summerfield and Bertrand Taithe

Centre for the
Cultural History
of War

The stomach for fighting

Food and the soldiers of the Great War

∼

RACHEL DUFFETT

Manchester University Press

Manchester and New York

distributed in the United States exclusively by Palgrave Macmillan

The right of Rachel Duffett to be identified as the author of this work has been asserted by her in accordance with the Copyright, Designs and Patents Act 1988.

Published by Manchester University Press
Oxford Road, Manchester M13 9NR, UK
and Room 400, 175 Fifth Avenue, New York, NY 10010, USA
www.manchesteruniversitypress.co.uk

Distributed in the United States exclusively by
Palgrave Macmillan, 175 Fifth Avenue, New York,
NY 10010, USA

Distributed in Canada exclusively by
UBC Press, University of British Columbia, 2029 West Mall,
Vancouver, BC, Canada V6T 1Z2

British Library Cataloguing-in-Publication Data
A catalogue record for this book is available from the British Library

Library of Congress Cataloging-in-Publication Data applied for

ISBN   978 0 7190 8458 4   *hardback*

First published 2012

The publisher has no responsibility for the persistence or accuracy of URLs for any external or third-party internet websites referred to in this book, and does not guarantee that any content on such websites is, or will remain, accurate or appropriate.

Typeset in Minion
by Servis Filmsetting Ltd, Stockport, Cheshire
Printed in Great Britain
by CPI Antony Rowe Ltd, Chippenham, Wiltshire

This book is dedicated with much love to my daughter,
Emily Donoghue

Contents

List of figures

Preface and acknowledgements

In March 2010, thanks to the seemingly limitless contacts of my friend John Wren the curator of the London Scottish Regimental Museum, I was fortunate enough to meet with Staff Sergeant Mark Hillier, the Unit Catering Manager at the Regimental Restaurant of the 1st Battalion Grenadier Guards. My arrival at Wellington Barracks, a military enclave in the heart of London, coincided with that of around forty Guardsmen in full dress uniform. They had just returned from the morning's ceremonials organised as part of the State Visit of the President of South Africa. I stood by as, complete with towering bearskins tucked under their arms and boots with the kind of polish on them that outshines even clichés, the soldiers raced up the stairs in pursuit of lunch. Watching them, I couldn't help but feel that their hungry enthusiasm was an echo of their predecessors in the Great War, whose eating I had been researching for the last four years. The opportunity to meet the man who was responsible for satisfying the troops' hunger was, for someone whose interest is the significance of food to the rank and file soldiers of the First World War, very exciting. A chance to discover how the feeding of the modern British Army compared to the provisioning processes of the early twentieth century.

The restaurant in which I sat with Staff Sergeant Hillier was a long way distant from the hastily constructed mess halls that were more familiar to the massed ranks of the 1914–18 war. Aside from the obvious differences in decor, most striking was the wide range of foods available: choice, other than Hobson's, had not been a feature of those earlier mealtimes. Apart from its clientele, there was little to differentiate the restaurant from any major company's canteen, and indeed, as a large number of civilian contractors were also eating there, even the diners were not exclusively military. The army's provisioning arrangements are now managed in conjunction with private enterprise, and, just as the venue and customers reflect civilian experience, so do the pressures on the food budget in these financially challenging times. However, the difficulties of feeding hungry men and women on a limited sum are not new, as the constraints listed in the military's official statistics indicate: brawn and sausages were far more likely to be on the menu than chops or steak. Much of what Staff Sergeant Hillier described was familiar; nutritional knowledge may have moved on and the soldiers' expectations of variety increased, but the centrality of food to the troops' physical and psychological performance remains the same. His energy and enthusiasm were infectious, evident in the obvious pride that his team took in their impressive product. From salad to curry and much else in between, it all looked good and the food I tried tasted good – better than much that is served in similar establishments.

Staff Sergeant Hillier explained that the professionalism that he and his team brought to the job could, at times, be countered by an unpredictability in their diners that had little to do with the actual food provided. He recounted an experience from his time on active service in Kosovo, when the troops had been having a particularly difficult time. Using the best of their stores, their knowledge of the men's favourite foods and a great deal of effort, he and his staff had organised a 'really great' meal for the soldiers. The feedback was wholly positive: the diners were delighted, relished the food, and 'awesome' was the overwhelming consensus. A few months later, after the unit had moved back to England, Staff Sergeant Hillier remembered the success of the special meal in Kosovo and decided to serve it again. The same food was prepared by the same cooks and served to the same men only to be met by a decidedly unenthusiastic response and a number of complaints.

Staff Sergeant Hillier commented upon the different physiological and environmental factors. The soldiers were at rest in their home barracks rather than undertaking the demanding physical work required in Kosovo, and of course there were fewer alternatives to army rations in the remote areas of the former Yugoslavia than there are in London with its myriad of fast-food opportunities. Nevertheless, these were not the only reasons that Staff Sergeant Hillier felt had determined the drastic change in the food's reception. He stressed that mealtimes on active duty, with all its attendant dangers and uncertainties, are important sites of companionship and mutual comfort; they deliver far more to the participants than mere calories. He believed that the presence or not of extreme external pressures had the power to shape the men's perception of what they ate in a manner that had very little to do with the contents of their plates. This ability of food to transcend the physiological, to assume a position where its emotional and social aspects become as important as its nutritional value, is a challenge to army cooks, but a source of endless fascination to anthropologists, sociologists and historians.

The unpredictability of food's reception in the contemporary army reflects the experiences of the preceding century. The First World War rankers were equally susceptible to their rations becoming a locus for feelings and concerns that were not directly related to the quality of the food. The calories provided by the British Army have barely altered over the years, although their form has changed more radically: the stir fries and fajitas on the menu at Wellington Barracks would have been unrecognisable to the men of earlier conflicts. The central question of eating has remained a constant: how can something that is on the one hand so utterly tangible and physically fundamental remain so elusively abstract and psychologically complex? The multi-nuanced nature of food consumption has a particular savour when its context is a military world peopled by conscripts and volunteers of rapidly fading enthusiasm; the difficulties of satisfying the millions of British soldiers of the First World War cannot be underestimated. While the book is an examination of the army's provisioning efforts, the details of its ration scales, the recipes and logistics of supply, it is also the story of the rank and file soldiers' experience, their responses to the food. The men's accounts indicate that their hunger was not for calories alone, sometimes it was a longing driven by more than purely physiological appetites. Food has the power to evoke memories of past meals and previous dining companions, and significantly for the army, it comes to symbolise the level of care and concern that a provider has for those it feeds. This is the story of food's ability to entwine the practicalities of nutrition with the mutability of feelings; its role as the connective tissue between the military and its men, home front and battle field, body and soul.

This book began life as a PhD thesis undertaken at the University of Essex, so first and foremost I must thank my two supervisors: Professor Michael Roper and Professor Steve Smith. Doctoral students count themselves fortunate to be able to rely on one excellent supervisor, for inspiration, encouragement and a regular injection of academic rigour; I was lucky enough to have two and I cannot thank them enough. A special 'thank you' to Mike, whose inspirational teaching in the first weeks of the MA course at Essex confirmed for me that 'doing history' was indeed everything I had always hoped it would be. Attending his classes on the emotional experience of war really was a pivotal point in my life, when what had been a lifelong interest began its metamorphosis into focused academic research. I am grateful to him, and also to Anne, Alice and Thomas, for their friendship and the non-history companionship that they have afforded me. My work benefited enormously from the scrutiny it received from Dr Peter Gurney over the course of my PhD. I thank him for his insightful observations and also for the suggestions he offered on readings and avenues of exploration that would otherwise have passed me by. Lisa West in the History Department at Essex has always been very generous with her time and expertise and it has been much appreciated. The comments of Professors John Walter and Joanna Bourke have also served, I hope they will agree, to strengthen the arguments I had sought to develop. Rose Matthews, who is much missed by her former colleagues at Essex University, deserves special thanks as her enthusiasm for my research and ability to find diverse audiences for it has presented me with opportunities that I could not have imagined. Thanks also to Ina Zweiniger-Bargielowska, who has been particularly helpful in shedding light on the post-Boer War concerns regarding the health of British manhood. I am grateful to Clare Makepeace of Birkbeck College for sharing her knowledge of the soldiers' sexual behaviour on the Western Front; the reading suggestions and pre-publication sight of her journal article have been very helpful.

I also owe a debt of gratitude to my fellow graduate student Deirdre Heavens not just for the companionship we have shared over countless coffees and her sterling support at times when the combined responsibilities of research, teaching and family have proved challenging but also for her extensive knowledge of local archives. The Stopher family letter collection at the Ipswich Records Office proved to be a treasure trove of information on soldiers from a rural background, material that is relatively hard to find amongst the overwhelmingly urban working-class accounts whose preponderance in the archives reflects the demographic of the ranks. I am grateful to the Suffolk Records Office at Ipswich for the use of the Stopher letters and Oliver Coleman's diary and also to their colleagues in Bury St Edmunds for the inclusion of material from the Suffolk Regimental Collection. I also thank Ian Hook the curator of the Essex Regimental Museum at Chelmsford for access to its archive and permission to use it here. I am especially grateful to Ian for sharing his great expertise in military history with me; this was so helpful at the beginning of my research when I knew more about the theory of army life than I did the practice – Ian helped me to redress the balance. My friends at the Western Front Association have been similarly helpful, and I thank Bill Fulton for sharing his family's war history as well as his knowledge with me. A very special 'thank you' to Alan Wicker and his wonderful collection of postcards. Alan has an extensive archive and several of his 'food specials' are, with his generous permission, reproduced here. I am also grateful to Alan for spotting cards for my own collection at the sales he regularly attends.

A 2009 symposium on 'Food and War in Nineteenth and Twentieth Century Europe' in Paris organised by the International Commission for Research into European Food History proved significant in extending my knowledge of other national experiences of army rations during the First World War. Special thanks are due to Steven Schouten and Peter Lummel for sharing their insights on the German Army. I am especially grateful to Professor Derek Oddy whose intervention secured my invitation to the symposium; his generosity, expertise and encouragement have been invaluable. The event in Paris included a tour of the French Military Archive at the Château Vincennes and a chance meeting with Major Luc Binet of the French Army who works there. Major Binet's research interest is the field bakeries used during the Great War. He has a large collection of postcards of the different types and has kindly allowed me to reproduce one of them here. Closer to home, the aforementioned John Wren, curator of the London Scottish Regimental Museum, has been a mine of information and my research has benefited enormously from his enthusiasm and generosity. I am very grateful to both him and Major Stewart Young for access to the wonderful collection of material held in their archive on Horseferry Road; by their kind permission, a number of excerpts from the London Scottish accounts of the war are included in the book. Thanks are also due to Staff Sergeant Mark Hillier of the 1st Battalion Grenadier Guards at Wellington Barracks for both his time and the excellent lunch. In the summer of 2009 I organised an exhibit '100 Years of Rations' in conjunction with Colchester Garrison for their Military Festival. I received considerable help with the practicalities of my stand from RQMS Bob Walker of Merville Barracks. Even more importantly, I am most grateful to him for his insights into contemporary army catering and especially for the chance to examine the new multi-climate active service ration packs at close quarters.

The bulk of my research has been undertaken at the Imperial War Museum in London and the National Army Museum where the expert staffs have been unfailingly helpful: I recall the days spent in their Reading Rooms with unmitigated pleasure. I am very grateful to the Arts and Humanities Research Council for their funding, which was invaluable. Thanks to Brill Publishers for permitting the publication of material from my chapter 'A War Unimagined: Food and the Rank and File Soldier of the First World War', in Jessica Meyer (ed.), *British Popular Culture and the First World War* (Leiden, 2008). Also to Berg, publishers of *Cultural and Social History*, for the reproduction here of material from my article 'A Taste of Army Life: Food, Identity and the Rankers of the First World War'. I am also grateful for the helpful comments received from colleagues at the conferences in Newcastle and Warwick where the initial papers for these two articles were delivered. Thank you too to *BBC History Magazine* for allowing me to reproduce material from the article on soldiers' food, 'What Do We Want with Eggs and Ham?', which appeared in its December 2009 edition.

I am exceedingly grateful for the generosity of families in giving me permission to reproduce extracts from papers at the Imperial War Museum to which they hold the copyright. I would like to thank Sue Johnson for the papers of B. Britland; the Trustees of the Imperial War Museum for the papers of A.P. Burke; Maggie Alexander for the papers of H.R. Butt; William Fulton for the papers of Canon J.O. Coop; the Trustees of the Imperial War Museum for the papers of T.H. Cubbon; T.W. Dalziel for the papers of T. Dalziel; Elaine Morgan for the papers of W.M. Floyd; Alison Baines for the papers of C.R. Jones; Paul Jones for the papers of P.H. Jones; James Sambrook for the papers of A. Sambrook; Mrs Nicola Kent for the papers of Lieutenant W.B.P Spencer; and Paul Finch for the papers of D.J. Sweeney.

Every effort has been made to trace copyright holders and the author and the Imperial War Museum would be grateful for any information which might help to trace those whose identities or addresses are not currently known. It has not proved possible to trace the copyright holder for the papers of E.S. Bennett; W. Clarke; R. Gwinnell: J. Hollister; S.J. Hounsom; A.J. Jamieson; C. Jones; J.M. McCauley; A.E. Perriman and F. Rawnsley.

Many thanks are also due to the National Army Museum for permission to reproduce extracts from the papers of A.G. Beer; A. Down; R. Littler; 'M.G.F.'; J. Rose; E.C.H. Rowland; Mrs E.D. Stephens and D. Willison. I am also grateful to the Lincolnshire Regimental Museum for allowing me to use extracts from the diary of R. Clark, a copy of which is held at the National Army Museum. Andy Robertshaw of the Royal

Logistics Corp Museum at Camberley has kindly allowed me to reproduce a number of images from the museum's collection for which I am most grateful. Andy organises wonderful 'hands on' army cookery events using original equipment and would love to secure an Aldershot oven (or elements of it) for the museum – any information gratefully received.

I am most grateful to Bruce Bairnsfather's daughter, Barbara Bruce Littlejohn, for her kind permission to reproduce the cartoon 'His Christmas Goose' at Figure 5.2; thanks are also due to Mark Warby for his time and effort in liaising with the Bairnsfather family. The Donald McGill Archive and Museum has generously allowed me to reproduce his illustration 'More German Atrocities' at Figure 6.3, for which I thank them. I also wish to express my gratitude to the animal charity The Blue Cross for its kind permission to reproduce 'Good-Bye Old Man' at Figure 6.2; a picture that was commissioned by The Blue Cross Fund in 1916 in order to help raise money to relieve the suffering of war horses in Europe. Every effort has been made to trace the copyright holder of the image from *The War Illustrated* reproduced at Figure 6.1, but with no success and I would be very grateful for any information on this matter.

Finally, as in all aspects of my existence, I am grateful for the love and support of my family and friends, who have never let me forget what life is really about despite my unhelpful tendency to immerse myself in matters of food and war to the exclusion of much else. Special thanks are due to my patient husband and unpaid computer support manager, Gary, whose skills have enabled me to leave all technological aspects in his capable hands and whose encouragement helped me start along the path that has led here. My Mum, Ruth, and my sisters, Claire and Emma, have been the great constants in my life and I hope they know how much they mean to me. Emily, my darling daughter, reminds me every day what joy there is to be had in the world and she has given me a great deal; this book is dedicated to her. Finally, the book is also for my Dad, who was so dearly loved and is still so deeply missed. He showed me that all things are possible. I wish he were here to read it.

List of abbreviations

ASC	Army Service Corps
BEF	British Expeditionary Force
BSD	Base Supply Depots
CO	Commanding Officer
IWM	Imperial War Museum
MO	Medical Officer
NAM	National Army Museum
POW	Prisoner Of War
QMS	Quarter Master Sergeant
RAMC	Royal Army Medical Corps
SS	Army Stationery Services

1

Food and war

The Reverend Oswin Creighton, who served as a chaplain in the First World War, was immensely frustrated by the fixation with food he witnessed amongst the troops. After yet another disappointingly ill-attended church parade, he wrote in a diary letter home: 'It is really extraordinary the part played by the stomach in life. We are paralysed, absorbed, hypnotised by it. The chief topic of conversation is rations with the men, and food and wine with the officers.' One of Creighton's responsibilities was the management of the battalion's canteen and the enthusiasm he witnessed in the men's enjoyment of this facility was absent when it came to the religious aspect of his duties. The canteen that Creighton organised was exceedingly popular with the rank and file soldiers, or rankers. In an attempt to capitalise upon this captive audience, he twice arranged for the Sunday evening service to be held in the canteen, but became 'rather furious' as the men filed out when it began and returned for cocoa once it was over.[1] Creighton's spiritual aspirations for the troops were frustrated by their taste for what he regarded as baser physical needs, a preference that is strikingly apparent from an analysis of the writing of the soldiers. The men's letters, diaries and memoirs are replete with references to food: its quality and quantity, the squandering and pilfering of it, its purchase, preparation and consumption, and the voluntary sharing of this most precious resource amongst the men.

As Creighton indicates, eating was important to the officers as well, but the role of rank in differentiating military diet is clear from his letter: men got rations, officers food and wine. Army tradition and procedures reinforced this separation, visible in each link of the food chain, from the setting of rations scales for the rankers to their consumption in the barracks' mess halls. On occasion, the conditions of war compelled the two groups to share food supplies and dining space but this was unusual. It was not only the poor quality of the food that distressed the men but the lack of control they had over their diet. Whilst necessary in practical terms, the coercive nature of army feeding contrasted unfavourably with the freedom and relative luxury of the officers' messes.

Whatever a soldier's rank, the importance of food to the men has not been fully reflected in the writing of the war's commentators. It is as if the unarguable assumption that food *is* important has militated against an attempt to analyse *why* this is so. Perhaps it is the physiological necessity of food that has handicapped investigation. It is a self-evident truth that calories are required in the same way as oxygen, yet food is so much more than ingestion and digestion. Eating comes freighted with resonances, emotions and memories that could never be associated with breathing. Sidney Mintz points out that 'no other fundamental aspect of our behaviour as a species except sexuality is encumbered by *ideas* as eating'.[2]

This book aims to provide a history of the rankers' eating on the Western Front; an account that will explore both the challenges the army faced in feeding millions of men, and the reception its efforts received from the hungry soldiers. Life in other theatres of war will be used for contrast only. The campaigns in, for example, Turkey or Mesopotamia presented additional challenges of logistics and climate which will not be examined here. The book also seeks to demonstrate that the importance of food extended beyond the merely calorific; it can be understood as a medium through which the social and emotional experiences of military service were expressed.

It is clear that there were breaches between the army's published supply targets and ration scales, and the food the troops received. The exigencies of war, inefficiencies in the supply procedures, sometimes common theft by those in a privileged position, all resulted in shortfalls in the rations supplied to the rankers. However, even if the army had met all its targets, there was another gap that was even more difficult to bridge than the physical: the chasm between what the men wanted and were accustomed to eating, and that with which they were issued. Eating presents a complex and indivisible relationship between the physical and the psychological: 'when humans eat, they eat with the mind as much as with the mouth'.[3] Meals became a relentless indicator of the differences between the civilian and military worlds. Even for regular soldiers, there was little similarity between meals in the peacetime barracks and the iron rations consumed in the trenches of the Western Front. The difference was, of course, founded as much in the environment in which the food was consumed as it was in the actual ingredients supplied, if not more. The emotional significance of food combined with its fundamental physical and social importance to provide a locus within which the rankers expressed their concerns, fears and disappointments as well as their pleasure.

The decision to explore the rankers' relationship with food arose from an interest in the way in which men expressed the emotional experience of war. In more widely read accounts of the war, the images of destruction and suffering with which we are most familiar have their roots in the officers' accounts of the conflict. The letters of Wilfred Owen are an example of the horrors of the front line and contain deeply moving and revealing accounts of the trauma he endured. On 19 January 1917 he wrote to his mother, Susan, 'I have not seen any dead, I have done worse. In the dank air I have perceived it, and in the darkness, felt.'[4] The ability of Owen to convey the agonies of the First World War is indisputable and his literary gifts make his letters exceptional. Owen, Sassoon, Blunden and Graves, the established leaders of the canon of personal accounts of the conflict, were all officers and consequently the war they described was an officer's war. Reading Owen's letters, where the suffering he describes pierced even a sensibility somewhat desensitised by prolonged exposure to accounts of the conflict, led to a desire to discover how the rankers had written about their emotional states. The central questions were: how did men endure the unendurable and how did they express their fear in the face of such horror?

Initial research indicated that the quest for explicitly emotional material in the rankers' accounts would be unrewarding. Descriptions of emotional responses to frightening situations were, when present, brief and hardly illuminating. A. Stuart Dolden describes at length a difficult night-time journey through water-logged trenches up to an exposed front line dug-out a mere forty yards away from the German positions. During one night of his stay, the Germans raid an adjacent post, and Dolden, crouching in his trench close by, hears the details of the attack, which he later describes as a 'terrific shermozzle'. He also endured a lengthy and heavy barrage that seriously wounded men standing close to him, and cut off any possibility of retreat, or, in Dolden's words, '"Jerry" gave us a pretty hot time of it.'[5] Frank Hawkings's diary has occasional references to what he regards as the indescribable yet unforgettable nature of many of the sights of war. Yet situations that must have been terrifying are referenced by language that does not convey the acute fear of the reality: a man who had previously had his coat pierced by a bullet is made 'nervy' by the constant presence of sniper activity in the exposed trench.'[6] In *Fear: A Cultural History*, Joanna Bourke explores the difficulty that the men faced in converting their experiences into words; as one ranker wrote, 'the sights cannot be explained in writing. Writing is not my line.'[7] The archives of the Imperial War Museum indicate that whilst writing *was* the line of thousands upon thousands of rankers it was chiefly concerned with the more prosaic aspects of life. Like Bourke's soldier, descriptions of the emotional states that war induced were difficult to compose and infrequently seen. What the diaries, letters and memoirs lacked in explicit psychological and emotional analysis, however, they made up for in extensive and regular references to food. It appears to have had a very particular set of meanings for the rankers, a function of both their lowly position in the military and their prewar experience. In the primary physiological sense, the rankers, unlike their officers, were largely reliant upon the army's rationing procedures.

Food and the military

The British Army had long acknowledged the importance of food to its soldiers: the first attempt to provide a consistent ration was made during the last quarter of the sixteenth century.[8] Disappointingly, as David Smurthwaite points out, the aim of successive governments appeared to be to spend the minimum possible to avoid mutiny and to pass as much of the responsibility for feeding to the individual regiments as they could.[9] Between the nutritional failures of the Crimean War and the disappointments of the recruitment campaign for the Boer War, army reformers had given 'fluctuating and intermittent attention' to the health and living conditions of the common soldier.[10] The experiences of the former had generated a great deal of political attention: in the years 1855–67, seventeen Royal Commissions and nineteen War Office Committees sat to examine the supply and transport needs of the army. By the start of the First World War, a combination of experience gained in earlier difficulties and recent developments in nutritional science resulted in the army – at least on paper – professing a thorough and conscientious approach to the feeding of the rankers. *The Manual of Military Cooking and Dietary Mobilization,* the key reference book for army cooks, was updated and reprinted three times during the war, and numerous supplementary pamphlets were produced.[11] Additional army instructions repeatedly made it clear that the provision of regular hot food and drinks to the men was a central aspect of an officer's role: 'It is a matter of paramount importance that soldiers' food be carefully looked after, and this duty should be attended to by the officers themselves.'[12] In order to fight, a soldier had to be physically strong. Calories were critical, but there was also a recognition that food, or lack of it, had a psychological as well as physiological impact. After a later conflict, Brigadier Bernard Fergusson wrote that his experiences as a commander had convinced him that 'lack of food constitutes the single biggest assault on morale'.[13]

Senior commanders have repeatedly espoused the importance of food in a successful campaign, echoing Napoleon's original comment of an army marching on its stomach. In a lecture on 'Generalship' at Cambridge University in 1939, Field-Marshal Earl Wavell quoted Socrates to his audience: 'The general must know how to get his men their rations and every other kind of stores needed for war . . . should also . . . know his tactics; for a disorderly mob is no more an army than a heap of building materials is a home.'[14] Wavell, who had served in the First World War, said that his chief attraction to the quotation sprang from the order in which the responsibilities were placed: the provisioning and supply of troops was of far greater importance than the strategy and tactics. It is pertinent that John Baynes, who quotes Wavell in his study of morale, then proceeds to address the issue of food in markedly little detail. He is content to repeat that army food was good and, for many rankers, a great improvement on that which they consumed at home.[15] The attitude of Baynes, an ex-officer himself, is indicative of virtually all the commentary on food in the military histories of the conflict. The officers, or men of the officer class, who are invariably the authors of such narratives, adopt a confident, somewhat paternalistic tone when the subject of rations arises: nothing more than an admission of a degree of monotony is admitted. Army records do not permit a comparison between the subsequent macro-level figures on rations and supply, chiefly provided in the *Statistics of the Military Effort of the British Empire during the First World War,* and the daily deliveries to the fighting units.[16] The low-level records have been lost, as information on provisions was no doubt regarded as peripheral and therefore not retained. Neither were food and eating considered sufficiently important to warrant regular inclusion in the day-to-day official military records, such as the War Diaries. Even if records had survived that could unequivocally demonstrate the delivery of full rations to the soldiers, food's nutritional efficiency as determined by the military elite was rarely the measure against which its consumers assessed their satisfaction.

Despite the claims of army statisticians and historians that provisioning the men was unproblematic, there is contemporaneous evidence that all was not well with the soldiers' diet. In 1917, food was reported to the War Cabinet as one of the principal causes of troop discontent.[17] It was not necessarily shortages faced by the men themselves that caused concern. Bernard Waites has explored the influence of the shortages of food at home on the rankers serving at the front, concluding that it had a significant impact on their morale.[18] Problems with the ration are described in the accounts of officers, like Captain J.C. Dunn, who was categorical that, at certain stages of the war, the men received insufficient food.[19] Shortfalls, certainly in the eyes of the army and its historians, tend to have been obscured by the magnitude of the provisioning challenge. By 1918, the ration strength of the British Army on the Western Front had risen to nearly two million men, and, as no soldier appears to have starved, clearly the most basic objective was achieved. Somehow, a defensible and pragmatic view of the situation has metamorphosed into a highly complimentary assessment of the army's efforts. Perhaps the key to the confidence in the success of the rationing procedures lay in the implicit assumption that they were less important than other supply systems. Whatever officers such as Wavell might say about the critical nature of food, at the front the soldiers' rations were not the first priority, as will be explored later.

Rations and the historian

The delivery and consumption of food in the conflict have received little detailed analysis from specialist military historians. Strategy and tactics have been of far greater interest than studies of supply and logistics, and those on the latter have tended to concentrate on ordnance rather than rations. Even specialists writing on the Army Service Corps (ASC), which was responsible for much of the movement of rations and also for the training of many of the cooks, have given the topic little attention. The preference has been to concentrate on, if not ordnance, transport, whether motor or horse-drawn.[20] Other military historians have touched upon the importance of food. Gary Sheffield, for example, acknowledges its role in his study of morale in the trenches but does not explore the full extent of its significance. Food is a subject whose significance seems to have been accepted implicitly without specific analysis. For example, a recent and extensive account of army life has offered little on the subject: Charles Messenger's authoritative *Call-to-Arms: The British*

Army 1914–18 subsumes rations and catering into a brief entry in a chapter on 'Welfare and Morale' – fewer than a dozen pages in a book of over five hundred.[21]

Food on the home front has attracted considerably more attention, ranging from Sir William Beveridge's 1928 study of civilian Britain's eating experience during the war to Belinda Davis's more recent analysis of food on the German home front.[22] Beveridge's research informed J.M. Winter's wide-ranging *The Great War and the British People*,[23] which despite its discussion of food at home, offers relatively little on the soldiers' rations. The few historians who have specifically examined the role of food in the conflict have preferred to explore its economic or agricultural implications to the nation.[24] Food historians have also concentrated on the civilian population and when commenting on army rations have concurred with the official line: plenty of food, of a standard higher than the rankers would have eaten in their prewar lives.[25] Historians of nutritional science have concentrated upon what was for them a fascinating side effect of the conflict: the massed ranks provided excellent opportunities for the testing of new biochemical theories, especially those relating to diseases of vitamin deficiency.[26] Social historians have devoted a certain amount of attention to food, and Denis Winter's *Death's Men* contains fascinating references to the soldiers' eating both in the trenches and behind.[27] More recently, Richard Holmes's *Tommy* has offered an engaging narrative of the ordinary soldier's war service, but it does not explore the full story of either provisioning or eating.[28] John Ellis offered a tempting glimpse of possible food supply difficulties in his comment that 3,240,948 tons of food left England 'but nothing like this quantity ever got to the troops at the front'.[29] Sadly, Ellis does not provide a detailed analysis of where the food went. The overwhelming assumption, for both historians and the army statisticians, was that food was almost always available in one form or another and the men could be relied upon to use their initiative when rations did not materialise. In his recent book *The Last Great War*, Adrian Gregory restates the overwhelming consensus amongst historians: 'Many, perhaps most, soldiers were better fed in the Army than they had ever been in civilian life'[30] – an assertion that, as with earlier historians, appears to be based upon a comparison between the official daily calorie allowance and data on prewar working-class diets.

Ilana Bet-El's narrative of the war's conscripts offers a more detailed description of the rankers' food than many accounts. In her book, she identifies discrepancies between the army's official ration scales and the men's actual experience.[31] In addition, Bet-El touches upon the psychological aspects of the men's approach to their rations and acknowledges the impact that the rankers' expectations had on their perceptions of the food. The soldiers wanted the varied diet enshrined in the official records: day after day of tinned rations was unacceptable, even if it did have the same calorific value as the stew, vegetables and suet pudding prescribed in the dietary manual. The problem, as perceived by Bet-El, was that when food was scarce the men were concerned with its quantity, and when it was available they shifted to complaints regarding its quality.[32] Whilst this conclusion is generally true, the human relationship with food is more complex than such a statement implies: starving men will, in extremity, choose not to eat, as will be discussed in Chapter 5. Hunger was a feature of the First World War for many soldiers and in some circumstances it was deemed preferable to the food provided, usually the bully beef, which they found particularly repugnant especially when hot weather had turned it into an oily liquid. The existing historiography reveals a disparity between the highly positive perspective of the official statistics and military historians and the more negative comments that some social historians have collected from soldiers' accounts. The men could be vehemently critical of their rations but, as we shall see in later chapters, their antipathy was often contingent upon factors other than scarcity. Whilst shortfalls did occur, it is also clear that nutritionally acceptable rations could be equally despised by the rankers.

The criticism of unpalatable food raises issues of expectation, perception and the emotional significance of food; eating carries associations and feelings that have little to do with physiological need or biochemical content. This is an area that, in the context of war, has had little exploration, with the exception of Michael Roper's *The Secret Battle: Emotional Survival in the Great War*.[33] The book considers the role of food in cementing bonds of friendship in the trenches and emotional ties with those waiting at home. Roper, like Gary Sheffield, highlights the nurturing role that conscientious officers adopted in their relationships with the rankers. Central to the successful execution of such a role was a proper diet for the men; the paternal role of the officer embraced that most fundamental of parental tasks, feeding. In addition to the efforts of many officers to ensure a decent level of rations for their men, there are numerous examples of their concern extending to the provision of extras, such as sweets and chocolate, from their own resources.

The insight provided into the officer's lives and emotional states has rather overshadowed the less positive aspects of the paternalism they displayed. In the manner of the ex-officer John Baynes's study of morale, officers tended to adopt an uncritical approach to army supplies. A positive assessment was, of course, a necessary manifestation of their loyalty to their senior commanders, but, for the diligent junior officer, it was also strongly influenced by his laudable desire to ensure, and indeed believe, that his men's lives were as comfortable as possible. For officers like Lieutenant Sidney Rogerson, who professed that the rankers often ate better than he did, confidence in the ration may have owed more to their own need to feel the men were satisfied than an objective assessment of the diet and its acceptability.[34] An acknowledgement that the food was unsatisfactory and the men unhappy would have been threatening to the officers' fragile yet essential self-image as the protector of 'their' rankers. The soldiers' hunger would have been tangible and unavoidable evidence of their failure to fulfil the duty of care placed upon them.

Captain J.C. Dunn was unusual in his detailed appraisal of the men's food and it is probable that his role as a Medical Officer (MO) facilitated this more analytical approach. The position of MO conferred upon him an objectivity fed by both his scientific training and his distance from a direct and continuous relationship with a small group of soldiers.[35] Objectivity and medical knowledge did not always translate well into trench conditions: what was *best* for the men was not always either popular or tenable. A prime example was the conscientious MO who decided that the limited rum rations would be best employed as a rub for the men's sodden feet. He appreciated that the men would need a warming drink in the absence of the alcohol and offered them cocoa as a substitute. The outcry that resulted from his, no doubt medically correct but highly unpopular, decision was sufficient to cause him to revoke the order.[36] The majority of ordinary officers demonstrate a less scientific approach to their men's diet, but indicate a tendency to exaggerate the men's enjoyment of the food they ate. The officers' enthusiasm for food they did not eat is more marked than that expressed by the actual diners.

Beyond calories

The significance of eating in human behaviour is evident in other fields of study, most fundamentally in psychoanalysis where the work of Melanie Klein developed from her study of the first acts of consumption: the baby at its mother's breast.[37] Freudian psychoanalysis was founded on appetites of a different nature, although the link between sexuality and food is clear. John Coveney, in *Food, Morals and Meaning: The*

Pleasure and Anxiety of Eating, narrates the common ground shared by eating and sex.[38] Jack Goody has explored the way in which sexuality has superseded nutrition in society's analysis of the individual's motivations. Goody reiterates the arguments of earlier social anthropologists, such as Malinowksi, who in the 1920s criticised the 'exclusive, one-sided and unsound interest in sex' that dominated modern psychology.[39] The emphasis on sex had, Malinowski believed, resulted in the dismissal of the even more fundamental role of eating in determining human behaviour. The British anthropologist Audrey Richards points out that to eat is the most basic need, far exceeding in importance and urgency the sexual drive.[40] Goody, who starved as a Japanese POW in the Second World War, concurs; he writes that the hunger he endured during his imprisonment 'confirmed the dominance of culinary over sexual deprivation'.[41]

In anthropological studies, the human relationship with food has been used as a key determinant of the emergence of society. Claude Lévi-Strauss identifies the cooking of food as a demarcation line between nature and culture. His 'culinary triangle' illustrates the way in which the application of fire transformed food from a raw article of nature to a cooked artefact of culture.[42] The nutritional and social importance of the ability to convert the raw to the cooked has been recently reassessed by Richard Wrangham in *Catching Fire: How Cooking Made Us Human* where he cites Darwin who described cooking as 'probably the greatest [discovery], excepting language, ever made by man'.[43] The writing of food anthropologists reflects the division between food as a source of nutrition and food, and in particular meals, as a site of culture and society. Lévi-Strauss and Mary Douglas emphasise the social aspects of eating, interpreting its function as they would a language, one that uniquely identifies human culture and separates it from the natural world.[44] Others, for example Marvin Harris, remain unconvinced of this social emphasis and assert that the biological, nutritional fundamentality of food is the overriding factor for humans, as it is with all animals.[45] The soldiers' relationship with food during the First World War provides an opportunity to explore these two aspects of eating, which were intensified by the physical and emotional vulnerability to which the soldier was exposed. The rankers' experience embodied the two strands of experience associated with food, which, whilst driven by contrasting impetuses, were also interdependent and demonstrated 'an intimate interconnection between social person and biological organism'.[46]

Soldiers' experience of food in war conditions, particularly those in the trenches of the Western Front, is apposite in the context of Douglas's study of taboos, *Purity and Danger*.[47] Rankers' accounts vividly express the revulsion they felt towards unfamiliar food whose unappetising appearance had the added unpleasantness of suggesting the probability of digestive illness, a very real physiological concern. A. Stuart Dolden, who served as an army cook, described a meat delivery that smelled sufficiently bad for him to call for an inspection from the MO. The officer immediately condemned part of the consignment and ordered that the remainder be washed in permanganate of potash before cooking and serving to the men.[48] Dolden does not report whether such treatment made the meat edible in terms of either its consumers' health or their enjoyment of it. It seems likely that any stew produced would have been less than appetising, and in this instance, concerns regarding the unfamiliarity of the food would have been superseded by well-founded fears of contamination

Rank and writing

The rankers' repeated references to food in their letters home indicates how fundamental it was to the preservation and celebration of bonds with their families. The difficulties of emotional expression have been noted earlier, and perhaps this inability to articulate feelings of separation, anxiety and love in letters to their families gave the language of food a more telling significance in the men's correspondence. For many rankers, education had been limited and despite the aggregate improvements in literacy during this period, any form of writing remained a struggle.[49] The correspondence of William Hate, held at the Imperial War Museum, provides a touching example of the limitations of letter writing. The eighty letters to his mother are all remarkably similar: each opens with a virtually identical sentence and the remaining text is divided between listing the post he has received and specifying any further items he requires.[50] Julie-Marie Strange and Ellen Ross highlight the often unbridgeable divide between words and emotions in the working-class society from which the bulk of the rankers came, where grief, for example, was commonly expressed in a non-verbal fashion.[51] Civilian existence had not prepared the rankers for the discussion of feelings, through either their literary education or domestic life. In the absence of language skills and behavioural acceptability, emotions for many soldiers and their families were expressed in the context of eating, whether it was a homemade cake posted to a distant son or the memory of a shared meal. The significance of food in this respect was not exclusive to the rankers, it was important to officers as well, but perhaps it had a special resonance for those whose abilities to articulate their experiences were less developed.

Class was inextricably linked with military rank and, whilst the relationship between the two was not wholly synonymous, it is possible to draw general conclusions. At its most fundamental, rankers came from the working and lower-middle classes and their officers were rooted in the solid middle and upper classes. There were of course exceptions to this general rule, as Martin Petter's work on the lower-middle-class men who were temporarily elevated to the status of gentlemen by the conflict has highlighted.[52] Commissions were not the sole prerogative of the professional and upper classes and, as the war progressed, officers were increasingly recruited from a broader spectrum than before. Many historians have stressed the widening of the criteria for admission to the officer corps that resulted from the casualty-induced increased demand.[53] Clearly, this was the case as Petter's research indicates, but much of the evidence suggests that any meritocracy was limited

Less commonly, 'gentlemen rankers' formed a small but articulate minority. Indeed, the predilection of this educated and vocal group to write about their experiences may have encouraged commentators to believe that they were more numerous than in actuality, given that the number of memoirs they produced was disproportionately large.[54] Occasionally one did join the ranks and stay there, but more commonly it was a pathway to the commission more in keeping with his status. The Uppingham- and Oxford-educated Alfred M. Hale served eighteen miserable months as a private, and his memoir makes it clear just how extraordinary his position was amongst the masses. Hale bemoaned the regulations that excluded him from the first-class train carriages while in his uniform, his indignation exacerbated by his role as a shareholder in the Great Eastern Railway. Hale was also contemptuous of the condescension he experienced from officers who were astounded by his cheque book, a middle-class accessory rarely seen in the ranks.[55]

It is the officers' world of the conflict that has became the foremost evocation of the First World War; the poetry and memoirs of a small, gifted, literary elite have captured the public's imagination.[56] The unprecedented culture of reading and writing in the trenches, amongst rankers as well as officers, has been highlighted. Paul Fussell has written extensively on what he determines as the unparalleled literariness of all ranks who fought in the Great War.[57] Fussell argues that improved levels of education and the 'civilian' nature of the army, with its incorporation of rankers who would never have contemplated a military career in normal circumstances, resulted in soldiers whose standards of literacy were vastly superior to those that had previously served. There is much truth in his argument, but mainly because of the very poor quality of the prewar rankers. Fussell's case is rather undermined by his choice of examples, chiefly Private Stephen Graham, whom he described as 'hardly educated at all'.[58] The details of Graham's education have been obscured, but he was a freelance journalist before the war and dined with royalty during it.[59] In his memoir, Graham's own view of the literacy levels of the rankers contradicts those of Fussell as he writes that the men preferred to look at pictures rather than read and 'some even seemed a little troubled when they received long letters from their wives and sweethearts'.[60]

There is no book by a British rank and file veteran that has achieved the prominence of Erich Maria Remarque's *All Quiet on the Western Front*. Instead the many novels and memoirs written by ordinary soldiers after the war disappeared after their one and only printing, leaving little trace. An exception to this is Frederic Manning's *Her Privates We*, which whilst remaining in print has never had the wide readership of Sassoon's Sherston books or Graves's *Goodbye to All That*. Manning was a middle-class journalist and an able writer: an atypical ranker. His war experience as an ordinary soldier resulted in a book that devotes far more attention to the humdrum aspects of military life, the eating, drinking and sleeping, than the writing of officer veterans: the 'pity of war' seems to have been obscured by more pressing concerns. In her study of memory and the First World War, Janet Watson asserts that subsequent disillusionment was strongest amongst those who had regarded their involvement in the conflict as an act of service rather than a job of work. The disenchanted voices of the once idealistic young subalterns drowned out other more pragmatic accounts. The prosaic and workmanlike memoirs did not resonate with the public: 'ideas about war as work jarred with the post-war emphasis on disillusionment; they were too far removed from the vision of the war as a world of tragedy'.[61] The rankers' stories, in their presentation of a broader range of experiences and emotions rather than a concentration on the misery, have not conformed to their audience's prejudices and have slipped from the publishers' lists.

If professional writers such as Frederic Manning struggled to make the ranker's story marketable in the interwar years, then the accounts of working- and lower-middle-class amateurs had little hope of success. The nature and popularity of First World War memoirs has been a subject for debate for much of the post-Armistice era, from Douglas Jerrold's

The Lie About the War published in 1930 to Dan Todman's recent *The Great War: Myth and Memory*.[62] Such studies illustrate the changes in the tone of memoirs that can be attributed to subsequent events and shifts in public consciousness; changes that have influenced both the veterans' accounts of their experiences and the receptivity of their audience. For the working-class ranker, the rising interest in social history and the disillusionment with war of the Vietnam generation coincided with their own retirements in the 1960s and 1970s. Paul Fussell comments that, for Sassoon, remembering the war became his life's work.[63] In his preface to *Undertones of War*, Blunden writes of the irresistible force that compels him to revisit his war experience every day: 'I must go over the ground again. A voice, perhaps not my own, answers within me. You will be going over the ground again.'[64] The professional revisiting of their lives as soldiers was not an option for working-class men. Once the war was over, the majority of the rankers had to seek livings, most of which were outside the literary arena and, therefore, rarely paid for reflexivity. Many such men waited until their retirement before they wrote of their war experiences; as George Coppard said in the introduction to his 1968 memoir, 'a busy working life prevented me from getting down to it [writing]'.[65] The men found themselves with the time in which to write their autobiographies and a reading public who were interested in the lives of the ordinary soldier, particularly if they were related to a conflict that resonated with contemporary concerns about the exploitation of men in unjust wars. The enthusiasm for social history resulted in an increased popularity for the rankers' accounts, partly due to the reason for which they were originally shunned: the representation of the minutiae of their existence.

Memory sources present particular considerations for historians, and those that emanate from war experience have been especially well explored.[66] This book does not explore the 'cultural gap' between events and their subsequent recollection, but acknowledges that the rankers' accounts of the conflict cannot be factually accurate in every detail, any more than those of Graves or Sassoon. However, they offer a rich mine of descriptive information of life at the front, from which a social history of the men and their food can be constructed. In addition to the memoirs, a number of 'novelised accounts' are used as examples of rankers' experience, given that the boundary between memoirs and autobiographical novels is often difficult to discern. They were usually the product of rankers, such as Manning, who had professional literary skills and were able to construct a more complex literary framework for their memories.

The preface to the novels often carries a reference to the reality on which the narrative was founded. Manning's states that all the events described actually happened, and, although the characters were fictitious, he heard 'the voices of ghosts' when writing their conversations.[67] W.V. Tilsley wrote in his preface to *Other Ranks,* that 'none of the characters in this chronicle are fictitious'.[68]

Whilst many of the soldiers' memoirs were circumscribed by limitations in literacy or a lack of emotional expressiveness, their contemporaneous writing was inhibited by the more practical considerations of time and censorship. Leisure time was limited for the rankers, a restriction that officers acknowledged. Lieutenant William Ratcliffe criticised the constant activities men were subjected to: 'why a battalion which is out of the trenches for a rest can't stop forming fours and sloping arms for one day I don't know'.[69] Men had little time for writing and any letters that they did write were subject to censorship. Even the 'green envelopes', which men sought as a means of avoiding their officer's critical eye, could be opened and read by an anonymous censor at home. Acts of censorship were central to the intimacy and popularity with their men of which so many officers were convinced. Lieutenant Wilbert Spencer wrote to his father, 'I am getting to know my new men and I think they like me. Anyhow it appeared so in one of their letters which I had to censor.'[70] Spencer's views were echoed by many of the young officers, who did not appear to make a connection between their role as censor and the favourable comments of their correspondents. Men had to be careful in their letters home; food was a subject regarded as critical to morale, and criticism was forbidden. S.T. Eachus noted in his diary that 'One of our comrades has been awarded 21 days Field Punishment No. 1 for stating in a letter certain truths respecting the poor food, which has been our lot for some time'.[71] Fear of punishment for outspoken criticism of the rations was a concern, but so was the reaction of families should they realise their men were hungry. The soldiers exercised a degree of care towards their anxious families, for whom the knowledge that their sons and husbands were not being fed, in addition to the other privations of war, might have been intolerable.

Ilana Bet-El describes the restrictions on rankers' letter writing as reducing their descriptions of army life to 'a vague existence of eating in various climactic conditions'.[72] However, as seen in the letters of William Hate above, some sets of letters did not even rise to comments on the weather. References to eating, as long as they were not negative, were a suitable subject for correspondence with home, but the implication

1.1 Cooks in France, 1918

is that food was a subject to be resorted to when other avenues of communication had been denied. Perhaps the rankers *chose* to write about food, because it was a medium through which many aspects of their lives other than mere ingestion could be conveyed. Michael Roper in *The Secret Battle* explores the problems officer sons experienced in composing letters suitable to be sent to their mothers, circumscribed as they were not by censorship but by a desire, in the main, to conceal their suffering. He notes that clues could be found in 'omissions, abrupt changes of topic, things alluded to but ultimately left out and contradictory comments about their spirits'.[73] Emotional states could not be made explicit but were conveyed through other means. Avner Offer writes that 'Food is rich in codes of communication, memory and emotion' and, as we shall see in subsequent chapters, it was a richness that facilitated loving connections in the letters between the rankers and their families.[74] Food was also the subject of much humour in the army, and 'Eric', one of the cooks pictured in the postcard at Figure 1.1, wrote home to his parents joking about the lack of culinary skills in his unit: see Figure 1.2.

Diaries might have offered a private space in which those rankers who were so inclined could record their feelings and complaints but, in a similar fashion to letters, Army Regulations forbade the men from writing of matters of morale. A.G.S. Innes kept a detailed account of his first six months in France, but it ends abruptly with the explanation

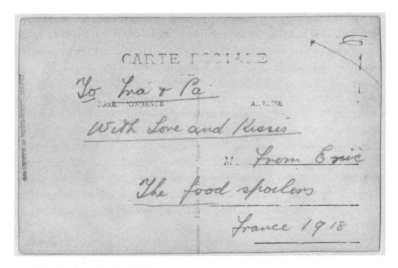

1.2 'The food spoilers', 1918

that he has now discovered it is an offence, and he is 'liable to be shot at dawn & very strict searches being conducted'.[75] Many diaries were little more than a long list of the men's movements around the Western Front, rather than insightful comments concerning their emotional states. Men wanted their families to know exactly where they were, fuelled by a desire for the synchrony explored in Chapter 5. Location was a prohibited subject for letters, which may partially explain why diaries became substitutes, filled with details of the men's movements. In the alien environment of the war, men sought to combat their feelings of displacement by concentrating on their physical, geographical position, as if a clear and unequivocal relationship between their body and the earth on which it stood would confer a similar equilibrium on their precarious emotional state. Regardless of the censorship of diaries and letters, comments on difficulties with the ration slipped through amongst the numerous other references to food and eating. However, it was later, in their memoirs, that the rankers were able to voice their most vigorous complaints about their rations.

Food, environment and control

The complex nuances of the human relationship with food are evident throughout the soldiers' accounts. Its consumption was an experience defined not only by the calories ingested or the format in which they were delivered but also by the environment in which meals were eaten. The revulsion that many soldiers experienced in the dirty, overcrowded mess halls is evidence of the significance to them of the proper, civilised manner of eating. Even when the direct fear of death or mutilation was absent, communal and comparatively uncomfortable living conditions ensured that the men remained inescapably conscious of their distance from the domestic comforts of home. The external pressures on the fundamental norms of the rankers perhaps came to increase the weight of significance on what might once have been regarded as the peripheral aspects of life. In the face of disorder and lack of civilisation, the necessity of decent table manners and clean cutlery assumed an even greater importance, representing as they did the vestiges of a more comforting prewar world.

General concerns regarding the strangeness of the environment, the contrasts between civilian life and the military, home and the trench, the kitchen table and the mess hall, became focused on failures in the ration. Eating can be both intensely pleasurable and yet fraught with danger, but it is at all times fundamental to the sense of self. If, as the eighteenth-century gourmet Brillat-Savarin said, 'we are what we eat', then eating food that cannot be readily identified has the power to undermine the individual's sense of identity.[76] The untried challenges us both biologically and psychologically; unfamiliar foods represent insecurity as they carry the potential to contaminate their consumer.[77] The challenge of new foods and tastes was one that the soldiers had to confront on a regular basis, whether it was the tainted meat that Dolden described or the strange mixtures contrived by the cooks when rations were short. The innate dislike or fear of new foods is counterbalanced with the boredom and resentment that results when humans are presented with a monotonous diet. Successful feeding is achieved through establishing a delicate balance between the two opposed forces that are fundamental to eating. Whatever equilibrium was or was not reached, the soldiers' involvement in its achievement was minimal: what they ate was, at least in terms of the official ration, outside their influence. The lack of choice was at the root of many men's dissatisfaction with army food, not only in the limited menu items on offer but, perhaps more fundamentally, as a symbol of the freedom they had surrendered. Sidney Mintz describes war as

> probably the single most powerful instrument of dietary change in human experience . . . Large numbers of persons are assembled to do things

together – ultimately to kill together. While learning how, they must eat together. Armies travel on their stomachs: generals . . . decide what to put in them.[78]

Given that war carries the possibility of violent and premature death, it may seem to be overstating the importance of food to regard it as a source of suffering on a par with the ultimate sacrifice. However, whilst the soldier lives, he eats; nothing, not even fear, and certainly not sex, could override food in his consciousness. A.W. Logue calculated that the average human spends around four hours and thirty-three minutes each day thinking about food and drink, far more time than is devoted to any other subject including sex.[79] Although it is impossible to quantify, the rankers' diaries, memoirs and letters certainly testify to their preoccupation with food. In common with other oppressed or enslaved populations, the ranker dreamed, even fantasised, about past and future meals as an escape from the hunger and misery of the present. In his study of the role of eating in remembering, David E. Sutton describes a cookery book compiled by women in Terezin concentration camp from their daily discussions about the preparation of food. 'Cooking with the mouth' as they called it, strengthened their determination to survive and was made vivid not so much by what they sought to escape but by that to which they longed to return.[80] Similarly, Sidney Mintz's study of Caribbean slaves includes an observation on the importance of food preparation to the psychological survival of plantation life. Mintz argues that cooking allowed the slaves to reassert their identity through creating dishes that referenced their past freedom. Meals became an act of creation that hinted at the possibility of a freedom slavery had denied them.[81] The pleasure that soldiers derived from preparing a meal or snack, sometimes a minuscule amount barely warmed over a candle in a mess tin, could seem disproportionate to both the delicacy of the dish and the calories it delivered. The delight they took in such acts is evidence of a reassertion of self and a note of defiance directed towards what they regarded as the oppression of the army hierarchy.

In general, the discipline and obedience required by the military left the ranker with few opportunities for self-determination, but food was one area where choices could be made and freedom, although limited, exercised. When there were no opportunities to supplement the rations, the choice could be as stark as choosing hunger over the bully and biscuit. While it is possible to make men march, drill, even go over the top, forcing them to eat is a more difficult proposition. Biological fears and the construction of identity ensure that ingestion is an acutely personal act. The military requirement of fit, motivated soldiers meant that their eating was an area that the army had to regulate and police, but it was also one in which the men found opportunity to resist control. It is ironic given the regulation and standardisation of the army ration, that it should have become a site of autonomy.

The book continues with an exploration of the military and civilian eating histories that were brought to the conflict. The army's successes and failures in the provisioning of its men during the sixty years between the Crimean and the First World War are considered. The ration scales and supply procedures developed to support a small peacetime army with limited experience of continental campaigns would be tested to the limit in the conflict. Of course, military eating was but one half of the equation that came together in the mess halls of 1914–18. The expectations and preferences that the millions of new soldiers brought to army food were as important in determining their response to provisioning as the rations themselves. The limitations of the civilian diet of much of the British working and lower-middle classes who were to fill the ranks after August 1914 will also be analysed. An understanding of the soldiers' peacetime dining is necessary in order to appreciate the often shocking contrasts that lay ahead in the barracks, camps and trenches.

The war created an army of mainly civilian soldiers. Men who would never have wished nor been compelled to join the army in normal circumstances found themselves in a world not of their choosing. The shock of the military environment was profound, and the home training camps were the site of the men's difficult transition from domestic familiarity to life in the ranks. The men's accounts indicate that army food was the locus in which the contrast between their past and present was repeatedly thrown into relief. Chapter 3 will explore this collision between the two eating histories and the role of food in the rites of passage necessary for consolidation into the military world.

Whatever criticisms the rankers may have levelled against food in the camps at home, the food a soldier consumed on British soil generally proved to be superior to that which he could expect on the Western Front. Distance and troop movement did not enhance army provisioning. In Chapter 4 the way in which the military fed its men is considered: the complex supply procedures that shifted vast tonnages of stores from the Channel up the line, the details of the official ration and the sometimes idiosyncratic recipe books the army produced. More privileged eating groups than the rankers existed within the army, people whose position was often resented by the men as much for their superior diet as for any other advantages. In the eyes of the rankers, the food that the ASC, the army cooks and the officers ate was all considerably tastier and more plentiful than the rations the men received.

The army was proud of its provisioning record, a view not necessarily shared by the soldiers: their responses to the rations on the Western Front are related in Chapter 5. For many rankers, poor-quality food, particularly when in the line, was an all too frequent occurrence, and one much commented upon in their own accounts. Clearly, the conditions of active service were not conducive to feelings of comfort and satisfaction, even if the food had been unfailingly satisfactory, and the complex emotions surrounding eating are identified. The chapter also considers the diet-related health issues with which the men struggled, in particular, the bad teeth and the persistent digestive disturbances.

The final chapter describes the eating alternatives to the ration that were available to the rankers, including parcels, canteens, meals in estaminets, or extra supplies scrounged from the army or civilians. Whatever the source of the food, its sharing was fundamental to the soldiers' experience and small groups of pals were formed, comrades with whom precious food resources were divided. For many of the rankers, the companionship they found amongst such pals was the only good thing to arise from their military service and much of this fellowship was centred upon the equitable division of food.

Food was the site of complex and, it must be said, frequently contradictory, emotional responses; for many soldiers, it represented the best and the worst of times. Each and every day it provided a locus where the men were confronted with both the disturbing breaks and the reassuring continuities of their new environment.

Notes

1 Laurence Housman (ed.), *War Letters of Fallen Englishmen* (Philadelphia, 2002), p. 79.
2 Sidney Mintz, *Tasting Food, Tasting Freedom. Excursions into Eating, Culture and the Past* (Boston, 1996), p. 8.
3 Alan Beardsworth and Teresa Keil, *Sociology on the Menu. An Invitation to the Study of Food and Society* (London, 1997), p. 52.
4 John Bell (ed.), *Wilfred Owen. Selected Letters* (Oxford, 1998), p. 215.

5 A. Stuart Dolden, *Cannon Fodder. An Infantryman's Life on the Western Front 1914–18* (Poole, 1980), pp. 144–5.

6 Arthur Taylor (ed.), *From Ypres to Cambrai: The 1914–1919 Diary of Infantryman Frank Hawkings* (Morley, 1974), p. 31.

7 Joanna Bourke, *Fear: A Cultural History* (London, 2005), p. 199.

8 David Smurthwaite, 'A Recipe for Discontent', in Marion Harding (ed.), *The Victorian Soldier. Studies in the History of the British Army 1816–1914* (London, 1993), p. 74.

9 Smurthwaite, 'A Recipe for Discontent', p. 74.

10 Carolyn Steedman, *The Radical Soldier's Tale* (London, 1988), p. 34.

11 *Manual of Military Cooking and Dietary Mobilization* (London, 1915), amended and republished in 1917 and again in 1918. Supplementary pamphlets include *The Cookhouse and Simple Recipes* (Army Stationery Services, hereafter SS, 606, 1916), *Cooking in the Field* (SS 615, 1917), and *Hints on Cooking in the Field* (SS 469, 1916).

12 *Manual of Military Cooking* (1915), p. 39.

13 Richard Holmes, 'Battle. The Experience of Modern Combat', in Charles Townshend (ed.), *The Oxford Illustrated History of Modern War* (Oxford, 1997), p. 205.

14 John Baynes, *Morale. A Study of Men and Courage* (London, 1987), p. xvi.

15 Baynes, *Morale*, e.g. pp. 42, 155 and 156.

16 *Statistics of the Military Effort of the British Empire During the First World War* (London, 1999), first published in 1920.

17 War Cabinet Minute 231, 12 Sept 1917, CAB 23/4, cited in J.G. Fuller, *Troop Morale and Popular Culture in the British and Dominion Armies 1914–1918* (Oxford, 2001), p. 61.

18 Bernard Waites, *A Class Society at War, England 1914–1918* (Leamington Spa, 1987), p. 231.

19 Captain J.C. Dunn, *The War the Infantry Knew, 1914–1919* (London, 1987), pp. 300 and 434, for example.

20 For example, Michael Young: *Army Service Corps 1902–1918* (Barnsley, 2000) and *Waggoner's Way* (London, 1993).

21 Gary Sheffield, *Leadership in the Trenches. Officer-Man Relations, Morale and Discipline in the British Army in the Era of the First World War* (London, 2000), p. 142, and Charles Messenger, *Call-to-Arms: The British Army 1914–18* (London, 2005).

22 Sir William Beveridge, *British Food Control* (London, 1928), and Belinda Davis, *Home Fires Burning. Food, Politics and Everyday Life in World War 1 Berlin* (Chapel Hill, NC, 2000).

23 J.M. Winter, *The Great War and the British People* (Basingstoke, 1987).

24 For example, Avner Offer, *The First World War. An Agrarian Interpretation* (Oxford, 1989).

25 For example, John Burnett, *Plenty and Want. A Social History of Diet in England from 1815 to the Present Day* (London, 1979), p. 271.

26 For example, J.C. Drummond and A. Wilbraham, *The Englishman's Food. A History of Five Centuries of English Diet* (London, 1964), pp. 431–442.

27 Denis Winter, *Death's Men* (London, 1978), see chapter 6 'Trench Life' and chapter 9 'Into Rest'.

28 Richard Holmes, *Tommy: The British Soldier on the Western Front 1914–1918* (London, 2005), see chapter IV 'Figures in a Landscape'.

29 John Ellis, *Eye Deep in Hell* (Abingdon, 1976), p. 125.

30 Adrian Gregory, *The Last Great War* (Cambridge, 2008), p. 282.

31 Ilana Bet-El, *Conscripts: Forgotten Men of the Great War* (Stroud, 2003), pp. 109–20.

32 Bet-El, *Conscripts*, p. 114.

33 Michael Roper, *The Secret Battle: Emotional Survival in the Great War* (Manchester, 2009), see, for example, chapter 2, 'Separation and support'.

34 Sidney Rogerson, *Twelve Days on the Somme. A Memoir of the Trenches, 1916* (London, 2006), p. 116.

35 Dunn, *The War the Infantry Knew*.

36 Helen B. McCartney, *Citizen Soldiers: The Liverpool Territorials in the First World War* (Cambridge, 2005), p. 137.

37 Melanie Klein, *Envy and Gratitude and Other Works* (New York, 1984).

38 John Coveney, *Food, Morals and Meaning: The Pleasure and Anxiety of Eating* (London, 2000), p. 11.

39 Jack Goody, *Cooking, Cuisine and Class A Study in Comparative Sociology* (London, 2000), p. 15.

40 Cited in Mintz, *Tasting Food*, p. 35.

41 Goody, *Cooking, Cuisine and Class*, p. 83.

42 Claude Lévi-Strauss, *The Origin of Table Manners* (London, 1978) p. 507. See also *The Raw and the Cooked* (London, 1970).

43 Richard Wrangham, *Catching Fire: How Cooking Made Us Human* (London, 2009), p. 127.

44 Mary Douglas, *Purity and Danger* (London, 1985) and 'Deciphering a Meal' in *Implicit Meanings. Essays in Anthropology* (London, 1975).

45 See Marvin Harris, *Good to Eat: Riddles of Food and Culture* (London, 1986), and Martin Jones, *Feast: Why Humans Share Food* (Oxford, 2007), for an exploration of the tensions between the two approaches.

46 Jones, *Feast*, p. 12.

47 Douglas, *Purity and Danger*, p. 4.

48 Dolden, *Cannon Fodder*, p. 79.

49 See Jonathan Rose, *The Intellectual Life of the British Working Classes* (London, 2001), for a discussion of the advances and limitations of literacy.

50 W.T. Hate, Imperial War Museum (hereafter IWM), 86/51/1.

51 Ellen Ross, *Love and Toil. Motherhood in Outcast London 1870–1918* (New York, 1993), and Julie-Marie Strange, *Death, Grief and Poverty in Britain, 1870–1914* (Cambridge, 2005).

52 Martin Petter, '"Temporary Gentlemen" in the Aftermath of the Great War: Rank, Status and the Ex-Officer Problem', *The Historical Journal*, 37:1 (March 1994).

53 For example, see Sheffield, *Leadership in the Trenches*, p. 33.

54 For example, Stephen Graham, *A Private in the Guards* (London, 1928), and Frank Gray, *Confessions of a Private* (London, 1920).

55 Paul Fussell (ed.), *The Ordeal of Alfred M. Hale. The Memoir of a Soldier Servant* (London, 1975), pp. 49 and 56.

56 Ironically, Owen's poetry that for so many symbolises the First World War experience was rejected for inclusion in the *The Oxford Book of Modern Verse* by its editor W.B. Yeats because 'passive suffering is not a theme for poetry'; Samuel Hynes, *A War Imagined: The First World War and English Culture* (London, 1992), p. 215.

57 Paul Fussell, *The Great War and Modern Memory* (Oxford, 2000), p. 156.

58 Fussell, *The Great War*, p. 155.

59 Graham, *Private in the Guards*, p. 79.

60 Graham, *Private in the Guards*, p. 173.

61 Janet Watson, *Fighting Different Wars. Experience, Memory and the First World War in Britain* (Cambridge, 2004), p. 20.

62 Douglas Jerrold, *The Lie about the War* (London, 1930), and Dan Todman, *The Great War: Myth and Memory* (London, 2005).

63 Fussell, *The Great War*, p. 92.

64 Edward Blunden, *Undertones of War* (London, 2000), p. xii.

65 George Coppard, *With a Machine Gun to Cambrai* (London, 2003), p. xv.

66 See, for example, Fussell, *The Great War*, pp. 203–220, on Robert Graves; Alistair Thomson, *Anzac Memories: Living with the Legend* (Melbourne, 1994), and Michael Roper, 'Re-remembering the Soldier Hero: The Psychic and Social Construction of Memory in Personal Narratives of the Great War', *History Workshop Journal*, 50 (2000).

67 Frederic Manning, *Her Privates We* (London, 1999), preface.

68 W.V. Tilsley, *Other Ranks* (London, 1931), preface.

69 John Laffin, *Letters from the Front, 1914–1918* (London, 1973), letter dated June 1916, p. 68.

70 Lieutenant Wilbert Spencer, IWM 87/56/1, letter dated 24.12.1914.

71 S.T. Eachus, IWM 01/51/1, diary entry dated 9.3.1917.

72 Bet-El, *Conscripts*, p. 135.

73 Roper, *The Secret Battle*, p. 64.

74 Offer, *Agrarian Interpretation*, p. 39.

75 A.G.S. Innes, London Scottish Regimental Museum.

76 Peter Scholliers, 'Meals, Food Narratives and Sentiments of Belonging in Past

and Present', in Peter Scholliers (ed.), *Food, Drink and Identity: Cooking, Eating and Drinking in Europe since the Middle Ages* (Oxford, 2001), p. 9.

77 Nick Fiddes, *Meat: A Natural Symbol* (London, 1992), p. 36.

78 Mintz, *Tasting Food*, p. 25.

79 Andrea Logue, *The Psychology of Eating and Drinking* (New York, 2004), p. 1.

80 David E. Sutton, *Remembrance of Repasts. An Anthropology of Food and Memory* (Oxford, 2001), p. 167.

81 Sidney Mintz, *Sweetness and Power. The Place of Sugar in Modern History* (New York, 1985).

2

Before the war

In 1899, Edwin Mole, who had enlisted as a ranker with the King's Hussars in 1863, reflected upon his army career. He vividly recalled his first day as a soldier in the barracks at Aldershot, the only new recruit in a room of fifteen men. The memory of the meal provided was especially clear: a plate of meat and a tin of potatoes were thrown down on the table and the men were left to help themselves. Mole noted that six of the more experienced men declined even to taste the food and, 'after a look at the dish, lit their pipes and went off to the canteen' where limited food but copious amounts of beer were available. The hungry new recruit tried to eat the meal but 'the meat and potatoes were both bad' and he was reduced to consuming the bread he had brought from home. Army rations had failed to meet the most basic expectations of this new recruit and his initial disappointment was not to be alleviated by subsequent meals.[1]

Historically, army food had always been regarded as poor, and the feeding of the rank and file soldiers was generally a haphazard and ungenerous procedure. The problems of the Victorian and Edwardian eras are evident from a range of sources: autobiographies such as Mole's; the repeated Government Enquiries; subsequent somewhat half-hearted army reforms; and popular literature. Rudyard Kipling in his 1892 poem *Tommy* included deficiencies in the ration as a key concern:

> You talk o' better food for us, an' schools, an' fires, an' all:
> We'll wait for extry rations if you treat us rational.
> Don't mess about the cook-room slops, but prove it to our face
> The Widow's Uniform is not the soldier-man's disgrace.[2]

The series of reforms and attempts at improvements, originally provoked by the failures of the Crimean War, were only partially successful and always hampered by the budgetary challenges imposed by the lack of government funding. Changes in army rations in the sixty years before the First World War reflected both the growing understanding of what constituted a productive diet, as developments in nutritional science progressed, and what the army presented as an increased sense of responsibility for the well-being of the men in its care. The first section of this chapter will review army provisioning in the prewar years, constructing a picture of the food and dining experience provided for its regular soldiers. Secondly, the civilian diet and eating habits of the men who would fill the ranks from August 1914 onwards will be explored. These two eating histories, their different diets and dining customs, would converge when the men of the working and lower middle classes exchanged their kitchens for the mess hall; a confrontation analysed in the following chapter.

Nineteenth-century rations

Official army rations were first fixed in the Army Regulations of 1813, no doubt as a result of the experiences of the Peninsular War. During this campaign, the military had attempted to feed the men in the traditional fashion. Meat was sourced 'from the hoof', by the slaughtering of the cattle that were driven alongside the marching soldiers. The failures in the system were much commented upon by the men in the available accounts, as they found the meat from the exhausted bullocks so stringy as to be virtually inedible. John Green of the 68th Durham Light Infantry described much of the meat offered as 'carrion', and Robert Knowles of the 7th Royal Fusiliers claimed that 'the meat is so poor that it would be burnt if exposed for sale in Bolton Market'.[3] The new regulations provided men with 1 lb of bread and 12 oz of meat per day,[4] although the prescribed weight of the meat applied to its raw state, which generally included a certain amount of bone, fat and gristle. Once it had been prepared, the men received considerably less than the overall weight implied. The ration lacked variety and was frequently short in energy values. E.J. Coss's analysis of the Peninsular War calculates that the food received by the men of the Roman Legions was more nutritious than that provided for the nineteenth-century British soldiers.[5] The inadequacies of the ration drove the underfed men to buy extra, but essential, food from their wages, and if that option were not available they were reduced to stealing it from the local population.[6] The soldiers' songs from this period contain numerous references to poor military food. In *The Rambling Soldier*, Roy Palmer reproduces a ballad from the mid-nineteenth century entitled 'The Hungry Army', a verse of which runs as follows:

> They served it out in a large tin can,
> A teaspoonful to every man;
> I got so fat I couldn't stand,
> To fight in the hungry army.[7]

Unaware of the true situation, some hungry recruits were no doubt tempted by the recruitment promise of 'free rations' when they decided to enlist. Men who enlisted in the ranks often did so because they were very hungry indeed: the military was not so much a career choice as a last resort for those who had exhausted all other options. An anonymous Kent soldier who joined up in 1891 explained he had done so because there were no alternatives: 'I chose a soldier's life because it seemed to be the only one open to me.'[8] Evidence indicates a close relationship between the price of bread and the enlistment rates of the British Army, where an increase in the former resulted in a rise in the latter. It appeared that it was the poorest in British society, those who relied almost exclusively on bread for nutrition, who were compelled by hunger to consider a future in the military.[9]

Rankers were paid around a shilling a day, a level that remained constant throughout the latter half of the nineteenth century, as pay rises were effected through the cancellation of deductions from wages to pay for additional food rather than an increase in the actual wage level. For example, at the time of the Crimean War, the minimum pay was a shilling a day, plus a penny beer money, less 4½d for rations.[10] Later in the century, the pay was still a shilling a day but the deductions for extra food had been withdrawn, increasing the men's disposable income. The necessity of soldiers using their meagre wages to feed themselves was much criticised. Veterans accused the army of being disingenuous, in that the 'free rations' it advertised applied strictly to the provision of meat and bread. All other items were classified as 'groceries': mustard, sugar, potatoes or the plum duff served on Sundays were all funded by deductions from the men's pay. Horace Wyndham, looking back on his military career, reflected that new recruits were not initially aware of this categorisation and were shocked that the items they regarded as staples were deemed 'extras'. Wyndham believed, somewhat bitterly, that 'a little more candour about this matter would be as well'.[11]

The additional payments the men made did not necessarily result in a full and varied diet, and inadequacies in the ration were highlighted during the Crimean War. The conflict prompted the army to review the full range of its strategies and procedures, from the use of cavalry charges in the face of artillery to the treatment of its sick and wounded. It was apparent from the general state of the soldiers' health that the rations supplied during the conflict were woefully inadequate. Private John Rose wrote home that while the men were given bread and meat each day 'it is not fit for men to use so sometimes we use it and other time we bury it and we have been half killed with work'.[12] J.C. Drummond calculated that scarcely 2,500 calories per day were provided when the conditions of active service demanded 3,500 to 4,500.[13] The high levels of disease on the campaign were clear evidence of the army's provisioning failures. A small saving grace, given the deficiencies in the rations, may have been the presence of familiar figures serving them. One of Roger Fenton's famous photographs of the war captures the arresting image of a crino-lined woman, hair neatly coiffed and clothes well-pressed, serving food to the men of the 8th Hussars, who are lounging outside their cookhouse. The photograph indicates the important role of women in the prepara-tion and serving of rations during the Crimean War; many of them had followed their men to the Crimea and provided both them and their bachelor fellow soldiers with the domestic support that was not always forthcoming from the army. Figure 2.1 dates from immediately before the war and shows the army cooks at work on manoeuvres. They are being assisted by the women on the right who are peeling the potatoes for the meal.

Wives cooked and washed for their husbands and nursed them if they were sick, and it seems that, should their man be killed, they maintained their position by the swift transfer of their affections to another. In the Peninsular War, John Green gleefully recalled there had been a widow who 'took up' with her sixth husband less than a week after the death of her fifth.[14] The role had attendant dangers, and a number of the women were killed in action in the Crimea; Mrs Maibee, a sergeant's wife, was fatally wounded by enemy artillery as she knelt by the campfire in order to prepare her husband's breakfast chocolate.[15]

Health problems

In addition to the deficiencies in quality and quantity found in the Crimean rations, the army compounded the men's health problems by

2.1 Army cooks on manoeuvres, c. 1850

its failure to supply important foodstuffs that were known to prevent disease. The role of vitamins, minerals and trace elements was not fully understood until after the First World War. Indeed that conflict facilitated research and nutritional evidence collected both in the army and on the home front helped to reveal their role.[16] Whilst the precise biochemical origins of vitamin deficiency remained unclear in the nineteenth century, a number of its consequences had been identified and their prevention understood. Foremost of these was scurvy, which had been successfully combated by the British Navy through the consumption of foods high in ascorbic acid since the experiments of Dr James Lind in the middle of the eighteenth century. Lind was not the first to make the discovery; indeed the Chinese were thought to have identified the solution to the disease as early as the fifth century.[17] While the ability to prevent scurvy was a significant achievement, its cause was to remain a mystery for some time to come; indeed, twenty years after the war in the Crimea in 1875, the Medical Society of Paris proposed that it resulted from a bacterial infection.[18]

An understanding of the role of anti-scorbutics in the diet was essential, but experience in the Crimean War proved that it was not merely a matter of knowledge: it was also an issue of planning and logistics. Scurvy was rife amongst the troops. Florence Nightingale noted that, of the transport of twelve hundred sick men which arrived at Scutari on 2

January 1855, 85 per cent were cases of acute scurvy. Lord Raglan, in an attempt to alleviate the problem, had twenty thousand pounds of lime juice shipped to the base at Balaclava, but it was never distributed. The failure to issue these stores was apparently a result of an administrative disagreement between the different corps within the army. They were unable to reach an agreement as to whether it should be issued as a 'medical comfort' or as an 'article of commissariat issue'.[19] The bureaucratic wrangling resulted in the juice remaining locked away in the stores for the duration of the war, together with supplies of dried vegetables which would also have proved invaluable in the treatment of the disease. The occasional innovative doctor was reduced to picking wild spinach in an attempt to improve his patients' diet.[20] However, it appears that the men did not always help themselves as, despite the shortage of fruit and vegetables, they could be unwilling to try nutritious, but worryingly new, foodstuffs. An issue of pumpkins, a relatively unusual vegetable for the British soldiers, was met with widespread objections as their unfamiliarity made them unpalatable.[21] The efforts of the chef Alexis Soyer, who initially travelled to the Crimea at his own expense, were valuable and the field stove he designed was widely used to provide hot food, and also clean boiled water, to the men. Unfortunately, Soyer's improvements were insufficient to compensate for the widespread army failures in provisioning. A subsequent enquiry into the conduct of the administration of supplies in the war was highly critical of the inability of the military to deliver necessary, and indeed available, foodstuffs to its men.[22]

The concerns precipitated by failures in the Crimea, where the five thousand soldiers killed through enemy action were eclipsed by the nineteen thousand lost to disease, resulted in the establishment of the Army Sanitary Commission in 1857. It was charged with reporting on a range of health matters, including that of diet.[23] The Commission was critical of the quantity of the meat ration and noted that the amount prescribed was all too often reduced to 7 oz of stringy, overcooked flesh once it had been thoroughly boiled, the only cooking method available in many barracks. The lack of consistency in the food provided across the army was of particular concern. In many units the food was painfully basic: bread and tea for breakfast, boiled beef and potatoes for dinner, and supper was merely tea with what, if any, bread remained from their daily ration. The Commission's report in 1858 stated it was the duty of the military 'to see that the soldier is supplied with and consumes a diet so composed as to keep him . . . in health and efficiency'; a responsibility which seems axiomatic, but obviously needed to be restated.[24] Following the

Commission's report, an extra 3½d per man per day was provided from central funds to finance the purchase of vegetables and condiments for the basic ration. It was left to the regimental authorities to purchase and supply the food, resulting in a variable degree of success. Historically, the regimental system of the British Army was founded upon independent units, each with their own particular customs and processes. They existed as a series of martial families where soldiers' loyalty and morale was nourished by their regiment's autonomy. Less positively, the individualism of the regimental system did not facilitate the easy imposition of a uniform approach to feeding soldiers across the military.

Despite the government's investigations and interventions, the level of nutrition remained low and army provisioning continued to be a matter of concern. In 1867, Lieutenant-Colonel Keane commented that an increase in the ration would be a much more effective recruiting tool than the addition to the military pension that was being mooted.[25] Keane's assessment identified the general recruitment problem the army faced: the life of a rank and file soldier was not one to which the majority of able and industrious men aspired. The hunger that drove men into the ranks fuelled the disdain with which much of the rest of society viewed the soldiers; David Silbey describes the popular view of the Victorian and Edwardian ranks as being 'the last refuge of the economically or socially incompetent'.[26] Albert Tucker, in his study of the late-nineteenth-century British Army, notes that the conditions to which the recruits signed up were only a slight improvement on those in the only other possible refuge open to many of them, the workhouse.[27] There appeared to have been little improvement since shortly after the Crimean War, when the research of Dr Robert Christison of Edinburgh University had demonstrated that the diet of the prisoners in Perth Gaol was more nutritious than that of British soldiers.[28]

Attempts at reform

The Cardwell Army Reforms of 1868–72 introduced significant changes, but the most influential of these related to matters other than diet, such as the removal of the outmoded and unhelpful practice of selling commissions. The reforms were lauded at the time, but were later criticised for failing to address the chief underlying challenge: to improve the status of the army and give it a 'positive and fundamental place in English society'.[29] Central to the lack of status was the continued disregard in which the army was held. The meagre levels of pay, together with the rankers' poor living conditions including their inadequate diet, were major contributory factors to this low esteem.

The unattractiveness of the army to working men resulted in the bulk of its recruits being drawn from the lowest and, consequently, the least well-nourished echelons of society. Whatever improvements the army may have attempted once the men were in the barracks, the privations of wider society were apparent in the poor nutrition and resultant physical underdevelopment of many of the working-class men who tried to enlist. In 1883, regulations had to be altered to reflect the limited physical stature of the available recruits and the minimum height for the infantry was reduced from 5 ft 6 in to 5 ft 3 in. Height requirements varied from corps to corps, and the more prestigious retained higher standards; for example, the Household Cavalry insisted upon a minimum of 5 ft 11 in. for its recruits.[30] The lowering of the height requirement for the infantry reflected a national drop in average male height in the latter half of the nineteenth century. Roderick Floud et al., in their study of height in history, ascribed it to the consequences of the 'Hungry Forties': children who had endured the lean years, or those born subsequently to the malnourished adults, reflected nutritional deficiency in their stature.[31]

Dissatisfactions with the army diet persisted and, in 1876, *Colburn's United Services Magazine* contained an editorial complaining that the rations were as 'insipid and wearisome' as those issued to criminals. The article also added that, given the unappetising official diet, it was unsurprising that a large part of the rankers' pay went towards buying extra food and, more worryingly, beer.[32] Traditionally, heavy consumption of alcohol had always been a feature of military life. Indeed it had once been a significant part of the official ration, as during the Peninsular War one-third of a pint of rum was supposed to have been issued to each man daily.[33] In later years, the soldiers had to create their own channels of supply, and William Robertson, who enlisted in 1877, noted that during his service the regimental canteen was 'a mere drinking saloon', offering little in the way of food or non-alcoholic beverages.[34] In 1901, another old soldier reviewing his career wrote that if he could give only one piece of advice to new recruits it would be to 'try and avoid the canteen as long as possible'.[35] Whatever the sober reflections of veterans, accounts indicated that drinking was a perennially popular activity. In addition, alcohol had a dual function: as well as its pleasing impact on the senses beer provided comforting additional calories, around two hundred a pint.

One strategy adopted in an attempt to ensure improvements and regularisation of the soldiers' diet was to enhance the training of army cooks. Previously the development of culinary skills had been left largely to chance, with mixed results. The poor meals produced by many army cooks meant that, even when there were no wives available to prepare food, men often preferred to do it themselves. In the Peninsular War, John Green boiled blood from the slaughtered bullocks to make a 'substitute for bread', although the similarities between the two foodstuffs are not immediately obvious. Green also writes that in extremity cooking was not always necessary, as he had seen a starving soldier eat raw tripe snatched from the cow being slaughtered in front of him.[36] In an effort to improve the meals delivered, a School of Cooking was established at Aldershot in 1870, and in 1889 the *Queen's Regulations and Orders* made it a requirement for each battalion to appoint Sergeant Cooks for training at the central school. These men would then be sent back to their battalions in order to educate and superintend others, thus ensuring a more rigorous and hopefully beneficial approach to the food served to the rankers.[37] In addition, the Regulations of 1889 stated that officers were now personally responsible for their men's food. It was their duty to inspect the kitchens daily in order to check the quality of the meals produced.

Success was not immediate, and on occasion the exigencies of active service presented challenges that even the most thorough training was unlikely to have anticipated. An officer writing home from Bulawayo in 1893 described the shortages of food experienced on patrol, which resulted in the killing of a horse in an effort to assuage the soldiers' hunger. The letter writer was to be disappointed as 'I couldn't tackle it, although I was fearfully hungry, as the piece reserved for me and my men was underdone . . . Underdone horse is disgusting.'[38] Later that decade, Horace Wyndham found the cooks on army manoeuvres in South Africa to be hopeless and 'absolutely incapable of preparing food in a palatable manner'.[39] In the spirit of fairness, Wyndham acknowledged it was not solely a matter of culinary training. The cooks' poor performance could be ascribed partly to the inadequacy of the equipment provided, and a shortage of coal for the ovens had further exacerbated matters. The success of reforms and changes to the regulations was limited, and difficulties in provisioning continued to be a problem. This was made evident in the War Office enquiry, *Report of the Committee on the Soldiers' Dietary*, published in 1889. The Committee was impressed by the quantity and quality of the rations provided by some units. It cited the Royal Irish Rifles, who were lauded for supplying their men with a range of additions from marmalade to split pea, but it regretted that such exemplary standards were not more widely evident.[40]

The desire of the army to formalise catering procedures resulted in the production of a number of manuals in a further attempt to disseminate standards. In 1899, the Quartermaster-General Colonel J.A. Boyd produced a *Supply Handbook for the Army Service Corps.*[41] The publication contains the lessons learned on the army's recent excursions in Africa: the Ashanti Expedition of 1895 and Earl Kitchener's 1898 progress through the Sudan. Its near three hundred pages are packed with information for successful campaigns in the region. The advice ranges from how to identify goat meat, to a colour plate illustrating the appropriate construction of a cattle laager. The rankers' ration scales printed in the *1899 Supply Handbook* indicated a continued reliance on the staples of meat and bread, with hardtack biscuit as a substitute for the latter.[42] Biscuit, made from flour and water and baked until dry, was popular with the army because of its longevity, but disliked by the soldiers because of its unyielding tastelessness. It is possible, through an examination of the two sets of ration scales, to identify a number of improvements made in the three years that separated the African campaigns. Primarily, the possibility of fresh vegetables was introduced in place of the original reliance on dried, and there was an addition of regular weekly distributions of jam and bacon. The changes might be interpreted as a combination of an improved understanding of the nutritional advantages of a varied diet, a reflection of the popularity of certain of the items in civilian diet and a more effective supply system.

The rations specified in the *1899 Supply Handbook* did not yet have their accompanying calorie values, as methods for the measurement of energy were still in the process of being developed. In the latter half of the nineteenth century, the work of German scientists such as Justus von Liebig had identified the key dietary building blocks of fats, carbohydrate and protein. It was not until the end of the century that an understanding of calories emerged when Wilbur Atwater, a professor of chemistry at Yale, constructed a calorimeter. Atwater's work proved the new thermodynamic model that was to inform the military's approach to feeding: food as fuel for the human motor. Atwater's research also made it possible to calculate the energy values of different foods. This was information that would shortly be adopted by the army in the detailed ration scales and calorie calculations used in the First World War. Biochemical knowledge remained imprecise, although Casimir Funk first coined the word 'vitamine' (a conflation of 'vital amine') in 1912, when he determined that trace elements must be an essential part of a healthy diet.

The Boer War

Before the trials of the First World War, the British Army endured another conflict which brought the fitness of the soldiers to the forefront of concerns regarding the health, and by association the diet, of the whole nation: the Boer War. Patriotism and enthusiasm for adventure inspired large numbers of men to volunteer for service in South Africa. The exact figures may be debated, but it appears that a worryingly high proportion of the prospective soldiers were deemed unfit. For example, of the 3,600 men who applied to enlist at York, Leeds and Sheffield between 1897 and 1901, nearly half failed the medical examination on the grounds that they were 'under-developed . . . diseased . . . [had] defective vision . . . and decayed teeth'.[43] Major-General Sir Frederick Maurice took a very bleak view of such statistics: he believed that only two out of every five volunteers were fit to serve and commented that it made the physical state of the nation 'a far more deadly peril than any that was presented by the most anxious period of the South African War'.[44] The stature and health of many of the working-class volunteers reflected a diet that relied heavily on bread and jam, rather than bone-building fats and proteins. The clear and widespread deficiencies amongst the available civilians resulted in a further reduction in the minimum height for an infantry-man: a drop of 3 in to 5 ft. The national figures echoed the disappointing experience in Yorkshire and it was calculated that around 40 per cent of volunteers were rejected.[45]

Failures in recruitment resulted in a government enquiry, published in 1904 as the *Report of the Inter-Departmental Committee on Physical Deterioration*. It is difficult to authenticate the veracity of all of the evidence presented to the Committee, given the variations between the standards of individual Medical Officers and the emotive nature of concerns surrounding the subject, but it is clear that British manhood had been put to the test and found wanting. The eugenically minded Major-General Sir Walter Knox was particularly concerned and declared that 'the physically deteriorated race of town-bred humanity was getting dangerously low in the scale of virility'.[46] Concerns were exacerbated by the knowledge that the pool of applicants had already been self-selected: only men who met, or were at least very close to, the widely advertised minimum height would have presented themselves at the recruitment offices.[47] J.M. Winter's research endorses the view that the situation was worse than the statistics indicated, as the hurried medical tests at recruit-ment centres were likely to have underestimated the full extent of the health deficiencies of the men.[48] As ever, the army remained the employer of last resort for many and, regardless of the flush of patriotism that pervaded British society, the majority of volunteers still came from the under-nourished working classes. Problems with recruitment persisted after the Boer War, and in the decade preceding August 1914 between 284 and 355 out of every 1,000 applicants were rejected for medical reasons.[49]

Supply matters

Aside from its revelation of national health problems, the Boer War also afforded the army the opportunity to test its logistical and supply procedures. Unfortunately, these too were frequently deficient; the distribution of provisions was irregular and troops were forced to march for days with little more than bully beef and biscuits. Tinned meat had been available since the beginning of the nineteenth century. The French government, perhaps with the provisioning of Napoleon's armies in mind, had offered a twelve thousand franc prize for anyone who could develop an alternative method of food preservation to the traditional methods such as smoking and pickling. In 1804 the prize was awarded to Nicholas Appert for his process which preserved food in glass containers by means of heat. In the following decade, experiments with tins had proved them to be cheaper, lighter and more durable and by 1820 the Royal Navy, leading the way for the British armed forces, was ordering large quantities of tinned meat for its sailors.[50] By the end of the century, army contracts had become a source of considerable profit for the British canning industry, even though imports from Argentina, the USA and Australasia dominated both military and domestic markets until after the First World War. The accounts for Henry Grant & Co. (London) indicate a five fold growth between 1892 and 1905 as a result of orders generated by the Boer War.[51] In many ways the tinned meat was an improvement on the fresh meat that had traditionally been available on campaigns: meat on the hoof was often stringy, as the soldiers of the Peninsular War had complained. In addition, the canned product as well as being tender could be eaten cold, saving time and fuel. These supposedly superior aspects were not always recognised by the soldiers, who much preferred (good-quality) fresh items. In his 1899 survey of army provisioning, Colonel Furse recognised that 'nothing will conduce to the health and strength of the fighting man as fresh bread and fresh meat'.[52]

The problems of supply in South Africa made the tinned meat and hardtack biscuit attractive to the military command, given that they took up far less storage space and could be stored virtually indefinitely. Meat had a particularly long life; it was on record that a can of meat carried by *HMS Fury* in 1824 was found to be perfectly edible in 1868.[53] Distribution remained a problem and, in an attempt to mitigate delays in provisioning, the first emergency ration pack was introduced during the Boer War. It was to be carried by every man and eaten only at the order of his officer.[54] The pack included two 4 oz tins, one of concentrated beef and one of cocoa; the inclusion of the latter reflected the popular view of cocoa as a nourishing foodstuff, with potentially medicinal properties.[55] However, the soldiers' accounts continued to reflect the difficulties in providing them with a varied, or on occasion adequate, diet. In May 1900, a Sergeant Hill wrote home, somewhat sarcastically, 'we are still on bully beef, biscuits and jam, but there is a rumour afloat that we are to have bread by next Christmas'.[56] A.F. Corbett paints a similar picture, but also conveys the delight in finding an abandoned Boer farm which provided a feast of roast goat and vegetables for his unit.[57] Even the wounded or sick men admitted to military hospitals, where the diet should have been enhanced by the addition of 'medical comforts' could go hungry. William Robertson remembered selling his £5 watch for just 30s to an orderly so that he might purchase some unduly expensive extra food from the selfsame man.[58] The experiences of these three soldiers were infinitely better than those of the men who endured the siege of Ladysmith. A. Down wrote of existing on ¾ lb of horsemeat and two biscuits per day and when supplies dwindled further on porridge made from ¼ lb of crushed meal, an item which had previously been used as animal fodder.[59]

Failures in ration supply in South Africa and the men's vocal dissatisfaction with the easily transportable but unpalatable bully beef and biscuit elicited improvements evident in the army's subsequent peacetime practice. Michael Young, the leading historian of the ASC, notes a new flexibility in the ASC's support of the 1903 manoeuvres of the 1st Army Corps. In contrast to the very basic provisions supplied in previous years, grocery rations were issued on the exercise. Items such as sausages, bacon, cheese, jam and milk were packed in various boxes for division between groups of five, ten, twenty or fifty men.[60] This required greater effort from the ASC in the storage and distribution of perishable items, but the positive impact upon soldiers' morale made the increased complexity of delivery systems worthwhile. Greater attention was also given to the quality of the products delivered to the men as the 1906 *Report of Inspections at Certain of the Meat Canning Factories in the United States of America as Affecting the Supply of Preserved Meat to the British Army* indicates.[61] Lieutenant-Colonel P.E.F. Hobbs travelled to Chicago to check that the tins of meat supplied by the American factories were being prepared in a proper fashion. The report does not explain its genesis, but perhaps the publication of Upton Sinclair's exposé of the meat packing trade in the same year fuelled the army's interest.[62] Hobbs had a number of complaints, in particular the inadequate separation of the factories' latrines from the areas of production, which in some places consisted of a mere 6 ft partition. He also points out that, although smoking was banned, chewing tobacco was not and notes that 'several cases of spitting on the floor occurred whilst the individuals were actually talking to me'. Hobbs was eloquent in his arguments for the provision of the best-quality tinned meat to the men, and his conclusion has a prescient tone given the role that bully beef was to play in the war to come. He insisted that the British Army needed to ensure the product was the 'best procurable for men to fight on and be one that is as little productive as possible of digestive derangement. No preserved meat can be too good which may someday be destined to be a means of getting efficient and cheerful work out of a fighting force.'[63]

Eating in barracks

The public concerns expressed regarding both the health of the nation and the feeding of its army gave added impetus to the long-running attempts to improve the meals provided in the rankers' barracks. Central to this was the introduction of a modern canteen system to improve upon the limited culinary skills and haphazard delivery of earlier years. *The Rifle Brigade Chronicle 1906* contains a lengthy article describing changes at its Winchester depot. A 'restaurant' system of messing had been introduced for the battalion in an effort to raise standards and provide the soldiers with a wider choice. Rather than each company making its own arrangements with the attendant waste, duplication of effort and generally poor results, a Sergeant Cook would draw rations and determine menus for some eight hundred men each day. Soldiers were issued with metal tickets, which could be redeemed for a two-course dinner from a relatively extensive menu. The sample menus offered ten options for the meat course, but the appearance of diversity may have been deceptive. A number of dishes appear to have been variations on a theme: 'Irish Stew, Tomato Stew, Curry Stew, Brown Stew, Stewed Steak'. Whatever the limitations in terms of the menus' reliance on boiled and stewed red

2.2 Mock execution of a cook, 1909

meat, it is clear from the bill of fare in the accompanying photograph that
the meal was a great advance on previous offerings. The improved menu
also includes an extensive list of vegetables and the inclusion of stewed
apples amongst the generally rather stodgy puddings. The new system
was popular with the men because of this wider choice and, in addition,
it was flexible as tickets not used on one day could be redeemed for extra
cold meat and pickles the next. The enthusiastic correspondent notes
that the system 'gives the soldier the best dinner I have ever seen supplied during my service'.[64] Further evidence of the improvement in army
rations is contained in *The Essex Regiment Gazette 1910*, where details
are provided of a French officer's visit to the 2nd Battalion at Curragh
Camp in Ireland. He was invited to tour the kitchens and mess halls and
was most impressed: 'The cooks are well up to their important duties. The
food is plentiful, appetising, and of excellent quality.'[65]

It appears that progress had been made and the rankers' food, at least
in some units, had reached a reasonable standard. Photographic evidence
confirms that not all cooks had earned the respect of their diners, as
Figure 2.2 indicates. The failures of those in charge of food preparation
remained a concern in the period immediately before 1914; at least here
it is treated with humour, a quality that was to become less in evidence in
the war years that followed.

In the years before the First World War, experiments were undertaken to test both the efficacy and the financial parameters of army rations. In 1906, the French Army had tested a low-protein diet with part of the meat ration being replaced by sugar; this had proved very successful in that the men displayed 'greater physical resistance to fatigue and sustained fewer accidents'.[66] There was no doubt an associated reduction in costs, as sugar was a cheaper commodity than the lean red meat required for fighting men. The British Army rations contained more meat than those of other European countries and, although in the years before the First World War there was a study to determine how this might be reduced, it was concluded that changes to the high-energy, high-protein diet would be inadvisable.[67]

Rank and rations

Subsequent chapters will explore what was, for many of the 1914–18 soldiers, a shocking contrast between domestic and army meals: a point of comparison that represented the polarities of their civilian past and military present. In order to determine the prewar diet of the rankers who served in the First World War, it is necessary to formulate certain criteria regarding the relationship between diet, class and rank. Eating in the British Army, whether in peace or war, was an experience determined by rank. In normal circumstances, officers' food was of limited concern to those in the War Office or General Staff who determined ration scales and supply systems. It was only on relatively few occasions, on active and distant front line service, that officers might be forced to rely solely upon army provisioning. Officers made their own arrangements, they had their own messes and paid monthly fees to cover the cost of the purchase, preparation and serving of meals. On certain occasions, at Christmas in particular, the officers as much as the army itself were regarded as a source of food by their men and the festive meal owed much to their generosity. William Robertson recalled the great feast provided by the officers at his Aldershot barracks in 1877, which 'included a variety of eatables never seen on any other day, as well as a liberal supply of beer'.[68]

Additional expenses such as these ensured that the rigidity of British society's class system in the Victorian and Edwardian eras was closely replicated within its army. Commissions were no longer bought and sold on an open market, but a private income was still considered a prerequisite, given the costs of the uniform, horses, food, drink and hospitality for the rankers. The amount required varied according to the prestige of the regiment, from £1,000 per annum in the Guards, £750 per annum in the cavalry, to £200 per annum in the infantry.[69] As we have seen, pay and conditions in the ranks ensured that those of the regular army were almost exclusively working-class in their composition. However, the constitution of the ranks would shift after war was declared in August 1914. Volunteers, and from January 1916 conscripts, were not as inflexibly restricted by class and the New Armies would provide a more inclusive reflection of British society than that of the prewar ranks.

The flood of men into the military ensured that the rankers of the First World War were less homogeneous in their prewar family, educational, employment and eating experiences than the peacetime regulars, but the prewar class divisions that separated officers from men largely remained. The ability of the ranks to reflect the diversity of the society from which they were constituted was limited, both by the relative proportions of the socio-economic groups from which they were drawn and by the underlying prejudices that continued to influence officer selection. J.M. Winter's analysis of enlistment rates to the British forces in 1914–16 indicates that these were proportionately higher among non-manual workers and professional men than among manual workers but the latter still outnumbered the former by a ratio of three to one.[70] In addition, because Winter's numbers cannot be disaggregated by rank, it is virtually certain that a far higher proportion of the men identified in his statistics as coming from the 'professions' and 'central and local government' were likely to have become officers in the army than those from 'industry' and 'agriculture'. Men from other than the working class and lowest echelons of the middle class did not generally remain as rankers for long. Rather, they passed through on their way to the commission for which their background had destined them. In the early years of the war in particular, it was often quicker for a keen middle- or upper-class eighteen-year-old to volunteer as a private soldier and obtain promotion from within the army, rather than wait for an entry-level commission to be forthcoming.[71] While Helen McCartney has emphasised the high standard of literacy required for some NCO posts, which attracted middle-class men with clerk's skills, the drift for most non-working-class men was upwards, away from the ranks.[72].

The occasional representative of the bourgeoisie did remain a private, and the 'gentleman ranker' was less of an oddity in wartime than in peace.[73] However, they remained atypical and it was the massed numbers of the working class, combined with the clerks and shop-workers of the lower middle class that constituted the bulk of the men. The ranks also reflected an urban bias, and J.G. Fuller notes the contrast between the French and the British Armies, where peasants made up around three-quarters of the former's infantry. This was a reflection of the agricultural predominance of a nation where, in 1911, 34 per cent of its working population was engaged in manufacturing and transport occupations, compared to 89 per cent in Britain. The British ranks came overwhelmingly from the cities: before February 1916 only 8.4 per cent of recruits came from agricultural occupations.[74]

Prewar civilian diet

The fact that the broadening of the social range of the ranks was relatively limited permits general assumptions regarding the diet of the majority of its members prior to their admission to the 1914–18 army. The problem with generalities is that they shroud complexities, and it is important to recognise that, despite the working-class, industrialised and urbanised bias of the ranks, 'working-class' was a label that covered a disparate body of people and a wide variety of very different households. Robert Roberts, brought up in early twentieth-century Salford, wrote that 'socially the unskilled workers and their families, who made up about 50 percent of the population in our industrial cities, varied as much from the manual elite as did people in the middle station from the aristocracy'.[75]

Exploration of the diet of the pre-1914 working classes is facilitated by the wealth of published investigations into their lives, as well as numerous memoirs and oral histories. Poverty attracted the interest of the Victorian and Edwardian middle classes; a vein of concern evidenced by the detailed reports of commentators, from Henry Mayhew, through Charles Booth, to Seebohm Rowntree. The attributes of extreme poverty were clear to those that cared to look: inadequate housing, limited sewerage, ragged clothing and dirt and disease all took highly visible forms. Hunger was less overt, although widely present and instrumental in causing much of the poor health endured. Sometimes the connection was explicit, and in 1890 starvation was recorded as the cause of death for a man found in St James's Park, London, after he had walked for five days from Liverpool in search of work.[76]

'"Normal" deprivation', as J.M. Winter terms it, was widespread. At the end of the century, Booth in London and Rowntree in York had assessed that almost one-third of the population lived in poverty.[77] Fifteen years later, a study by A.L. Bowley suggested little had improved;

27 per cent of children lived in 'families which failed to reach the low standard taken as necessary, for healthy existence'.[78] A number of contributory factors could make the difference between satiety and hunger: the age and number of the children in a family was critical, but the key factor was income. *Round About a Pound a Week* by Maud Pember Reeves, a member of the Fabian Women's Group, vividly illustrates the hardships faced by families in Lambeth living on this sum. A family with few children, reasonable rent, a mother who was an accomplished housewife and cook, combined with a husband in secure employment might be able to manage, but such a favourable set of circumstances was uncommon.

Rents were high in London and the South East; Philip Snowden reported that rents in the poor areas of Poplar and Stepney were the same as those paid by the wealthier artisans living in the leafier suburbs of Enfield and Chiswick.[79] Bowley noted that, in Reading, 67 per cent of rents exceeded 6s a week, whilst the largest employer in the area paid a maximum of 23s a week to its unskilled workers.[80] The result was that the poorest, on less than 15s a week, generally spent two-fifths of their income on rent.[81] The unreliability of wages was a difficulty for many: even if a man remained in his job, the work available to him and hence his pay could be summarily reduced by his employer. One woman described her husband's weekly income to the visiting District Nurse: 'They call it 32s . . . but I added it up last year and it averaged 22s 3½d.'[82] In this restricted existence, it was invariably the food budget that suffered. There was no elasticity in the payment of rent, as non-payment resulted in debt and then eviction, but people could, and did, eat a little less: 'less food all round, though a disagreeable experience, leaves no bill in shillings and pence to be paid afterwards'.[83]

There had been gains in real wages amongst the working classes from the middle of the nineteenth century onward. The benefits they might have delivered were negated by insanitary housing and a generally innutritious diet, as well as widespread disease.[84] Many of the problems identified by Friedrich Engels in 1844 still persisted: in particular, expensive, poor-quality food and the inability to prepare that which was available, because of inadequate kitchen facilities, the cost of fuel or lack of time due to the increased employment of women outside the home.[85] The relationship between deprivation and physical development was clear. A 1913 Manchester survey of five hundred twelve-year-old boys found that those from poorer areas averaged a height of 4 ft 4 in and a weight of 70 lb and those from wealthier areas, 4 ft 9 in and 82 lb.[86]

The concentration of the population into urban areas and the development of new food storage and transportation techniques resulted in a larger number of people being offered the same types of food. Gradually, the British working-class diet moved towards a higher degree of homogenisation. Within the range of this group and the lower middle class who abutted it, an increase in income resulted in the consumption of greater quantities of familiar ingredients, rather than in the choice of radically different foods. The meals of families on a higher income were generally similar to those of their less affluent neighbours, but were larger and incorporated more of the expensive items, primarily meat and additional fats such as butter, cheese and eggs. The British had never been famed for the variety of their cuisine: as Voltaire declared, 'the English have forty-two religions but only two sauces'.[87] Britain's prewar working class, even allowing for variations in income, reflected the dietary conservatism that had long been a national hallmark.

The constituent parts may not have varied widely, but the differences in quantity consumed between the richest and the poorest of the working classes meant that many of the dietary statistics produced during this period offer a rather bland picture, as the averages obscure the specific details of very different experiences. For example, figures produced in 1908 indicate that the weekly consumption of meat and bacon by the working class was 1 lb 9 oz per head, only 8 oz less than the average for the whole community.[88] However, evidence produced by social researchers working at that time indicates that for poorer families meat remained a luxury item: 'The children get a pound of pieces stewed for them during the week, and with plenty of potatoes they make a great show with the gravy.'[89] Meat was a rare commodity for many and Barry Reay refers to the 'enforced vegetarianism of labouring households'.[90] Clearly the better-paid members of the disparate working classes were eating meat in large quantities, well in excess of the average, while the poorest struggled by on scraps.

D.J. Oddy notes the dichotomy between strong economic indicators and actual nutrition when, in the late nineteenth century, rising food consumption accompanied increased levels of malnutrition.[91] In his article, Oddy collates 151 working-class family budgets for dietary analysis. The data were taken from the investigations of Booth, Rowntree and Dr Thomas Oliver, a professor of physiology in Newcastle's medical school. Oddy's analysis highlights the manner in which gross averages obscure the variations in consumption. For example, an average daily intake of 2,096 calories for the working class reflects a range where the hungriest families of unskilled workers, living on less than 18s a week, had an average daily consumption of 1,578 calories – a restricted diet that was in contrast to skilled workmen earning in excess of 30s per week, who averaged 2,537 calories a day.[92] Neither of these levels reached the 3,500 calories a day which Rowntree deemed necessary for a man in 'moderate work'. The total seems relatively high in twenty-first-century terms, but reflects the greater proportion of manual labour performed by this earlier workforce. Whatever the credibility of the target daily intake, any discussion of a 'working-class diet' must acknowledge the great nutritional range this spanned, from those who ate well to those who essentially went hungry.

Almost all of the quantitative dietary data measures consumption in terms of the family unit, without a breakdown of individual food intake within that unit. It is only Dr Oliver who presents detailed figures for the individual men and women in his survey. These statistics from the working class of Newcastle appear to represent a relatively well-fed population, with an average daily nutrient intake of 2,595 calories. However, when this average is analysed by sex it can be seen that, on average, men ate 3,321 calories per day to women's 1,870. Whilst their intake of carbohydrate was roughly similar, men consumed three times as much fat and more than double the amount of protein.[93] The particular impoverishment of women's diet was noted in the commentary of social investigators. Pember Reeves writes that 'only one kind of diet is possible, and that is the man's diet'; women and children ate what was left over.[94] The nutritional sacrifice that mothers made for their families was acknowledged in their own memories of the period. In a collection of oral histories from the time, Mrs Wrigley remembered, 'I have gone without my dinner for their [the children's] sakes and just had a cup of tea and bread and butter.'[95] J.M. Winter points out the apparent contradiction at this time between the relative fitness of miners and the high infant mortality rate in their communities. Winter concludes that the males' strong constitution was bought at the expense of their wives and children.[96] Marvin Harris represents this imbalance in purely practical terms as the only appropriate response. The man, who was generally the main breadwinner, had the greatest physiological need of calories and hence the first call on the limited amount of food his labours provided, as his health and energy were critical to the continued economic survival of the family.[97] Ellen Ross argues that the 'breadwinner effect' explanation is unconvincing, The demands of pregnancy and heavy domestic labour, which for many would have been supplemented by paid cleaning or laundry work, meant that women's nutritional needs were generally similar to their husbands'. Ross believes that the significant factor was the higher status of the male and the housewife's perceived need to appease, indeed favour, her husband. Even in families where there was no shortage of food 'the best was saved for father'.[98] Indeed in many households in England it appeared that cooking was done 'only for the father', and that the rest of the family existed on food that did not require the use of a pan and the application of heat.[99] The privileging of men at the family dining table, both husbands and grown sons, would have implications for the new soldiers when they found themselves part of an aggregated mass in the mess halls of the New Armies. The entitlement that was theirs in the civilian world could not be replicated in the exclusively masculine environment of the British Army.

Bread

The poor mothers' meals of tea and bread represent the linchpins of the working-class diet, and it would be difficult to over estimate the significance of bread. In 1892 the children of Bethnal Green were nourished almost entirely on bread: 83 per cent had no other solid food for seventeen out of the twenty-one meals in a week.[100] Confusingly, statistics for the period 1880–1914 indicate a fall in the consumption of the staple foods of the poor, bread and flour. The decline, accompanied as it was by an increase in the amounts of sugar and meat eaten, has been cited as evidence of increased wealth and improved diet amongst the working class.[101] Economic indicators such as these were not reflected in the qualitative evidence of the period, where bread consumption, particularly amongst women and children remained very high. It is likely that, as has been noted above, the aggregation of data has obscured the divisions between relative wealth and poverty. Evidence given to the 1905 Royal Commission on the Supply of Food and Raw Material in Time of War stresses that bread was fundamental to the diet of the poor. Any drop in wages resulted in an increase in its consumption as other more expensive foodstuffs were eliminated from their purchases.[102]

At this time, the introduction of roller-milling, which allowed the extraction of the dark wheat-germ with the bran, resulted in a paler flour which satisfied the public's demand for ever-whiter bread, although at the expense of nutritional value.[103] The preference for white bread was not based solely upon its social cachet, as it had significant advantages over the darker, heavier and sourer type. Firstly, its colour implied that worrying impurities had been removed and, secondly, it could be eaten on its own, without the need of expensive butter or cheese to make it palatable.[104] The darker variety was scorned and later during the war, when a government initiative introduced wholemeal bread, the diarist Reverend Andrew Clark recorded a village woman's complaint: 'Fancy bringing English people to eat that stuff. It ain't fit for pigs.'[105] The resentment she felt would be echoed in the response of the soldiers to the biscuit that the army substituted for the bread ration. Bread was the staff and stuff of working-class diet and the absence of such a profoundly familiar and comforting food elicited angry responses in the disappointed men, as subsequent chapters explore.

The widespread availability of cheap white bread ensured that the taste for it spread to regions which had traditionally obtained their carbohydrates elsewhere. Oatmeal had been key to the Scottish diet but its popularity declined rapidly in the face of competition from the mass-produced loaf.[106] Social reformers in Lambeth, who tried to encourage the consumption of the nutritionally superior porridge rather than bread, met great resistance from mothers who had neither the fuel nor the time to carefully stir cooking oatmeal – nor of course, the money for the extra milk and sugar required to make porridge palatable.[107] In addition to the pressures on finances and the time available for cooking, much of the new housing hurriedly created for the influx of workers to industrial centres lacked adequate cooking facilities. Traditionally, houses had been built with a solid, functional range or even a bread oven, but these expensive design features were not incorporated into the new, cheaper developments. In 1898, only one home in four that had a gas supply also had a cooker.[108] Pember Reeves comments upon both the lack of ovens and the fact that those available required enormous quantities of coal or gas to cook properly.[109] A 1906 survey of the village of Corsley by Maud Davies reveals that wives cooked only once or twice a week and it was 'exceptional to find a woman who cooked every day'.[110] Indeed, the 'gross inadequacy' of cooking facilities was recognised as a direct cause of the inadequate nourishment of the population by the 1904 Committee on Physical Deterioration.[111]

Lack of cooking was reflected in the increased consumption of white bread, which, although it could be eaten alone, usually had something spread upon it, although this was rarely the expensive butter. Margarine, first produced in 1869, was initially made with animal fats and highly unpalatable, but the substitution of hydrogenated vegetable oils for suet, developed at the beginning of the twentieth century, made it more acceptable.[112] The changes in production resulted in margarine becoming more widely available, but its flavour was not widely enjoyed and it remained relatively unpopular. In rural areas where the better-off families would keep an annual pig – or at least a part share in one – lard was the favourite spread. Flora Thompson remembered hers being flavoured with rosemary and that the men of the village topped theirs with mustard.[113] Fresh herbs were not widely available in urban areas, so, in order to improve the taste of cheap fats, treacle, jam or plain sugar were spread or sprinkled on top. For many, butter, margarine and lard were expensive luxuries and bread was generally consumed with a sugary spread without the addition of fat. Indeed, the working class ate much of their fruit as jam, and its production, which had once serviced a luxury market, had grown to become 'the backbone of the fruit industry' by the end of the nineteenth century.[114] The importance of jam in the working-class diet would be evident in the criticisms voiced in the army during the First World War. The unpopularity of the ubiquitous 'plum and apple' indicated that availability was only part of the issue and that flavour was equally significant.

Vegetables and meat

Fresh fruit and vegetables constituted a small part in the diet of the majority of the working class. Myths concerning food were prevalent, and summer diarrhoea was directly attributed to the consumption of fruit and vegetables in season at the time, rather than its true bacteriological source.[115] The nutritional necessity of fruit and vegetables was not understood and they were regarded as peripheral to a healthy diet. Wilbur Atwater, who had identified the method for the measurement of calories, regarded fruit and green vegetables as 'water rich' and unnecessarily extravagant purchases on a limited income.[116] Significantly, such foods were ineffective in relieving hunger, a prime requirement of those on restricted incomes, Vegetables, other than potatoes and the occasional onion or celery for flavouring, were not regularly consumed. In this nutritional area there was a clear division between the urban and the rural, with higher levels of vegetables being consumed by the latter, a certain amount of which may have been grown by the families themselves. The proportion of home-grown food was lower amongst rural families than might be expected: Barry Reay calculates that, on average in his sample, it constituted only one-twelfth of the total food consumed.[117] Research suggests more vegetables were consumed in northern England, a lingering reminder of the traditional favouring of the stew or soup pot over the frying pan. Elizabeth Roberts's oral histories of Lancashire families indicate that, when meat was unavailable, vegetable or potato hotpots were eaten as alternatives.[118] In terms of nutrition, potatoes were an important source of ascorbic acid for the working classes, and Magnus Pyke notes that it was potatoes, not green vegetables, which had protected the British population from ascorbic acid deficiency.[119] The truth of Pyke's assertion can be confirmed by the 1917 outbreaks of scurvy in Manchester, Newcastle and Glasgow, which resulted from the nationwide shortage of potatoes.[120] Potatoes and bread were used to add carbohydrate-laden bulk to meals. Similarly, it was common to eat a suet or batter pudding at the start of the meal in order to take the edge off the appetite before the more meagre serving of meat or gravy.

Meat had always occupied a very particular place in the British diet, regardless of class. The anthropologist Nick Fiddes ascribes this significance to the fact that 'meat tangibly represents human control of the natural world', a potent symbol of superiority achieved through killing and consumption.[121] Social anthropologists recognise the special importance of meat for many cultures: in certain Amazonian tribes there is a specific word for 'meat hungry' which is more extreme than ordinary hunger.[122] A pyramid demonstrating the hierarchy of food shows fruit, nuts and seeds at the bottom, and ranges through vegetables, dairy products and fish to meat at its apex. There is an additional hierarchy within the category of 'meat', where red meat occupies the peak position, ranked above white and processed meat.[123] The British diet had long reflected a desire for meat. In 1562 Alessandro Magno, a Venetian merchant, commented incredulously of Londoners: 'it is almost impossible to believe that they could eat so much meat in one city alone'.[124] In 1902 a survey by the Statistical Society showed that Britain was the heaviest meat-eater in Europe with 122 lb per head per annum consumed, compared to Germany's 99 lb or Sweden's 62 lb, although much of this was consumed outside of the working classes.[125] Meat was traditionally seen as the food of free men, not slaves. Beef in particular, with its 'John Bull' connotations, was in the eighteenth and nineteenth centuries 'popularly regarded as the very basis of English liberties'.[126] A.L. Bowley notes that 'a workman would sacrifice part of the defined necessaries in favour of a meat diet',[127] although, all too often, it was his wife and children who made the greater sacrifice.

The range of meat available reflected the spread of income within the working classes, as well as the urban–rural divide. The poaching of rabbits was a popular choice for those living in the countryside: 'it was a wonder we didn't grow fur', as one Cumbrian woman recalled.[128] Urban dwellers had fewer, and often less palatable, alternatives. Robert Roberts describes the butcher shops of Salford, which ranged from the purveyors of quality beef to those that sold 'slink', the flesh of prematurely born calves, and 'braxy', the meat of sheep that had died of disease.[129] Bacon was the most common meat consumed. It was not particularly cheap, but it had several advantages: it kept well, important in homes without storage facilities; it was easy and quick to cook; it had a strong taste; and it could be cut very thin. These were important qualities as they permitted a relatively small amount to add a disproportionate degree of flavour and pleasing fat to a meal. Bacon required a simple frying pan to prepare it, an important point as it was not just the limitations in ovens and ranges or the cost of their operation that restricted cookery. The limited culinary apparatus available in many homes consisted of 'one kettle, one frying-pan and two saucepans, both burnt'.[130]

The popularity of meat, and of course its nutritional importance as a source of protein, had ensured its central position in army rations and, as we have already seen, the difficulties of supplying fresh meat had been resolved in part by the increasing use of the tinned product. The development of ships with refrigeration systems in the last quarter of the nineteenth century provided another alternative, as supplies of fresh meat could now be transported from the USA and Australia. However, the quality of the meat was 'consistently low if not bad' and it was generally sold at those street markets which catered to the poor.[131] Frozen meat also entered the market, but was regarded with suspicion by both civilians and the military: the army's *1899 Supply Handbook* records that frozen beef was excluded from the ration as 'the process of thawing . . . renders it unnutritious'.[132]

While tinned meat was welcomed by the army, at least by those responsible for the logistics of supply, the British working classes were less enthusiastic, and canned foods were generally regarded with suspicion; as one woman commented: 'she [mother] wouldn't have any tinned stuff, she said it would poison you'.[133] In the 1870s there had been riots at two workhouses that had introduced tinned meat, which had been deemed 'stringy and tasteless' by the inmates.[134] There appears to have been a class dimension to the consumption of canned foodstuffs, in that the first of such products were aimed at high-income groups. An illustration from *Mrs Beeton's Book of Household Management* depicts sixty tins, and the emphasis is clearly on the more sophisticated diners, those who ate 'galantine of wild boar's head' and lobster.[135] The acceptance of tinned food was further hampered by the delay in the production of a tin opener, which did not appear until 1858. Soldiers generally had a bayonet to hand, but domestic consumers had had to rely on a hammer and chisel or the willingness of the local grocer to perform this service for them.[136] While the more prosperous families might have had a tin of fruit or salmon for a festive tea, canned food remained relatively unpopular, with the notable exception of tinned milk.

Meat, in any form, was not a mainstay of the working-class diet, but fats were even more rare and eaten in very small quantities. They were expensive and Oddy calculates a weekly mean of 4.9 oz per head for the working class.[137] Magnus Pyke writes of the 'almost mystic significance' attached to fat. The mystical aspects of foodstuffs may be difficult to prove, but fat is the most highly concentrated source of calories in the diet and as such holds a great allure for the hungry.[138] The specifically individual 'mouth feel' of fat is particularly pleasing to the palate, and research suggests that it may have a positive emotional impact, as a very low-fat diet can negatively influence an individual's psychological well-being.[139] Whatever the psychological and physiological connections that may be attributed to fat, little was consumed, but it was a highly prized food as an antidote to the carbohydrate that formed the bulk of the diet.

Relishes and other supplements

'Relishes' were central to the diet of the poor. These were additions to meals that brought a richness or savour that was absent in the usual dreary foodstuffs: herring, bacon, mustard, pickles, cheese and eggs were all popular. In wealthier families the women might also share the relish. Children were rarely included in such dietary treats and thought themselves fortunate if they were given scraps, such as the top of a parent's boiled egg.[140] For those who had money, the variety of food sold on the street was extensive, including 'sheep's and pig's trotters, fried fish, roast potatoes, ham sandwiches, hot peas, hot soups, hot puddings, hot gingerbread, all kinds of cakes'.[141] The purchase of a complete ready-to-eat meal for the family, rather than these extra treats and relishes, was unusual. The exception to this was fish and chips, and by 1914 there were approximately twenty-five thousand chip shops in Britain.[142] John Walton describes how early disparagement of their use, countering as it did the Victorian ideal of home cooking within the domestic sphere, dissipated as fish and chips developed into a family meal, consumed at home, rather than an accompaniment to a working man's drinking evening.[143] Within the Lancashire communities that Elizabeth Roberts investigated, fish or pie and chips had become acceptable convenience foods in families where there was little time for cooking.[144] Resistance to ready-cooked dishes rested on the fact that their quality was uncertain: 'you never know what you are getting'. In addition, home cooking was bound up with identity: a good mother prepared her family's meals from scratch.[145] Both these factors were likely to have implications for the men who joined the ranks of the First World War, where the provenance of much of the mass catering would be unknown. If home-cooked food had a special significance for women, it was likely to have had a similar reception amongst the husbands and sons for whom they cooked.

Eating in restaurants was not a facet of working-class family life. John Burnett could find no evidence of women eating outside the home in cafés or restaurants, and one could assume the same applied to their children.[146] Working men, if they could not return home to eat, generally took a cold lunch to their workplace. Some companies provided a room where food from home could be reheated and eaten, but few of them offered works canteens: there were barely a hundred in existence in 1914.[147] In this period, only the very largest and most keenly paternalistic of employers such as Cadbury's or Tangyes, a Birmingham engineering firm, were able to provide their workforces with lunches at subsidised rates.[148] Those workers on a higher income might take a weekday lunch at coffee shops and eating houses, but this was more prevalent amongst the clerks of the lower middle class.[149]

Appetites that could not be satisfied with food were regularly suppressed with hot drinks. The most popular of these was tea, the annual consumption of which grew from 1.9 lb per head in 1851 to 6.5 lb in 1911.[150] The establishment of tea as the drink of the people was institutionalised in the army's *1899 Supply Handbook*, which states that 'tea may be regarded as a national beverage, and is much appreciated by the soldier'.[151] Tea had the ability to convert a cold meal, that is bread and jam, into a hot one with an accompanying increase in the levels of satisfaction and comfort derived from that meal.[152] Children also drank tea, as little fresh milk was consumed, given its high price and chequered nutritional history in urban areas. The town dairies of earlier years had been notorious for their lack of hygiene and the contamination of their product, with, for example, the TB bacillus or faecal matter.[153] Improvements in transportation and distribution meant that milk from country farms could be delivered to urban areas rapidly, but tinned condensed milk remained widely popular because of its sterility and extra sweetness. However, as the cheaper varieties were made from skimmed milk, they lacked the full nutritional value of the fresh product and damaged children's physical development. General Booth of the Salvation Army despaired of the working-class diet and pronounced that 'tea and slops and beer take the place of milk and the bone and sinew of the next generation are sapped from the cradle'.[154]

Beer remained the favoured drink of many adult males. Robert Roberts's father regularly bellowed at his family 'Beer is my food!' and to satisfy his appetite he drank four quarts a day.[155] There was some substance to his claim: beer, unlike tea, had traditionally provided additional calories to the working-class diet, just as it had for the regular soldiers. None the less, the consumption of beer declined from the end of the nineteenth century onwards, partly as a result of the efforts of the temperance movement. The picture of a drunken, feckless working class had been drawn by a number of commentators who wrote of children whose diet would have been adequate if the parents had not squandered their income on alcohol.[156] Others demonstrated a sensitivity to the pressures of poverty; the Committee on Physical Deterioration noted that the poor often drank to 'get the effects of a good meal. They mistake the feeling of stimulation after alcohol for the feeling of nutrition.'[157]

Even allowing for the limited availability of foodstuffs and financial constraints, the working-class diet of this period appeared particularly unadventurous. The pattern of eating was monotonous, and variations between each day's meals could generally be ascribed to the gradual dwindling of the week's budget: families ate better closer to pay day. The exception to the general dreariness of the diet was Sunday dinner. In most families, where at all possible, a piece of meat, or extra bacon, would be purchased for Sunday dinner. The disproportionate expenditure on this one meal had less to do with improvidence than with a desire to eat well and fulfil the need to escape the nutritional oppression of poverty, if only once a week. The memory of the Sunday meal 'allowed even the very poor to feel like respectable human beings all week long'. Even if the extra food was not available it was important to keep up appearances; one child remembered his mother rattling the pots and plates at the appropriate time for Sunday dinner preparations despite the fact that they had nothing to cook. It was important that the other tenants remained unaware of the family's privations.[158] In a similar fashion, food was used to mark celebrations such as Christmas and Easter, which became true feast days for many impoverished families. Alice Foley remembered the joy of Easter Sunday, not for any religious fervour but because it was the only time she was given a whole egg for breakfast.[159]

Living from hand to mouth resulted in repeated trips to the local shop – three times a day was not unusual. These shopping trips provided children with the opportunity to run errands for extra food as only the wealthier families could afford to pay for such help, so payment in kind was gratefully received. Jack Lanigan got extra bread by fetching 2 lb loaves for neighbours and, when a loaf was 'short', the 'make-weight' slice cut from another loaf by the baker became his tip.[160] Lanigan also remembered standing at the factory gates at the end of the day and asking the homebound men "'Ave yer any bread left master?'" Any remnants of the workers' lunches were taken home to share with his brother and mother.[161] Scrounging and begging were commonplace and, as children lived most of the waking hours not spent at school on the street, they quickly learnt where to pick up stale bread or over-ripe fruit left over from market stalls.[162] Rural areas also offered numerous opportunities for finding extra food. Depending on the season, the children picked hawthorn shoots, sorrel leaves, blackberries and sloes in the hedgerows or stole peas, grain and turnips from the fields.[163] The resourcefulness acquired as boys would stand the grown men in good stead when they found themselves in a military world whose privations could be mitigated by individual initiative.

In an effort to alleviate hunger, some schools in the poorer areas had provided breakfast.[164] The 1906 Education Act (Provision of Meals) introduced school dinners, formalising the charitable initiatives already in existence, and by 1911 more than two hundred thousand children were receiving them free of charge.[165] However, well-meaning endeavours did not meet with unequivocal gratitude, as the eating habits of the poor could be sufficiently entrenched to override nutritional benefits. A 1908 survey of children in Bradford revealed that many of the school meals served – shepherd's pie, fish and potato pie, Yorkshire cheese pudding – were unfamiliar and hence unpopular amongst the young diners. The children were used to little more than bread, margarine and tea and often rejected alien tastes until they became used to them.[166] Resistance to new foods, whatever their dietary superiority, prefigured the response many soldiers would have to the massed catering of military life, where calories could exert a less powerful attraction than the desire for familiar food.

The serving of familiar foods did not overcome the difficulties of institutional eating; the environment itself appeared to blunt appetites. Anna Davin cites several prewar reports which suggest that the food served in pauper schools and convalescent homes was not always well received, despite its calorific superiority to the home diet. Children were unenthused by the plain, wholesome cooking and prone to leave much of it on their plates.[167] It appeared that it was not *only* the familiarity of foodstuffs that determined their acceptability but also the circumstances in which they were consumed. Neophobia is strengthened at times of anxiety and illness; it seems likely that the pupils of pauper schools or children convalescing after serious illness were more likely to be subject to unhappiness and physical weaknesses, thus increasing their resistance to the meals provided.[168] One contemporary reporter was certain that emotion was a determinant of appetite and wrote, 'food eaten with pleasure nourishes far better than a superior diet eaten, for any reason, without enjoyment'.[169] It was clear that, whatever the quality of the meals provided, hospitals, schools and, as we shall see later, armies struggled to please their consumers.

The poorest of the working class could be particular about the way in which they consumed meals in their own kitchen. A table covering was desirable, although often it was an old newspaper, which worked well as no one cared if it got dirty and it could be used to light the fire the next day. Meals might be inadequate and the surroundings poor, but they were still a critical medium for the expression of familial care and cultural beliefs. Indeed, for many, meals were a matter of survival rather than recreation and this imbued them with a significance that John Burnett describes as 'almost sacramental'.[170] Children frequently ate standing at the table, primarily because of a shortage of furniture, although Robert Roberts writes that in some families not sitting was regarded as 'good for moral fibre'.[171] Etiquette demanded that they remained silent: eating was a serious matter, to be undertaken reverentially. Despite the widespread lack of comfort, the shared utensils and insufficient food, children were expected to be grateful for what they had received. A rudimentary grace was common, particularly perhaps when enquiring ladies like Maud Pember Reeves were present.[172] Whilst recollections of shared childhood meals were voiced by many, Anna Davin's research indicates that it was not a universal practice but was dependent upon numerous factors including regular hours, reliable income and sufficient space to accommodate the whole family.[173]

Lower-middle-class eating

The eyes of contemporary social commentators had been focused upon the experience and behaviour of the working classes, a focus that lingered in the subsequent attention of historians and the publishers of memoirs and oral histories. The relative wealth of material available affords some insight into the food the working classes consumed and the manner in which they ate. Similarly, the banquets and fine dining of the upper classes and the solid bourgeoisie have attracted interest, but the home dining of the lower-middle-class has not been investigated. Obscurity was a quality that pertained to much of their existence and explicit analysis or accounts of their eating are rare.[174] It is likely that the diet of the lower-middle-class clerks and their peers did not differ drastically from that of the artisans, with the already stated exception that dining outside the home was more common. Fuelled by the demand amongst the growing mass of clerks, shop-workers and shoppers, the first Lyons Teashop opened on Picadilly in 1894 and heralded the rapid growth of the chain: between 1895 and 1914 a new teashop opened on average every six weeks,[175] However, eating out as a family, rather than with colleagues or friends, was still relatively unusual, as evidenced by the memorable nature of the first time Richard Church ate 'in public', as an eight-year-old at an Italian restaurant in Clapham.[176]

Paul Thompson's account of the life of Sidney Ford offers an insight into the precarious nature of lower-middle-class existence. Ford's family had aspirations but the employment difficulties experienced by his clerk father meant that their income was low and occasionally uncertain. True to the 'keeping up appearances' philosophy of their class, the Fords did all they could to maintain a respectable address and the rent costs this entailed were compensated for by a restricted diet. Ford's descriptions of food are reminiscent of working-class accounts: 'the meals were rather sparse, two penn'orth of bones stewed down into broth with peas and lentils . . . we didn't seem to run to joints'.[177] Limited incomes and high aspirations ensured that the working-class principles of thrift were applied to the lower-middle-class diet. Starch provided the backbone of daily consumption and every scrap of food was consumed, even if it took several days. Mr Pooter, the archetypal clerk, reached the limits of his thrift when his stomach revolted at blancmange for breakfast, an unpopular dish that had lingered on the meal table for the preceding three days.[178]

Mr Pooter was the epitome of the hen-pecked husband, and the Grossmiths' satire reflects contemporary concerns regarding the feminisation of lower-middle-class men. Their loss of manliness was a perceived result of their appropriation of 'women's jobs and a worrying predilection for domesticity. The absence of muscular masculinity amongst the clerks further fuelled concerns regarding the physical degeneration of British manhood, which had centred upon the more obvious problems of working-class under-nourishment. The lower middle classes' retreat into a sedentary and physically undemanding life, at both work and home, generated concerns about their fitness, as did the excess consumption and resulting obesity of the established middle class.[179] The extent of Mr Pooter's exercise was an occasional ride on a 'Liver Jerker', but he did demonstrate an energetic enthusiasm to engage in a range of domestic chores.[180] While his tedious conversations with the butcher and grocer owe a debt to literary licence, evidence suggested that lower-middle-class men were more likely than their working-class contemporaries to share the household tasks traditionally undertaken by women. An Edwardian advice manual warned men there was no room for masculine false pride on a clerk's salary; they should not be too proud to assist their wives with the shopping in order to take advantage of lower food prices near their places of work.[181] Sidney Ford's father was 'prepared when necessary to cook' and Richard Church's was happy to share some of the domestic burden, if not the cooking, certainly the washing-up.[182] It appears that the ingredients of home-consumed meals of much of the lower-middle-class did not differ radically from those of the working class, but there was an added dimension of the greater involvement of men in the process.

Whatever generalisations are made about eating on the grounds of class, they are just that. What families ate was determined not just by income, region and the availability of ingredients but also by the expertise of the cook and the facilities available. Add to this list the differing palates and personal preferences of the individual and the possible dining permutations are virtually endless. Allowing for the variations between households, what we can be sure of is: a significant portion went hungry; there was an emphasis on starch, particularly bread; fat, fruit and vegetables other than potatoes were not heavily consumed; and meat was more of a flavouring than a central part of the meal, excepting Sunday dinners and feast days. Military provisioning, at least by 1914, aimed for a higher standard. The British Army felt the impact of increased nutritional understanding and new dietary ideas more quickly than the ordinary family, whose lives and meals were generally beyond the immediate reach of the machinery of the state. The military's main concern, a reflection of contemporary biochemical knowledge, was to provide sufficient energy values for its soldiers in order to ensure that they would be able to perform their duties properly. The delivery of calories, regardless of medium, was paramount.

The army's concentration on the purely physiological aspects of eating would be problematic to the rankers who joined after August 1914. Unlike the prewar regulars they were not drawn almost exclusively from the poorest and hungriest levels of society. For them, the army was not a destination of last resort but a choice or a compulsion created by extraordinary circumstances, a situation that created a different set of expectations from those of the peacetime soldier. This chapter has created a picture of the two eating worlds, the military and the domestic, that would confront each other in the mess halls of the New Armies. It was only reasonable for institutions such as the army to base its provisioning upon the available nutritional knowledge: feeding soldiers was, and still is, regarded as more of a science than an art. However, the powerful influences which accompany the biological aspects of eating did not disappear because a war was being fought. Food retained its power to signify a wealth of feelings and associations as well as convey energy values. Primarily, for many of the new rankers, food had been a fundamental signifier of maternal and uxorial care. Numerous working-class families struggled for survival and it was mothers and wives who were at the forefront of this domestic battle. It was the women who selected food purchases, cooked them and then fed them to their children and husbands, the former often fed from their mother's own plate, as Ellen Ross notes: 'meals signified maternal service'.[183] In a world where there was little time or perhaps ability to explicitly articulate affection within the family, food was used to demonstrate love. Flora Thompson recalled that, just before she left home for her first job, her mother gave her a specially baked treat to eat between meals. Food was short in their home and anything outside of the usual meals was a highly unusual occurrence and Flora, feeling the moment of the gift, 'had a sudden impulse to tell her mother how much she loved her . . . [but] all she could do was to praise the potato cake'.[184] Amongst the working class, love was often given and received through the medium of food and the rankers took this lesson, literally learned at their mother's knee, into the alien military world of the First World War.

Notes

1 H. Compton (ed.), *Edwin Mole: The King's Hussar. The Recollections of a 14th (King's) Hussar During the Victorian Era* (Driffield, 2008), p. 31.

2 Rudyard Kipling, in M. Harrison, C. Stuart-Clark and A. Marks (eds), *Peace and War: A Collection of Poems* (Oxford, 1989), p. 73.

3 John Green, *A Soldier's Life 1805–1815* (Wakefield, 1973), p. 71, and E.J.

Coss, *All for the King's Shilling: An Analysis of the Campaign and Combat Experiences of the British Soldier in the Peninsular War 1808–14* (PhD Thesis, Ohio State University, 2005), p. 144.

4 Alan Ramsay Skelley, *The Victorian Army at Home. The Recruitment and Terms and Conditions of the British Regular, 1859–1899* (London, 1977), p. 63.

5 Coss, *All for the King's Shilling*, p. 160.

6 See Green, *A Soldier's Life*, p. 149, for a description of theft from a bakery and also his unwillingness to catch the culprits out of sympathy for their plight as he also knew 'what it was to be hungry and scarce of provisions'.

7 Roy Palmer, *The Rambling Soldier: Life in the Lower Ranks, 1750–1900, through Soldiers' Songs and Writings* (Harmondsworth, 1977), pp. 79–81.

8 Palmer, *The Rambling Soldier*, p. 61.

9 Coss, *All for the King's Shilling*, p. 113.

10 Palmer, *The Rambling Soldier*, p. 63.

11 Horace Wyndham, *The Queen's Service* (London, 1899), p. 32.

12 National Army Museum (hereafter NAM), 2000-02-94, letter from John Rose, undated.

13 Drummond and Wilbraham, *The Englishman's Food*, p. 395.

14 Green, *A Soldier's Life*, p. 102.

15 Annabel Venning, *Following the Drum* (London, 2005), p. 122.

16 For example, see the Cabinet Committee on Food Supplies report of December 1916 which reflects the debates around the nature of 'vitamines', but does acknowledge their role in maintaining health. Cited in James Vernon, *Hunger: A Modern History* (Cambridge, MA, 2007), p. 92.

17 Reay Tannahill, *Food in History* (London, 2002), p. 227.

18 Hans J. Teuteberg, 'The Discovery of Vitamins: Laboratory Research, Reception, Industrial Production', in Alexander Fenton (ed.), *Order and Disorder: The Health Implications of Eating and Drinking in the Nineteenth Century and Twentieth Centuries* (Edinburgh, 2000), p. 257.

19 Colonel G.A. Furse, *Provisioning Armies in the Field* (London, 1899), p. 169.

20 Yuriko Akiyama, *Feeding the Nation: Nutrition and Health in Britain before World War One* (London, 2008), p. 118.

21 Furse, *Provisioning Armies*, p. 297.

22 See *Report of the Commission of Enquiry into the Supplies of the British Army in the Crimea 1856*, Drummond and Wilbrahim, *The Englishman's Food*, p. 396.

23 Furse, *Provisioning Armies*, p. 169, and Skelley, *The Victorian Army*, pp. 63–64.

24 Skelley, *The Victorian Army*, p. 64.

25 Roderick Floud, Kenneth Wachter and Annabel Gregory, *Height, Health and History: Nutritional Status in the United Kingdom, 1750–1980* (Cambridge, 2006), p. 54.

26 David Silbey, *The British Working Class and Enthusiasm for War 1914–1916* (Abingdon, 2005), p. 16.

27 Albert V. Tucker, 'Army and Society in England 1870–1900: A Reassess-

ment of the Cardwell Reforms', *The Journal of British Studies*, 2:2 (1963), p. 112.

28 Smurthwaite, 'A Recipe for Discontent', p. 81.

29 Tucker, 'Army and Society', pp. 110–112.

30 *The Army from Within*, by the Author of 'An Absent Minded War' (London, 1901), p. 7.

31 Floud et al., *Height, Health and History*, p. 305.

32 Skelley, *The Victorian Army*, p. 65.

33 Green, *A Soldier's Life*, p. 71.

34 T.H. McGuffie, *Rank and File. The Common Soldier at Peace and War 1642–1914* (London, 1964), p. 34.

35 Author of 'An Absent Minded War', *The Army from Within*, p. 9.

36 Green, *A Soldier's Life*, p.155.

37 Howard N. Cole, *The Story of the Army Catering Corps and Its Predecessors* (London, 1984), p. 34.

38 NAM 91-01-72, letter from 'MGF', 20 (?) December 1893.

39 Wyndham, *The Queen's Service*, p. 149.

40 Skelley, *The Victorian Army*, p. 65.

41 Colonel J.A. Boyd, *Supply Handbook for the Army Service Corps* (London, 1899).

42 Boyd, *Supply Handbook*, pp. 161–163.

43 Deborah Dwork, *War Is Good for Babies and Other Young Children. A History of the Infant and Child Welfare Movement in England 1898–1918* (London, 1987), p. 15.

44 Floud et al., *Height, Health and History*, p. 306.

45 Burnett, *Plenty and Want*, p. 271.

46 Tim Travers, *The Killing Ground. The British Army, the Western Front and the Emergence of Modern War 1900–1918* (Barnsley, 2003), p. 40.

47 Floud et al., *Height, Health and History*, p. 63.

48 J.M. Winter, 'Military Fitness and Civilian Health in Britain during the First World War', *Journal of Contemporary History*, 15:2 (1980) p. 214.

49 Silbey, *The British Working Class*, p. 43.

50 Alfred Plummer, *New British Industries in the Twentieth Century* (London, 1937), p. 229 and Andrea Broomfield, *Food and Cooking in Victorian England: A History* (Westport, CT, 2007), p. 18.

51 W.J. Reader, *Metal Box: A History* (London, 1976), p. 24.

52 Furse, *Provisioning Armies*, p. 292.

53 Plummer, *New British Industries*, p. 229.

54 Anthony Clayton, *The British Officer. Leading the Army from 1660 to the Present* (London, 2006), p. 119.

55 J. Othick, 'The Cocoa and Chocolate Industry in the Nineteenth Century', in D.J. Oddy and Derek Miller (eds), *The Making of the Modern British Diet* (London, 1976), p. 86.

56 Young, *Waggoners' Way*, p. 38.

57 A.F. Corbett, *Service Through Six Reigns: 1891–1953*, cited in McGuffie, *Rank and File*, p. 243.

58 McGuffie, *Rank and File*, p. 406.

59 NAM 1969-10-19, letter from A. Down, February 1900.

60 Young, *Army Service Corps 1902–1918*, p. 17.

61 *Report of Inspections at Certain of the Meat Canning Factories in the United States of America as Affecting the Supply of Preserved Meat to the British Army* (London, 1906).

62 Upton Sinclair, *The Jungle* (New York, 1906).

63 *Report of Inspections at Meat Canning Factories*, pp. 12 and 38.

64 *The Rifle Brigade Chronicle 1906*, Essex Regimental Archive, Chelmsford, Essex, pp. 66–71.

65 *The Essex Regiment Gazette 1910*, Essex Regimental Archive.

66 L. Margaret Barnett, 'Fletcherism: The Chew-Chew Fad of the Edwardian Era', in David F. Smith (ed.), *Nutrition in Britain: Science, Scientists and Politics in the Twentieth Century* (London, 1997), p. 20

67 David F. Smith, 'Nutrition Science and the Two World Wars', in Smith (ed.), *Nutrition in Britain*, p. 143.

68 McGuffie, *Rank and File*, p. 80.

69 Clayton, *The British Officer,* p. 109.

70 J.M. Winter, *The Great War*, pp. 34–37.

71 E.g. A.P. Herbert: see Reginald Pound, *A.P. Herbert: A Biography* (London, 1976); Frederick James Hodges, *Men of 18 in 1918* (Ilfracombe, 1988); Henry Williamson, *The Wet Flanders Plain* (Norwich, 1987).

72 McCartney, *Citizen Soldiers*, p. 41.

73 Baynes, in *Morale*, his analysis of the 2nd Scottish Rifles, noted that he could find 'no trace' of the gentleman ranker within that unit before 1914 and that they were largely confined to the cavalry.

74 Fuller, *Troop Morale*, p. 149.

75 Robert Roberts, *The Classic Slum: Salford Life in the First Quarter of the Century* (Harmondsworth, 1971), p. 13.

76 Richard Tames, *Feeding London: A Taste of History* (London, 2003), p. 188.

77 J.M. Winter, 'Military Fitness', p. 237.

78 A.L. Bowley and A.R. Burnett-Hurst, *Livelihood and Poverty. A Study in the Economic Conditions of Working-Class Households in Northampton, Warrington, Stanley and Reading* (London, 1915), p.47.

79 Philip Snowden, *The Living Wage* (London, 1912), p. 41.

80 Bowley, *Livelihood and Poverty*, pp. 18 and 35.

81 Bowley, *Livelihood and Poverty*, p. 79.

82 M. Loane, *The Queen's Poor: Life as They Find It in Town and Country* (London, 1998), p. 14.

83 Maud Pember Reeves, *Round About a Pound a Week* (London, 1913), p. 132.

84 Floud et al., *Height, Health and History*, p. 305.

85 Friedrich Engels, *The Condition of the Working Classes in England* (London, 2005), pp. 104, 107 and 165.

86 F.B. Smith, *The People's Health 1830–1910* (London, 1979), p. 177.

87 Annette Hope, *Londoners' Larder: English Cuisine from Chaucer to the Present* (Edinburgh, 1990), p. 131.

88 Betty McNamee, 'Trends in Meat Consumption', in T.C. Barker, J.C. McKenzie and J. Yudkin (eds), *Our Changing Fare: Two Hundred Years of British Food Habits* (London, 1966), p. 90.

89 Pember Reeves, *Pound a Week*, p. 97.

90 Barry Reay, *Rural Englands: Labouring Lives in the Nineteenth Century* (Basingstoke, 2004), p. 77.

91 D.J. Oddy, 'Working-Class Diets in Late Nineteenth-Century Britain', *The Economic History Review*, 23:2 (1970), pp. 314–315.

92 Oddy, 'Working-Class Diets', p. 319.

93 Oddy, 'Working-Class Diets', p. 320.

94 Pember Reeves, *Pound a Week*, p. 144.

95 Margaret Llewelyn Davies (ed.), *Life As We Have Known It: By Co-Operative Working Women* (London, 1982), p. 63.

96 J.M. Winter, 'Military Fitness', pp. 239–240.

97 Harris, *Good to Eat*, p. 240.

98 Ross, *Love and Toil*, p. 33.

99 Derek J. Oddy, 'The Paradox of Diet and Health: England and Scotland in the Nineteenth and Twentieth Centuries', in Fenton (ed.), *Order and Disorder*, p. 47.

100 Drummond and Wilbraham, *The Englishman's Food*, p. 331.

101 See discussion in D.J. Oddy, 'A Nutritional Analysis of Historical Evidence: The Working-Class Diet, 1880–1914', in Oddy and Miller (eds), *The Making of the Modern British Diet*, pp. 214–215.

102 *Supply of Food and Raw Material in Time of War: Royal Commission Report* (London. 1905), p. 39.

103 Burnett, *Plenty and Want*, p. 140.

104 Following the first Adulteration of Foods Act in 1860, *The Lancet* had regularly sampled the content of bread. In 1872, it calculated that 50 per cent of the loaves sold were adulterated but by 1884 this had been reduced to 2 per cent; see Tames, *Feeding London*, p. 192, and John Burnett, 'Trends in Bread Consumption', in Barker, McKenzie and Yudkin (eds), *Our Changing Fare*, p. 62.

105 James Munson (ed.) *Echoes of the Great War. The Diary of Reverend Andrew Clark, 1914–1919* (Oxford, 1985), entry dated 2.12.1916. The woman's grievance was also influenced by the further association of wholemeal bread with the black, rye bread eaten by the German enemy

106 R.H. Campbell, 'Diet in Scotland. An Example of Regional Variation,' in Barker, McKenzie and Yudkin (eds), *Our Changing Fare*, p. 58.

107 Pember Reeves, *Pound a Week*, p. 58.

108 P. Brears, M. Black, G. Corbishley, J. Renfrew and J. Stead, *A Taste of History: 10,000 Years of Food in Britain* (London, 1997), p. 275.

109 Pember Reeves, *Pound a Week*, p. 59.

110 D.J. Oddy, 'Food, Drink and Nutrition', in F.M.L Thompson (ed.), *The Cambridge Social History of Britain 1750–1950* (Cambridge, 1990), Vol. 2, p. 257.

111 Stephen Mennell, *All Manners of Food. Eating and Taste in England and France from the Middle Ages to the Present* (Oxford, 1985), p. 263.

112 Walter Gratzer, *Terrors of the Table. The Curious History of Nutrition* (Oxford, 2005), p. 106.

113 Flora Thompson, *Lark Rise to Candleford* (London, 1984), p. 29.

114 Angeliki Torode, 'Trends in Fruit Consumption', in Barker, McKenzie and Yudkin (eds), *Our Changing Fare*, p. 122.

115 Drummond and Wilbraham, *The Englishman's Food*, p. 379; although there was clearly a degree of truth in such fears, given the use of manure as a fertiliser and the unlikelihood of thorough washing prior to eating.

116 Coveney, *Food, Morals and Meaning*, p. 74.

117 Reay, *Rural Englands*, p. 77.

118 Elizabeth Roberts, *A Woman's Place. An Oral History of Working Class Women 1890–1940* (Oxford, 1984), p. 157.

119 Magnus Pyke, *Townsman's Food* (London, 1952), p. 163.

120 John K. Walton, *Fish & Chips & the British Working Class 1870–1940* (Leicester, 1992), p. 158.

121 Fiddes, *Meat*, p. 2.

122 Harris, *Good to Eat*, p. 26.

123 'lean meat provides the highest quality of protein and has a moderate fat content with desirable unsaturated fatty acid composition' in D.A. Booth, *Psychology of Nutrition* (London, 1994), p. 78, and Roy C. Wood, *The Sociology of the Meal* (Edinburgh, 1995), p. 5.

124 Tames, *Feeding London*, p. 7.

125 Burnett, *Plenty and Want*, p. 203.

126 Cited in Fiddes, *Meat*, p. 64.

127 Cited in Oddy, *A Nutritional Analysis of Historical Evidence*, p. 225.

128 Reay, *Rural Englands*, p. 76.

129 Robert Roberts, *Classic Slum*, p. 115.

130 Pember Reeves, *Pound a Week*, p. 56.

131 Broomfield, *Food and Cooking in Victorian England*, p. 87.

132 Boyd, *1899 Supply Handbook*, p. 28.

133 Elizabeth Roberts, *A Woman's Place*, p. 159; see also Anna Davin, 'Loaves and Fishes: Food in Poor Households in Late Nineteenth-Century London', *History Workshop Journal*, 4 (1996), p. 169.

134 Smith, *People's Health*, p. 207.

135 Reproduced in Reader, *Metal Box*, p. 1.
136 Broomfield, *Food and Cooking in Victorian England*, p. 18, and Laura Mason, 'Everything Stops for Tea', in C. Anne Wilson (ed.), *Luncheon, Nuncheon and Other Meals: Eating with the Victorians* (Stroud, 1994), p. 79.
137 Oddy, 'Working-Class Diets', p. 318.
138 Pyke, *Townsman's Food*, p. 130.
139 Logue, *Psychology of Eating*, pp. 268 and 130.
140 Alice Foley, *A Bolton Childhood* (Manchester, 1973), p. 26.
141 Julian Franklyn, *The Cockney: A Survey of London Life and Language* (London, 1953), p. 89.
142 Gerald Priestland, *Frying Tonight: The Saga of Fish & Chips* (London, 1972), p. 76.
143 Walton, *Fish & Chips*, pp. 164–167.
144 Elizabeth Roberts, *A Woman's Place*, p. 158.
145 Davin, 'Loaves and Fishes', p. 171.
146 John Burnett, *England Eats Out: 1830 – Present* (Harlow, 2004), p. 107.
147 Burnett, *England Eats Out*, p. 110.
148 Sir Noel Curtis-Bennett, *The Food of the People: The History of Industrial Feeding* (London, 1949), pp. 189–190.
149 Richard Church fondly remembered the taste of a 'baby's head' in an eating house on his first day at work – a 'baby's head' was a steak and kidney pudding. *Over the Bridge* (London, 1974), p. 238.
150 P. Mathias, 'The British Tea Trade in the Nineteenth Century', in Oddy and Miller (eds), *The Making of the Modern British Diet*, p. 91.
151 Boyd, *1899 Supply Handbook*, p. 166.
152 Burnett, 'Trends in Bread Consumption', in Barker Mekenzie and Yudkin (eds), *Our Changing Fare*, p. 62.
153 See Edith Whetham, 'The London Milk Trade, 1900–1930', in Oddy and Miller (eds), *The Making of the Modern British Diet*, p. 68, and Dwork, *War Is Good*, p. 97.
154 William Booth, *In Darkest England and The Way Out* (London, 1890), p. 62.
155 Robert Roberts, *Classic Slum*, p. 120.
156 George R. Sims, *How the Poor Live and Horrible London* (London, 1889), pp. 21–24.
157 Oddy, 'A Nutritional Analysis', p. 227.
158 Ross, *Love and Toil*, pp. 39 and 29.
159 Foley, *Bolton Childhood*, p. 26.
160 John Burnett, *Destiny Obscure: Autobiographies of Childhood, Education and Family from the 1820s to the 1920s* (London, 1984), p. 97.
161 Burnett, *Destiny Obscure*, p. 95, and see also Robert Roberts, *Classic Slum*, p. 117.
162 Davin, 'Loaves and Fishes', p. 172.
163 Flora Thompson, *Lark Rise*, p. 169.

164 Kathleen Dayus, *Her People* (London, 1982), p. 15.

165 Drummond and Wilbraham, *The Englishman's Food*, p. 409.

166 Burnett, *England Eats Out*, p. 115.

167 Davin, 'Loaves and Fishes', pp. 176–177.

168 Gerald Bennett, *Eating Matters: Why We Eat What We Eat* (London, 1988), p. 177.

169 *Report on Poor Law Schools 1873–4*, cited in Davin, *Loaves and Fishes*, p. 177.

170 Burnett, *Destiny Obscure*, p. 58.

171 Robert Roberts, *Classic Slum*, p. 117. Margaret Visser has suggested that, in addition to ensuring small children could reach the tabletop, standing may have been regarded as good for the child's digestion: *The Rituals of Dinner* (London, 1992), p. 49.

172 For example, 'Thank Gord fer me good dinner', Pember Reeves, *Pound a Week*, p. 89.

173 Davin, 'Loaves and Fishes', p. 168.

174 Geoffrey Crossick, 'The Emergence of the Lower Middle Class in Britain: A Discussion', in Geoffrey Crossick (ed.), *The Lower Middle Class in Britain 1870–1914*, (London, 1977), pp. 11–60. There is little, if any, attention to diet in other studies, including Lawrence James, *The Middle Class: A History* (London, 2006), David Lockwood, *The Black Coated Worker* (Oxford, 1989), and Alan Kidd and David Nicholls (eds), *Gender, Civic Culture and Consumerism: Middle Class Identity in Britain, 1800–1914* (Manchester, 1999).

175 D.J. Richardson, 'J. Lyons & Co. Ltd.: Caterers and Food Manufacturers, 1894 to 1939', in Oddy and Miller (eds), *The Making of the Modern British Diet*, p. 167.

176 Church, *Over the Bridge*, p. 75.

177 Paul Thompson, *The Edwardians* (London, 1992), p. 85.

178 George and Weedon Grossmith, *The Diary of a Nobody* (London, 2006), p. 92.

179 See Ina Zweiniger-Bargielowska, '"The Culture of the Abdomen": Obesity and Reducing in Britain, circa 1900–1939', *Journal of British Studies*, 44 (2005), pp. 239–273.

180 Grossmith, *Nobody*, a tricycle, p. 70.

181 J. Hammerton, 'The English Weakness? Gender, Satire and "Moral Manliness" in the Lower Middle Class 1870–1920', in Kidd and Nicholls (eds), *Gender, Civic Culture and Consumerism*, p. 169.

182 Paul Thompson, *Edwardians*, p. 86, and Church, *Over the Bridge*, p. 116.

183 Ross, *Love and Toil*, p. 27.

184 Flora Thompson, *Lark Rise*, p. 379.

3

First taste: eating in the home camps

Percy Stopher was born into a poor rural community, near Framlingham in Suffolk. He and his two cousins, George and Albert, worked as agricultural labourers before volunteering for the Western Front. Percy's first taste of army life was at a training camp near Hastings, where he spent almost six months converting his farming experience into skills more appropriate for an infantryman. During that time he wrote many letters home: to his parents, sister and cousin Ethel, to whom he appears to have been very close. The Stopher boys' education was limited, and Percy's correspondence was mainly a list of items he wanted posted to him and complaints about them being unforthcoming. However, in the midst of this emotionally opaque narrative, he gives us a glimpse of the bewilderment that his new life in the military engendered. He wrote to Ethel on 2 June 1915: 'we get very little food at times and at the best it is not very comely, I don't think you can realise what a change of life this is to me.'[1] The transformation of Percy's life was overwhelming, and it is hunger and eating that act as the point of reference through which his general distress and uncertainty are communicated.

On a practical level, his disappointment in the rations reflected the experience of many new recruits; food was frequently found wanting in both quantity and quality. But Percy's letter offers an insight into the wider significance of food to the new recruits. Food was a source not purely of physical energy but also one of psychological comfort. 'Comely' is an intriguingly feminine adjective to employ in a description of food, but it has an additional meaning of 'proper and seemly'. In the context of army rations, it indicated a set of associations that were far wider than the mere 'taste' or presentation of the meals. For Percy, military feeding lacked the peacetime eating attributes he so valued: food was scarce, it did not look or taste good, and perhaps just as importantly it was, as we shall see, unseemly. It was confusingly different from that to which he had been used and was all too often consumed in a rough and dirty mess hall surrounded by strangers. It was an environment that lacked all semblances of both proper table etiquette and domestic family life.

John Burnett claimed that 'for millions of soldiers ... wartime rations represented a higher standard of feeding than they had ever known before'.[2] His discussion of First World War food in *Plenty and Want* concentrates on the civilian diet and it appears that his perspective on the success of military provisioning was founded solely upon the stated calorie levels of the official ration scales. Burnett's view has been echoed by other historians, including David Silbey and Correlli Barnett, the latter believing that as 'one third of the British Nation lived their entire lives in the slums' the conditions of military service were relatively luxurious.[3] The difficulty lies in the concept or definition of 'feeding'. It is true that the army rations scales, as we will see, were higher in calories than the civilian diet of many of the new recruits, but this was not the sole criterion upon which the soldiers' satisfaction rested. The military judged itself to have discharged its duty to the ranks via the provision of a nutritionally sound diet, at least by the standards of the day. Men such as Percy Stopher, however, displayed considerable dissatisfaction with both their rations and the manner in which they were served and eaten, often regardless of their calorific value. There were times when the army failed to deliver the stated ration and the men's hunger was unavoidable and, of course, those occasions lodged in the men's memories in a way that successful provisioning did not. A key point at which army provisions were found most wanting was during the men's initiation into military life; the alienation and uncertainty that was common to men's first experience of their martial existence appeared to have been vented on the rations. The dismay at their new-found situation was expressed through a critique of provisioning, rather than complaints about the exhausting harshness of the drills or fearful intimations of what a future in the trenches held. The men could have complained about the discomfort of the boots, the stiffness of the uniform, the lack of sleep, the relentless drills, the myriad of regulations and orders that now governed every aspect of their lives and of course, on occasion, they did. And yet, it was the medium of food that was returned to repeatedly as the gauge by which their experience was measured. Sidney Mintz has described eating 'as a basis for relating oneself to the rest of the world', for these civilian soldiers in this new and alien environment, their dislike of its food was evidence of their inability to assimilate easily into army life.[4]

The rankers had been separated from their jobs, friends and families; they were segregated in training camps and struggled to incorporate themselves into the military. Ilana Bet-El describes the troubling rites of passage facing the civilian soldiers: the loss of a name to an army number, the uniformity of clothing, the unfamiliarity of the drill all contributed to the sense of alienation they experienced.[5] Bet-El explores the differing response to the military of those who volunteered in comparison to those who were conscripted. She states that, for the former, joining the army was 'an expression of personal desire'.[6] However, as Adrian Gregory points out, volunteering often had less to do with an act of free will than a response to extreme social pressure.[7] Bet-El suggests that conscripts had an expectation that the army should provide for all their physical needs, given that it was institutional compulsion that had forced them into a position of dependency.[8] In fact, the responses of the volunteers do not appear to have been radically different: they too had high expectations of the military, but for different reasons. They believed that, having willingly sacrificed their freedom, it was only just that the army should reward them with a proper level of care. Whether through choice or mandate, the new soldiers found themselves in a disturbingly unfamiliar world and sought the reassurance of decent living conditions.

Eric Leed has illustrated how the trauma of war experience 'often lay in a profound sense of personal discontinuity'.[9] For the rankers, meals were a thrice-daily indicator of this discontinuity, of the differences between civilian and military life. What and how men ate in the army camps was a constant reminder of what they had left behind: the accustomed foods eaten in a familiar environment with family or friends. The act of eating, its very repetition, generated an association with past acts of consumption; as Mary Douglas suggests, 'each meal carries something of the meaning of all the other meals'.[10] Whether it was a meal with a special resonance such as Christmas dinner or Sunday lunch or just an everyday breakfast, eating evoked memories of past meals, of different foods and alternative settings. The men had a fundamental expectation that proper food should be provided, given the sacrifices already made and the far greater ones that lay ahead. Rations in the camps were the recruits' first taste of life as a soldier and they carried with them far more than mere calorific concerns, bridging as they did the needs of both body and psyche. It was at this intersection between the physical and the emotional, the individual and the institutional, that men judged the success or failure of the army in fulfilling its part of the contract that had been made between them.

Feeding the new armies

The challenge the army faced in housing, clothing and feeding its recruits was enormous, particularly at the beginning of the conflict, when it was ill-prepared for the influx of new soldiers. In the early summer of 1914, the regular British Army consisted of 247,432 officers and men, against an authorised establishment of 256,798.[11] In the six weeks between 4 August and 12 September 1914, 478,893 men joined up, motivated by a complex cocktail of duty, patriotism, economic need and the pursuit of excitement.[12] By the end of the conflict, over 5,700,000 men, volunteers and conscripts had served in the army. The vast majority of these recruits had no peacetime military aspirations and their presence in uniform was as a result of war-engendered enthusiasms or state coercion. The challenge of victualling the vast numbers that rushed to enlist was enormous. The military's peacetime recruitment and training procedures were not ready for this overwhelming response to the request for manpower at the outbreak of the First World War.

In *Kitchener's Army*, Peter Simkins provides a detailed and revealing analysis of the lack of preparedness of the army to house, clothe, feed and train the volunteers. Whilst training could be deferred and uniforms improvised, the men would always need to be housed and fed. Accommodation was less problematic, as it could either be commandeered from those local homeowners who had a spare bedroom or improvised through the use of public buildings. When the space in private houses and corporation properties had been filled, tented camps were created in parks and fields. When Alfred Bigland, the MP for Birkenhead, headed the call for a creation of a Bantams regiment in the town in the autumn of 1914, he was unprepared for the response. Bigland had anticipated eleven hundred volunteers, but two thousand arrived; he managed to resolve the problem by converting the Town Hall into a dormitory.[13] It was more common to engage the help of the local population and at the start of the war as many as 800,000 new recruits were billeted in this way at any one time.[14] The provision of food, however, presented greater challenges: supplies were limited, logistics undeveloped and demand unrelenting.

The experience of Robert Cude, a twenty-year-old volunteer from south London, was typical. When Cude arrived at the depot in Canterbury on 9 September 1914, the army was unready to welcome him. He wrote in his diary, 'here, if we were expected, no steps were taken to receive us, and so no food awaited us and no sleeping accommodation'.[15] After a night spent in the open, he was sent to Purfleet where, as in Canterbury, there was little food and he spent an equally uncomfortable night in a hastily erected tent. After three days of makeshift accommodation and inadequate rations, he and his fellow recruits approached the officers and demanded that, as the army was unable to feed them, they should be allowed to return home. The authorities agreed and the men were given three days' leave, while steps were taken to improve the situation. Cude and his pals were infuriated by the army's failure in its duty. It was an anger that was further inflamed by the presence of armed sentries at the gates of the camp, there to prevent men leaving without permission; a forcible reminder of the freedom the hungry volunteers had willingly surrendered. Their country had called, they had answered and their trust in receiving the most basic of human requirements in return had proved misplaced.

A lack of preparation was evident across the country, from Deepcut Barracks in Aldershot where the one hundred and fifty places for new recruits were swamped by the arrival of one thousand men, to the Shrewsbury depot of the King's Shropshire Light Infantry, which had anticipated around two hundred and fifty newcomers but was sent fifteen hundred.[16] The army was unable to provide for the huge influx of men and the experience of Denis Willison, who volunteered in Derby in August 1914, was not unusual. He wrote in his diary that he spent the first week of his military life sleeping on a concrete floor and living principally on gooseberry jam.[17] Frederick Gale, who enlisted with the Essex Regiment at Warley barracks on 10 September 1914, kept a detailed diary for the first two months of his service. Gale was painstaking in his recording of the fine details of the meals he was served at his training camp. As a grocer by trade, he appears to have had something of a keen professional interest in the rations provided. He found the ubiquitous breakfasts of bread, margarine and tea unappetising and resented the long queues in the mess hall. The situation in his camp near Harwich was especially bad in his first days there. On one occasion the meat for dinner ran out completely, leaving those last in line to make do with potatoes and gravy.[18] Gale did note a gradual improvement, and three weeks later was able to write, 'We had a very nice dinner today. We had meat, potatoes and kidney beans. It was quite a luxury to get two vegetables.'[19] It seemed that, after initial struggles, camp organisation had risen to the challenge.

The situation had been at its most critical in the winter of 1914–15, when the influx of men was at its highest, but problems continued beyond the initial first rush. When Eric Hiscock enlisted in October 1915, lack of accommodation caused the adjutant to billet him at home, which had the distinctly unmilitary advantage of a cup of tea in bed from his father every morning.[20]

Although Hiscock was particularly fortunate, the soldiers who were billeted in private homes tended to have a more comfortable introduction to army life than those living in the training camps. M. Watcyn-Williams remembered with fondness the 'cosiness and semi-privacy of good billets', qualities rarely ascribed to barrack rooms.[21] Billeting was unpopular with the homeowners, whose patriotism did not appear to overcome their dislike of having unwanted guests forced upon them. The low esteem in which the regular army was held fed their reluctance. One new recruit remembered the lady of the house's exclamation of relief when he arrived and she discovered he and his roommates were volunteers: 'Oh! I thought you were common soldiers.'[22] Aside from the less institutionalised nature of the accommodation, there were dietary benefits too, with the continued availability of home-cooked food. The Mayor of Preston recalled that men who were billeted in the towns and villages could be more certain of their breakfast than those sleeping in barracks.[23] Some of the billeted men were fed in the local camps, but many ate all their meals at their billets, where food was prepared from supplies delivered to the households by the army. However, given that during the first winter of the war there were hundreds of thousands of troops in billets, the supply of food to households became a time-consuming and logistically challenging task. In addition, officers, such as Captain G. Christie-Miller, thought that delivering slices of bacon and slabs of meat to the billets was not only tedious but a task that was 'beneath the dignity' of soldiers.[24] The army reached similar conclusions and the procedures were changed in favour of an allowance being paid to the householder for the purchase of food. However, this system was open to abuse from those who collected the money, only to invest the bare minimum of it in food for their billettees.[25] The fairest and most cost-effective solution was for the army to feed the men itself and it embarked upon a programme of mass catering on a vast scale.

The purchasing of food was of critical importance. At the declaration of war, the army had moved swiftly to put into place the controls necessary to ensure that the military's priority in the food markets was clearly established. The assertion that military need ranked above that of the civil population was not unanimously acknowledged. When war was declared, a rash of panic buying broke out and food supplies came under pressure as people hoarded goods. A London journalist recorded, in a diary entry for the day after war was declared, the early closure of several food shops in his Clapham neighbourhood after they had been emptied by anxious shoppers.[26] H. Cartmell, Preston's Mayor, was compelled to issue a warning bulletin to the town, which stated 'we must condemn the selfishness, almost criminal, of those who have been appropriating the commodities of life to the detriment of the community'.[27] Many producers regarded the high prices on the home market as a far more attractive proposition than the filling of relatively low-priced army contracts. General S.S. Long, the head of the ASC, was quick to step in and forcibly clarify the priorities. When civilian contractors in Bristol and Liverpool were uncooperative, he requisitioned their meat supplies and informed the Parliamentary Financial Secretary at the War Office that an Act of Parliament must be passed that would enable the army to appropriate foodstuffs when necessary. The Member of Parliament concerned initially told General Long that this was impossible. When Long explained that he had already taken such action, the prospect of hefty compensation claims for the illegal seizure of foodstuffs proved a powerful incentive for the government and the demand was met that evening.[28]

Food disturbances in the training camps

The army had established its right of access to food supplies, but, although the principle had been accepted, it would take time for the necessary provisioning processes to be established and in the interim men still went hungry. Anger regarding food shortages was at the root of many of the acts of disobedience, both collective and individual, that were reported during the war. Hunger protests on the home front have been better documented, particularly later in the conflict when rising prices resulted in hardship for many families.[29] Less widely reported have been a number of instances where lack of food provoked disturbances amongst the soldiers, references to which can be found in the men's accounts. One of the earliest, and best-tempered, of such outbursts was described by Lieutenant-Colonel T.M. Banks and Captain R.A. Chell in their account of life with the 10th Essex. In the first days of the war, over a thousand new recruits arrived without notice at Shorncliffe Downs, where food supplies were limited. The hungry men became increasingly agitated, as they explained, 'We didn't come down 'ere to be blinkin' well starved. We came to fight Germans.' The officer in charge, a Captain Heppel, tried to persuade them that he was doing his utmost to obtain food for the unexpected arrivals. Fuelled by hunger, the men's anger continued until the frustrated officer declared 'Well, boys . . . if you don't believe that I'm doing my damnedest, I'm ready to fight each one of you in turn until you do.' His offer, although unable to address the volunteers' hunger, defused the volatile situation and the men began to laugh and gave a rousing cheer for the brave Captain.[30]

The 10th Essex's experience, atypically, ended in humour; other descriptions of similar situations found little cause for amusement. Incidences of indiscipline related to food were usually localised and resolved by the officers without recourse to the army's disciplinary procedures. However, a swift resolution was not always possible and a court martial ensued from a disturbance at Upwey Camp, Dorset, in November 1914. A sergeant had withheld cheese from the unit's rations and resentment erupted into a drunken brawl. During the violent incident, one soldier was shot and a Corporal Amey was injured when struck from behind with a 15 lb piece of cheese.[31] On occasion, it was local dignitaries rather than the army that stepped in to resolve the conflict. The inability of the military to meet the demands of the influx of men occasionally resulted in an organised street protest. H. Cartmell writes of how, on 11 September 1914, around two hundred and fifty recruits had marched through the town protesting their situation. The men carried a banner which read 'No Food, No Shelter, No Money' and demanded to be sent back home to their villages in south Wales. The new volunteers were miners, accustomed to good wages of around £2 per week, and they did not take kindly to the hunger, discomfort and poverty of Kitchener's Army. Cartmell, as Mayor, took the lead and he and his peers dealt with the situation themselves, rather than involve the police. The protestors were invited to the Town Hall, where they were treated to a good meal and had the opportunity to explain to the local dignitaries that the hardships caused by having been in Preston for two weeks without any pay. Arrangements were made by the Mayor and his colleagues and money was distributed to the men in the form of subsidies, to be repaid once the payment of official wages had been established.[32]

Regardless of problems with pay, it was sometimes the quality of the food alone that could act as a trigger for acts of protest. In 1915, at a rather spartan camp in Tidworth, Hampshire, the hungry recruits became convinced that the civilian contractors responsible for the catering were stealing their rations. One morning the sausages served at breakfast appeared to be off; this proved to be the final insult and 150 men reacted by placing the plates and sausages on their beds, standing to attention next to them and refusing to 'fall in' despite the NCOs' orders.[33] Food has a long tradition as a focal point for the expression of anger, as E.P. Thompson's work on the food riots of the eighteenth century so clearly illuminated. Thompson argued that food riots were not an irrational, spasmodic response to hunger, but a manifestation of a belief in the right of the hungry to be fed by those that had plenty.[34] In this military marketplace, the men were offering their labour, and ultimately their lives, to the army and they maintained the belief that this entitled them to certain rights, the chief of which was to be fed. The anger of new recruits, certainly at the start of the conflict, was fuelled by the knowledge that neither their officers nor the civilian population were compelled to go hungry. Shortages of food fired the men's sense of injustice and caused significant unrest.

At the outbreak of the war, food was not the sole source of the rankers' grievances; the disorganisation and lack of supplies were evident in matters of accommodation, uniform and weaponry. The army had a limited reserve of clothing and its suppliers were not equipped to cope with a massive increase in orders. Consequently, men were forced to wear their own clothes and boots; the latter presented a real problem in that the soles soon gave out and the new rankers were reduced to practising their slow marching on grass.[35] A national shortage of khaki resulted in uniforms of various hue and design, including the blue serge of the Post Office, a level of improvisation that was resented by many men. The new soldiers were keen to demonstrate their patriotism and felt it to be undermined by the rag-bag nature of their appearance, just as they resented rifle training with wooden weapons.[36] More seriously, inappropriate clothing compromised the men's health. The lack of army greatcoats and proper boots meant that men had no protection against the rain during exercises and parades. Wet feet and bodies would not have been such a problem had the men returned to warm, dry barracks, but the lack of accommodation meant that a cold, damp tent was the more likely option. The missing clothing and inadequate living conditions in many camps were likely to have been exacerbated by the poor diet, and the accumulation of factors resulted in a number of outbreaks of disease in the winter of 1914–15. A measles epidemic killed eighty-five men at Bedford, cerebral meningitis was rampant at Halton in Bucks, and pneumonia and pleurisy were widespread.[37] Increased rates of pneumonia were directly related to the army's inability to keep the men dry, and, by

January 1915, 1,508 cases had been recorded amongst men at the training camps, and of those 301 had died.[38]

Whilst problems of contagious disease continued throughout the war, an inevitable side-effect of large numbers living in close proximity, improvements in uniform provision and the rapid creation of barracks meant the men were less likely to contract pneumonia or pleurisy once the initial problems had been rectified.[39] Outbreaks of disobedience resulting from poor accommodation, such as that described by Oswald Sturdy, who was invited to join a strike in the South Wales Borderers against the inadequate tents, petered out.[40] An additional casualty of the initial overwhelming of the army's systems, as the volunteers in Preston had discovered, was the payment of wages. However, procedures were swiftly put in place and the men's pay, admittedly somewhat low, was soon being distributed regularly. Food was an issue that continued to exercise the men, even after the bulk of the army's supply procedures appear to have stabilised. Unlike training, uniform and accommodation matters, where short-term problems could be weathered, there was little margin for error in provisioning and it did not take long for a shortfall in food supply to make an impact.

Fulfilment of food promises?

Ironically, the prospect of regular and plentiful food may have been an incentive for some who enlisted: an opportunity to satisfy a hunger that was as much physical as it was patriotic. Certainly for the hungrier men, the Recruiting Sergeants' promise to the inhabitants of the Salford slums of the unparalleled treat of 'meat every day!' was seductive.[41] Popular recruiting songs extolled the virtues of the military diet:

> Come on and join Lord Kitchener's army
> Ten bob a week, plenty of grub to eat.[42]

The assertion that army rations were a key attraction rather raises the question that, if this were the case, why had the hungry men not joined up before the declaration of war? The army was not at full strength in the years preceding August 1914, so the option to enlist in the pursuit of meat had been present in peacetime. It would seem that, in ordinary circumstances, the rations were not sufficiently appealing to attract the men from their civilian freedoms, but the wave of patriotism and enthusiasm that swept the country at the declaration of war provided the extra impetus that tipped the balance in favour of enlistment. The excitement generated by the war had made the soldier an 'object of acclaim rather than derision'.[43] Men who might previously have preferred to live with hunger, rather than join the ranks of the unrespectable, changed their minds in the face of the general war fervour. In addition, the need for soldiers, inescapably pressing at the start of the war when the regular army was conspicuously failing in the retreat from Mons, meant MOs were likely to have been less exacting in their standards and were prepared to take the poorest and hungriest, who might well have failed the peacetime standard.

There is evidence that a number of the men who rushed to enlist at the start of the war *were* motivated by hunger. One hopeful recruit reported being pushed to the back of the enlistment queue in an office in Dundee by a crowd of eager unemployed men, who told him that he should make way for 'us lads wi'out jobs'.[44] George Coppard recalled that several of the men he enlisted with on 27 August 1914 were 'near-tramps', whose main interest was to get a hot meal.[45] Edward Casey, a new recruit from a particularly poor background, said he had volunteered in order to get some decent food and described himself as 'almost a dwarf' he was so under-nourished.[46] For many men, whilst they may not have been in quite the straitened circumstances of Casey, their new lives at least offered the prospect of the prized daily serving of meat. Robert Roberts writes that local recruits, returning home on leave from the camps, were 'Pounds – sometimes stones – heavier'.[47] H.T. Bolton, who enlisted in September 1914, wrote with satisfaction in his diary that his weight had increased from 9 stone 6¾ pounds to 11 stone during his stay at the training camp. Whether or not this was due to the ration alone was debatable, as he also noted that he left camp several times a week in order to get an adequate meal, in contrast to those which were served in the mess hall.[48] Some men, who volunteered at the outbreak of war into an unprepared and disorganised army with limited drills or exercise, lived lives of leisure and R. Clark wrote in his diary, 'I believe that with all the lying about we do, we must have gained pounds in weight.'[49]

The army's ration scales certainly appeared generous, particularly at the beginning of the war when all soldiers, whether at home or abroad, received the same amount of food. In August 1914, each man was entitled to around 4,200 calories a day, which included: 1 lb 4 oz of meat, the same weight of bread, 3 oz of sugar, 4 oz of bacon, 3 oz of cheese and 8 oz of vegetables. The scale was impressively precise. It began with the essential components of the men's diet – meat headed the list – and moved through the carbohydrate, fats and dairy to the condiments. Soldiers

Table 3.1 British Army daily ration scales, 1917–18 (Statistics of Military Effort of the British Empire, p. 586)

	Frontline *(4,193 calories)*	*Lines of communication* *(3,472 calories)*
Bread	16 oz	14 oz
Meat	16 oz	12 oz
Bacon	4 oz	3 oz
Vegetables	9⁶⁄₇ oz	8 oz
Sugar	3 oz	2 oz
Butter or margarine	⁶⁄₇ oz	1 oz
Jam	3 oz	3 oz
Tea	½ oz	½ oz
Cheese	2 oz	2 oz
Condensed milk	1 oz	1 oz
Rice	–	2 oz

were entitled to a daily twentieth of an ounce of mustard and one thirty-sixth of an ounce of pepper. However, the initial generous levels were soon amended as the army was quick to realise it could not sustain such supplies to all. On 21 September 1914, the ration was reduced for soldiers at home camps, while maintaining the higher levels for those on active duty abroad. The main areas of reduction were protein and fats; the meat ration was reduced to 1 lb, cheese to 1 oz and the supply of bacon halved. The army's account of provisioning explains that despite the difficulties in maintaining the nation's food supplies, adjustments were made only after careful consideration and the troops always received the best of what was available. In the case of cheese, the reduction in the ration was 'decided with the consent of the medical authorities', giving a scientific credibility to the change. The shortages in the supply of cheese resulted from the loss of Dutch imports, which were countered by the Board of Trade taking over all imports from New Zealand, Australia and Canada. Once the army's requirements had been fulfilled, the remainder of the cheese was passed to the civilian population.[50] The philosophy for differential reductions within the overall scale dependent upon the soldier's position was not made explicit, but was no doubt founded upon the belief that those under the greatest stress and pressure should receive the most plentiful food. The first reduction in 1914 signalled the start of a downward trend in the ration scales that was to continue throughout the war, influenced by prevailing food conditions, poor harvests and world shortages. The brunt of the savings were borne by the men in the home camps, who, by May 1918, found their daily meat allowance reduced to 8 oz. Even those in the front line trenches were affected, and found that their meat ration had shrunk from 1 lb 4 oz of fresh meat each day to 1 lb. The details of the daily scales for the last two years of the war are shown in Table 3.1.

The ration scales for 1917 are reproduced in the *Statistics of Military Effort of the British Empire* alongside those of other countries. The figures for the British Army compare relatively favourably with those of other nations. The best fed were the Americans, who received an extra 500 calories daily, in the form of increased fats and a daily allowance of 1 lb 4 oz of potatoes. The British meat ration equalled that of the Americans, and that figure of 1 lb 4 oz (meat and bacon combined) exceeded that of the other nations, most significantly the German which was just over half the figure at 10½ oz. The Anglo-Saxon emphasis on meat is clear, with the French, Germans and Italians all having larger bread issues than the British and Americans. The French field ration had a slightly higher calorie intake, which can be attributed to the daily distribution of 0.88 pint of wine, an addition of which many British soldiers were jealous.[51]

The records suggest that, while provision was made for the different ethnic groups that the War Office was responsible for feeding, such as the Sikh troops brought from India to serve on the Western Front, no allowance was made for special dietary requirements within the British Army. It appears that, for example, vegetarian soldiers, and Orthodox Jews, would have been compelled to become non-observant for the duration or have gone very hungry. An exception to this was the three Jewish Battalions of the Royal Fusiliers recruited in Palestine, who were specifically granted the right to kosher food by the War Office.[52] At least one vegetarian refused to compromise his views and managed to survive the war without resorting to flesh, noting that 'during my period of Army service I failed to consume at least half a ton of meat that was due to me in rations'.[53] However, this contributor to *Vegetarian News* was a doctor in the RAMC and, as will be seen in subsequent chapters, officers had far more flexible feeding arrangements than the men. Vegetarianism was not widespread throughout British society and the available evidence indicates that its proponents were almost exclusively from the middle and upper classes. Clearly, this was not a major problem amongst the rank and file soldiers, but the absence of kosher products is likely to have been a more significant issue.

Army cooking

In addition to the detailed ration scales, the army produced a manual that contained not only recipes for the cooks but a complete one-hundred-day menu schedule for use in the camps. The main aim of the plan was not so much to ensure a pleasing variety for the men, but to make certain that the cookhouses made the most economical use of ingredients. Following the menus ensured that the leftovers from one day could be readily included in the next day's dishes. The recipes in the publication, the *Manual of Military Cooking and Dietary Mobilization*, sound relatively enticing.[54] On closer examination, they prove, in the tradition of army food, to be variations on a single theme: the theme was meat, whether boiled, fried, stewed, braised, steamed or roasted. Even 'Sea Pie', which sounds like a welcome break for even the most ardent carnivore, proves to be meat stew with a pastry crust. The recipe for the optimistically named 'Fish Paste' is four tins of sardines mixed with eight tins of bully beef.

Many of the recipes appear decidedly unpalatable, and the *Manual* is based upon the assumption that the full range of foodstuffs would be available to the cooks. Ultimately, the variety of the menus and the official ration scale were undermined by the small print, which states that the army reserved the right to replace any item should the need arise. This it frequently did: for example, rabbit, although never officially included in the scale, was, according to army records, issued as an 'occasional substitute for the meat ration'. Statistics demonstrate that during the war, the army collected £123,192 from the sale of 5,649,797 rabbit skins, which suggests something a little more frequent than the official 'occasional'.[55] Rabbit, as indicated in the previous chapter, was a food eaten widely by the poor. The rankers presented with it, although they might have preferred steak, appear to have readily accepted the meat and it was not a significant cause for complaint. The substitutions that provoked the greatest outrage were hardtack biscuit for fresh bread and tinned bully beef for fresh meat. It was hard for even the best cook to make the greasy and salty bully taste like anything other than the oleaginous foodstuff it was.

When it came to making the most of the available ingredients, much depended upon the camp cooks; a talented and energetic team could really enhance the men's satisfaction with their meals. Unfortunately, talent and energy in the cookhouse were often in short supply and their competence was frequently called into question. The performance of the cooks is considered in greater detail in the following chapter, where it can be seen that disparagement of them was at its harshest on active service. At the front, their unpopularity was caused by a combination of both the poor meals they produced and their relative safety, or at least as it appeared to the front line infantryman. Nevertheless, anger concerning the cooks' failures is also apparent at the men's first point of contact with them in the training camps. Walter Holyfield of the 10th Essex complained in a letter to his mother from a camp in Aldershot, 'our cooks are manuals; they'll turn a lump of the finest steak into a rough chip of mahogany in no time at all'.[56] Criticism, although widespread, was not universal, and some men were more appreciative than Holyfield. Sid Liddell was very enthusiastic and described a meal of stewed rabbit and pork with stewed mixed fruits and custard provided by his unit's cooks, whom he regarded as 'really splendid'.[57] Even in the safety of the home camps, cooks held a position of considerable privilege, and their proximity to food supplies was a benefit much envied by other hungry soldiers. Cooks had access to whatever food was available and, aside from the personal benefits – whether to their stomach or pocket, as cooks were notoriously active on the food black market – it gave them a position of power over the men they were supposed to support. At its worst, this power assumed an air of brutality. F.A.J. Taylor was disgusted by the behaviour of a cook at his training camp. Unable to separate a large lump of dried dates, the man threw them up into the air above a group of hungry rankers, in order to enjoy the spectacle of the soldiers fighting over them.[58]

The scramble for food

The meals provided in the home camps tended to be of a higher standard than those served in France and Flanders, despite the fact that the rations were less generous. This was because the kitchens were static, the men came to the food, rather than the other way around and the lines of supply were at their shortest. As we have seen, the recruits' accounts contained plenty of criticism but also some fulsome commendations. In the middle ground, there were men like Charles Cook, who wrote home from a camp at Dover with the measured assessment that: 'the grub all along has been pretty fair'.[59] However, the actual content of the meals provided was only one factor in the rankers' determination of their acceptability. The circumstances in which they were consumed appears to have been given an equal importance by many of the novice soldiers. John Jackson, who volunteered in September 1914, recalled the struggle to get food for his first breakfast at a camp in Inverness Castle: 'It was simply a wild scramble, such as respectable people could not imagine, and a very rough introduction to army life. It was no use waiting til the scramble had subsided. That only meant we should get nothing, so, like hundreds of others had to, I scrambled for food.'[60] Jackson's concern was not merely the shortage of food but the rough behaviour required in order to secure any of it. The mess hall was the site of his first confrontation with, as he viewed it, the uncivilised nature of army life, in contrast to the 'respectable' existence that had preceded it.

Jackson's disgust was repeated in numerous soldiers' accounts; on occasion it was accompanied by a degree of bemusement. R. Gwinnell recalled his camp near Bristol: 'there seemed to me to be plenty of food, but this fighting one's next companion for a dinner, I could not understand for a long time'. His memoir does not indicate how he reached the understanding he suggests in the earlier passage, nor offer an analysis of the motivation behind the scramble for food that was freely available. Gwinnell's account suggests that it was matter of acceptance of the differences inherent in a military life rather than a particular insight into their origins. His brother Dick, who was in the same camp, was even more disgusted and after the experience vowed that he would never use the mess hall again, but Gwinnell's pragmatic response was: 'I pointed out that as we had joined the army the only thing was to get used to it, with all its unpleasant sides, and the quicker the better.'[61] Even in the presence of a sufficiency, it seems men were anxious that they might not be served and were prepared to push and shove in order to guarantee a meal. Speed was of the essence. Joseph Murray, who trained at a camp in Blandford, Wiltshire, noted in his diary that there was 'plenty to eat if you were not particular what you ate' but 'you had to be quick'.[62] Murray and his pals facilitated their speedy arrival at the breakfast table by sleeping in their uniforms, although this was a decision founded as much upon the temperature of their hut as it was on hunger. Fast eating in the mess hall was not new: it had never been a venue for leisurely dining and one nineteenth-century veteran had reckoned that ten minutes was usually enough time for dinner.[63] An educated, middle-class ranker, Frederic Keeling, was sickened by the behaviour and living conditions that he witnessed in his training camp, where '*l'homme moyen sensuel*' will fight for food when there is plenty to give everyone a good meal'.[64] Keeling describes the actual food as 'excellent': as this was in an article that he wrote for *The New Statesman*, his enthusiasm may have been coloured by the desire to present a positive view to those still waiting to enlist.[65] Ivor Gurney was appalled by camp existence and commented as he left for France: 'Thank God we leave camp tomorrow! In it we have suffered all the horrors of slum life.'[66] The fighting for food in the presence of sufficiency was perhaps indicative of the uncertainty of the world in which the new recruits found themselves, where the supply of the most basic of life's requirements was thrown into doubt. Perhaps, too, there was an element of masculine display in the behaviour; some recruits may have felt that visible aggression in any aspect of military existence was appropriate and indicative of how 'proper' soldiers behaved.

Initiation into the army was a period of, at best, struggle and discomfort and, at worst, distress and alienation. The training camp was central to this rite of passage. In the camp, men were segregated from their normal lives, in a liminal community. They were set apart from both the norms of civilian life and an ordinary military existence, in order that they might be prepared for their future as soldiers. Victor Turner's description of the liminal period in *The Ritual Process* reads like a template of life in the training camps: the requirements of passivity, humility, implicit obedience to instructors and the acceptance of arbitrary punishment without complaint.[67] Army life and its expectations were impressed upon the new recruits at the meal table, as well as on the drill square and the firing range. The food traditions of the army, from the free-for-all of the barrack dining hall to the complex protocol of the officers' mess, reflected the significance of eating as a central factor in the establishment of a military identity. Arnold van Gennep wrote: 'the rite of eating and drinking together . . . is clearly a rite of incorporation'; in the army it also functioned, at least initially in the training camps, as a rite of separation.[68] The shock many rankers experienced at the uncouth behaviour in the mess hall, a roughness that was not directly related to the quantity of food available, helped to disengage them forcibly from their civilian past. Forty years later, a soldier remembered his own National Service as a time of crisis, but believed that, if ordinary men were to be rapidly converted into good soldiers, 'you must first strip them of their ordinary manhood – and regular bullying and humiliation do that faster and more efficiently than other means'.[69] The eating rituals, together with the stark living conditions and the harsh instructors, were an integral part of the ordeals and humiliations which effected the dissolution of their previous status and the creation of their new identity as soldiers. Situations in the training camps where men had to fight for the fundamentals of life, such as food, forcibly distanced them from the behaviour and customs of their earlier civilian existence.

The soldiers' accounts indicate that concerns regarding uncivilised behaviour at mealtimes, such as those of Ivor Gurney and Frederic Keeling, were not the prerogative of recruits from middle-class homes. It was probable that men from the roughest working-class backgrounds found little to fear in camp life. Their civilian existence was likely to have prepared them for a cut-throat environment, where it was 'every man for himself, the survival of the slickest'.[70] For many men, however, military life bore little resemblance to that which they had known before. J. McCauley, a working-class man from the Isle of Man, describing how he felt at the end of his initial training, wrote of his camp experience, 'I had grown hard ... my hold on the civilisation and the ordered life I had been used to was weakening'.[71] Indeed, such a loosening of the bonds of civilisation was necessary if men were to do the uncivilised and disordered things that war demanded of them. John Jackson, whose 'scramble' for food at Inverness was quoted above, experienced the shortage of adequate provisions at two levels. Firstly, his sense of justice was roused by the army's inability to fulfil its duty and feed him. Secondly, he was angered, perhaps to an even greater degree, by his forced reduction to brutish behaviour in order to get any food at all. Matters did not improve at his next camp in Aldershot, where, he wrote: 'We became more like animals than humans, and only by scrambling and fighting like dogs were we able to get food to eat'.[72]

Jackson's experience was shared by George Coppard, who wrote shortly after his arrival at his training camp, 'I realised that I had left the simple decencies of the table at home. One had to hog it or else run the risk of not getting anything at all.'[73] C. Jones was equally disgusted and wrote to his wife: 'I had to use my fingers for the meat and potatoes and drink the gravy out of the plate.'[74] It is not surprising that food and the manner of its consumption should have become the focal point for concerns of justice and respectability. The disgust that many soldiers experienced in the grubby rapacity of the mess hall was evidence of the importance of proper modes of eating. Table manners have been described as 'signs of our renunciation of the savage within us'.[75] The pressures and expectations of war made the visible signs of a more civilised and gentler environment especially important. The symbolism of knives and forks has been identified as playing a critical role as a buffer between the individual and the frightening and uncontrollable events circling around him. Claude Lévi-Strauss asserts that eating utensils 'moderate our exchanges with the external world and superimpose on them a domesticated, peaceful and more sober rhythm'.[76] For the new recruits, the desire for moderation of the alien military world was great and the loss of peaceful domesticity profoundly felt.

Table manners

The work of Norbert Elias further illuminates the importance of table manners as a set of rituals that separate man from the animals; to ignore them is to behave like 'wolves or gluttons'.[77] Interestingly, Elias notes how conditions in the trenches enforced a breakdown of peacetime taboos: for example, eating with hands or knives only, rather than the full battalion of cutlery. He writes, 'the threshold of delicacy shrank rather rapidly under the pressure of the inescapable situation'.[78] *In extremis*, table manners were abandoned, but Elias does not fully explore the distress many soldiers felt at their loss. Rather, he focuses upon the fragility of such refinements, as if they were willingly swept away by men who regarded them as unnecessary constraints. In fact, their absence was frequently mourned and the men's longing for spoons, forks and table coverings rather proves Elias's proposition regarding the power such accoutrements had to signify civilisation. Interestingly, Elias identifies a 'close parallel between the "civilising" of eating and that of speech'[79] – a relationship manifest in the men's accounts of the initial shock of army life, where swearing and eating were the twin cornerstones of their complaints. F.E. Noakes hated the 'army language' at his training camp.[80] George Herbert Hill was initially terrified by the aggressive language of his Sergeant, who 'was constitutionally incapable . . . of speaking without coming out with fearful oaths'.[81] The coarse language remained a constant of army life and Hill notes that the new recruits not only became inured to hearing it but rapidly began to use it themselves.

Dirty mess halls and inadequate cutlery, like swearing, appeared to be constant features in the military and were commented upon by new recruits for the duration of the conflict. Soldiers such as George Coppard and John Jackson joined up in the late summer of 1914, when the quantity of the rations, regardless of their quality and variety, was severely compromised. Whilst the supply of food improved after the initial problems, the shocking contrast between mealtimes at home and the mess halls remained a concern for recruits throughout the war.

Norman Gladden trained in 1916 and remembered that, whilst the food was adequate, the crockery and tables were dirty and 'the atmosphere stank of stale food and crowded humanity. It was not a place to dally in.'[82] Frederick Hodges, who joined up in the winter of 1917, commented that 'table manners were non-existent' in his training camp.[83] Frank Gray, another 1917 recruit, recalled, rather superciliously, the need to wipe one's plate with bread 'in order to prevent a collision between cold mutton grease and hot plum-duff'.[84] The unalterable unpleasantness of the mess hall indicates that the quantity of available food, as experienced in the opening months of the war, was only part of the problem. The lack of cleanliness of plates and crockery was much commented upon, and occasionally the subject of humour as a postcard from the popular series 'Sketches of Tommy's Life' demonstrates. Soldiers in camp are shown wiping their cutlery on the ground and the caption reads 'You clean your knife and fork by shoving them in the sand, here at Base, It's much better than washing them.'[85]

For most men it was not amusing and the indignity of being forced to eat in an improper fashion disturbed and angered them. The revulsion expressed by the First World War rankers was not new and it was not purely a function of either the weight of numbers or the seeping brutality of the conflict. Soldiers, it seemed, had always eaten like this, and it had traditionally caused offence to the raw new recruits. In 1890, Horace Wyndham had been shocked by his comrades cutting meat on the bare table and using their fingers in such a way as to render cutlery 'almost superfluous'.[86] An abandonment of the tools that permitted men to transcend animal eating to a state of civilised dining had always been a shocking attribute of army life.

The concerns regarding the lack of propriety were common, implying perhaps more elaborate domestic dining arrangements than historians of the prewar working classes have described. The lower-middle-class rankers, many of whose civilian lives had been predicated upon their class ethos of 'keeping up appearances', were no doubt used to a neatly laid table and proper use of the cruet, but such refinements were beyond the reach of the poorer working-class families. Evidence suggests it was the attempt, the actual ambition, to eat respectably that was important, not necessarily its successful execution, against which lack of income frequently militated. Many of the rankers, although they might have known hunger, would also have experienced the chronic struggle to sustain 'respectable behaviour' in the face of it. Ellen Ross in her research into the families from which many of the recruits came, wrote of the importance of the manner in which meals were presented: 'if the food was served and eaten properly, [it signified] respectability for everyone at the table'.[87] As described in Chapter 2, social researchers such as Mrs Pember Reeves had commented upon the importance placed upon table manners in many poor households. Flora Thompson remembered how 'good manners prevailed' at the meal table: other than 'please' and 'thank you', children were expected to eat in silence; a tranquillity that must have contrasted sharply with the rough noise of the mess hall.[88]

Consequently, the scrum at army mealtimes, where at its worst men might have to fight for food, was, for many new recruits, the antithesis of their prewar experience. Although not for all. Kathleen Dayus, born into a very poor and deeply unrespectable Birmingham family in 1903, described her first hop-picking trip when, confronted with the laden tea table provided by the farmer's wife, 'we all made a mad dash for the food ... what we couldn't eat we filled our pockets with for later.'[89] A number of the rankers' disapproving, or sometimes shamefaced, accounts suggests that some of the men may have reacted as Dayus did to her sumptuous tea when confronted with army rations; the sight of unfamiliar plenty triggered a reflex survival mechanism. Hunger had not made the poorest sanguine about the guarantee of future meals; rather it had impressed upon them the need to secure food supplies as decisively as possible, whenever they became available. Interestingly, this reaction has been confirmed by the results of a 1961 research project on children's relationship with food. It was found that, for those brought up in homes where it was scarce, food provoked feelings of anxiety and a sense of deprivation. Children with the possibility of hunger displayed a greater propensity to hoard surpluses whenever they could. The results also suggested that those raised in homes where food was abundant and their food needs were easily gratified developed a psychological predisposition to share food.[90]

The objectivity of modern researchers may have determined a certain set of behaviours, but the accounts of the First World War recruits passing judgement on the unsettling behaviour that surrounded them at mealtimes seem to have arrived at a different conclusion. Many rankers believed that the very fact that food had been in short supply at home was the key to sharing it fairly, of it having been distributed in the visibly equitable manner they so fondly recalled. It is probable that the men, both in their actual experience and in their memories of it, tended to imbue family life with a level of comfort and respectability it may not have had in actuality, but was to develop later in contrast to army feeding. R. Gwinnell, when confronted with men fighting for food in his camp 'like pigs at the trough', recalled, 'however little food we had at home . . . it was always shared to each one to the minutest fraction – and it had to be eaten in the proper fashion of course'.[91] Gwinnell's recollections support historians' assertions that working-class life provided good training for the army; a man from such a background would have experienced a certain degree of material deprivation and would also have been used to sharing limited resources.[92] The clear and accepted rationale that underpinned the sharing of the family's meals may have helped to mitigate any unrelieved hunger that followed them; at least the hungry boy or young man knew that his discomfort was shared in equal part by the other members of his family – although, as noted in the preceding chapter, a hungry man was a less common feature of working-class life than a hungry woman or child, given that the working male usually received the best food. Therefore, for some recruits, it may have been that the contrast between home and the camps was especially shocking because of the loss of the privileges to which they had been accustomed at family meals. The transfer to the wholly masculine world of the army may have found the men unprepared for the enforced equality of mealtimes, where they no longer held the elevated position in the food chain that had been conferred upon them by their mothers and wives in civilian life.

The unrelieved masculinity of the mess hall was an additional unfamiliar aspect for the recruits; there was no mother or wife present to impart an ameliorating femininity to the proceedings.[93] Indeed the absence of women may have been strange for army regulars as well. Before the war, it had been common practice for soldiers' wives and children to live with them in a blanketed-off corner of the barrack room. In addition, the women frequently cooked, as well as laundered and mended, for the room's other occupants in exchange for accommodation and a share of the rations.[94] For the majority of First World War rankers, given their age profile, it was mothers, rather than wives, that were missed. A good number of the volunteers were young; a significant group of them, like the sixteen-year-old George Coppard, were below the official age of enlistment and found themselves in the training camps after a knowing Recruiting Sergeant had advised them, following an initial refusal, to 'come back tomorrow when you're eighteen'. Immaturity, particularly when combined with a sheltered civilian working environment, made the alien testosterone of the training camps very unsettling. The junior clerk George Herbert Hill, another underage recruit, found the sight of men ladling the stew out 'roughly' very off-putting and said that this, together with the strong, stewed tea and 'too thick' slices of bread, 'compared oddly with ... mother's housewifely care'.[95] The lack of familiarity with the meals, their setting and preparation was problematic. Charles Darwin, credited with initiating the psychological interest in the origins of disgust, commented that 'it is curious how readily this feeling is excited by anything unusual in the appearance, odour or nature of our food'.[96] For the new recruits, much was unusual, not least the presence of men in the kitchen. Walter Holyfield described the cooks to his mother as 'manuals' and this picture of unskilled labourers misplaced added to the soldiers' uneasiness. Cooking was not men's work, and the juxtaposition of what for most men had always been two separate worlds was unsettling. Masculine hands touching the food were inappropriate. Paul Rozin has explored the 'law of contagion', how those preparing food can irredeemably contaminate it: 'when someone you don't like touches your food, they are "in" it somehow'.[97] In *Other Ranks*, W.V. Tilsley describes the disgust evoked by the 'filthy fingers' of an army cook dispensing the breakfast bacon by hand – a disgust that reached new heights when later diners noted that the man's hands had become 'pinkly, greasily clean' after regular dips into the fat-filled bacon pan.[98] For the rankers, food preparation had generally been the responsibility of the familiar, feminine figures of wives and mothers; now the provenance of their meals was uncertain, created by men they did not know and undermining their confidence in the safety of its consumption.

Food and privacy

Almost everything about army eating was unhappily different for the new soldiers, and for some, even if the mess hall had been clean, the crockery and cutlery in place, the dining companions polite and the rations tasty, the requirement to eat in the presence of large numbers of other men would have been disturbing. Anna Davin's exploration of the negative effect that institutional feeding had on children's appetites was discussed in Chapter 2; it is an impact that the new soldiers may well have experienced. Eating with anyone other than family appears to have been problematic for many of the working class and for some their homes were not open to visitors at all. Kathleen Dayus recalled her mother would not 'have any neighbours in our house unless it was essential. She said they only came to see if you'd got more than them', and the 'more' for Dayus's mother referred to food as well as possessions.[99] Whilst this may have been the main point of entertaining at home for the middle and upper classes, those with little did not wish to advertise their deficiencies, even to those who were in a similar position. Concerns in this area were not related purely to the embarrassment that poverty could engender; Robert Roberts observes that, when there was plenty, 'many families had queer inhibitions about the very process of eating'; meals would be served only when any visitors had left and sometimes the door would be locked and left unanswered until the food had been cleared away, and that men especially did not like to be observed eating.[100] As described in Chapter 2, employers sometimes provided a room where food from home could be reheated and eaten by their employees. The North-Eastern Railways Company had such a facility and its long dining tables were split into individual places with ten-inch-high dividers, in order that the men could eat in relative privacy. John Burnett attributes this desire for seclusion to a reticence regarding the quality of the meal rather than any embarrassment at eating in public, although, it is difficult to see how the two could be separated.[101] Gerald Bennett has offered an anthropological reason for the preference for private dining. Our hominid ancestors were most vulnerable at the moment of eating as they were static and the smell of dead flesh attracted predators. Bennett suggests that human's primitive anxieties and ambivalence about eating in public ensure that when eating out we are still drawn to public restaurants with cave-like dining rooms, offering an atmosphere of privacy and preferably flickering candles, whose flames evoke the protection of the prehistoric fires.[102]

The privacy associated with mealtimes may have a connection with the long-acknowledged link between food and sex, which together have been regarded as at the centre of the 'problem of pleasure' since antiquity.[103] The working classes may not have had many opportunities to indulge in the sensual pleasures of the table, but they did appear to afford eating a similar degree of intimacy to that which they gave to sexual activity. Meals in the home were both discreet and discrete: to be eaten by the family alone, away from the eyes of strangers. Limited crockery and cutlery meant the items often had to be shared; siblings might drink from the same cup and mothers feed children from their own plates. The necessity of sharing combined with the intimacy of the family environment to make such actions acceptable. The camp mess hall was the antithesis of family togetherness and its occupants were forced to eat in large groups, with little influence over their choice of dining companions. One of the important freedoms the men had surrendered in the army was that of choosing with whom they ate. It was only later in the lines of the Western Front that they were able to reassert the right to determine their own commensality, in the small groups of pals they formed to share rations and parcels.

Sources indicate that not all the men ate in the mess halls. B. Britland, whose training camp contained a significant number of regulars, wrote home that 'the new recruits go into the large dining room for their meals, whilst the old soldiers have theirs in the barrack rooms'.[104] It may be that the regulars wished to keep their distance from the overwhelming numbers of civilian soldiers, whose lack of military bearing must have been irritating to the old hands, but perhaps they too found the massed dining offensive. The canteen systems discussed in Chapter 2 that the most forward-thinking units, such as the Rifle Brigade, had introduced shortly before the war were not universally implemented. Many of the regulars would have been accustomed to eating in smaller groups in the barrack rooms where they also lived and slept. A number of late nineteenth- and early twentieth-century photographs demonstrate the cramped conditions of rankers' accommodation, and depict men eating meals on their beds as the table space in the centre of the rooms was usually inadequate for all the occupants to sit and eat at the same time.

Rankers' mess halls did not feature in every new camp. Lord Kitchener believed the costs of hutment, which were estimated as £15 per man, were far too high and ordered that every possible reduction should be made. One way in which the authorities acted to save money and speed completion was the elimination of mess halls from many establishments, facilities that Kitchener regarded as a 'luxury'.[105] Picture postcards, such as that in Figure 3.1, taken in the Eastbourne area in March 1915, illustrate the alternative to the mess hall. The group of men are eating crowded around a table in a hut, where most of the space is taken up by beds, bedding, packs and uniforms. To eyes accustomed to more spacious living conditions, it might be interpreted as an environment hardly conducive to civilised consumption. In fact it was both a more traditional approach to army dining, and for many of the new soldiers its relative privacy may have been preferable to the situation in the more populous mess hall.

The men were deprived not just of the dining environment to which they had been used in civilian life but also of the familiar food they had shared at home. The difference in diet was often particularly unsettling at breakfast time. Walter Holyfield wrote to his mother from his camp in Aldershot of the horrors of tripe and onions for breakfast. Holyfield was hungry but was appalled by strangeness and unfamiliarity of army food:

3.1 Hut dinner, Eastbourne area, 1915

'You know how they change our grub about from saveloys for breakfast to fish and plums for dinner.'[106] M. Watcyn-Williams vividly recalled the anger he felt at his barracks, when he 'was one of hundreds who refused to parade because of the stinking tinned herrings supplied for breakfast'.[107] Watcyn-Williams's complaint is an interesting example: fish for breakfast is a British tradition and a middle-class man such as he was likely to have eaten kippers, that is smoked herrings, for breakfast in his civilian life. Herrings in their unsmoked state, however, were regarded as anathema, yet scientifically and nutritionally the foods are very similar. But for the new recruits they were deemed poles apart. The difference in response may be related to the presence or not of the smoking process, which gives a fish a longevity absent in its fresh state and acts as a reassurance to its consumer that the food will not have a deleterious impact on his digestion. Fish is one of nature's most perishable foods and has a 'fragile freshness'. Refrigeration has only a partial ability to extend its life, given its relatively limited effect on the enzymes and bacteria that make good fish go bad.[108] It is also noteworthy that both of the soldiers were criticising camp breakfast, the meal that is perhaps most sensitive to one's eating equilibrium. Mrs Beeton declared that 'the moral and physical welfare of mankind depends largely on its breakfast'.[109] While she could hardly be accused of understatement, in a more measured vein modern nutritionists have emphasised breakfast's importance as the dietary foundation of the day's activity. Its significance is reflected in the comments of the soldiers: for example, in a letter home, Ernest Boughton described a good breakfast as a 'magic rite, it makes the world paradise again!'[110] The satisfaction of the hunger with which many men must have awoken given that tea or supper was a negligible meal in most camps, was a matter for celebration. Margaret Visser asserts the inappropriateness of 'anything fancy' for breakfast as we feel 'fragile and unadventurous just after the daily trauma of getting out of bed'.[111] In addition, the men's usual civilian breakfasts of bread and tea would have left them ill-prepared for the more esoteric early morning menus served in the mess halls.

The new soldiers appear to have been in a permanent state of 'fragile unadventurousness' when it came to trying new food, regardless of the timing of the meal. The traditional narrowness of the working-class diet has already been explored, and its restrictive nature underpinned the culinary conservatism displayed by the men. Just as the institutionalised children of whom Anna Davin writes longed for familiar food, so the recruits in their unsettling new environment found their longing for 'comfort food' increased.[112] Clearly the new and relatively brutal conditions of the training camps were exactly the type of surroundings guaranteed to reinforce a longing for familiar dishes. Food had the potential to serve as a commonly understood and reassuringly prosaic language in the men's communications with their families, as will be seen in Chapter 6. However, food's role as a signifier of emotional need as well as a physiological necessity imbued it with an additional register, particularly between sons and their mothers given the fundamental bond that had once tied them together as child and nurturer.[113] In their letters home soldiers tended to be circumspect in their criticism of army life, unwilling to exacerbate the worrying absence from their families further by drawing attention to something as profoundly distressing to a mother as a hungry child.

The expression of dissatisfaction with rations in terms of their unfamiliarity, as in Walter Holyfield's letter describing tripe for breakfast, was less perilous than the revelation of shortages, which would make hunger explicit. Soldiers were often keen to reassure their mothers that they were eating well in their new lives. B. Britland described his camp Christmas dinner at great length and in some detail, even down to which parts of the turkey he ate ('leg and a bit of body'). He signs off by assuring his mother that 'I am still keeping in the best of health and getting as fat as a pig', an unflattering but no doubt soothing image to a concerned mother.[114] Charles Cook wrote at considerable length to his parents describing the food in his camp at Dover:

The dinners have mostly been stew or roast beef with potatoes and haricot beans or peas, and the last two days we have had cabbage. The breakfasts have been bacon, liver, cold bacon, tinned fish (this has now stopped though), and kippers. Tea is either jam or cheese with bread, and today we had some cake. I have bought fruit (apples, bananas and walnuts) cocoa, and tea and cakes regularly.[115]

Cook's experience was considerably better than many soldier's, and he may well have been pleased by the curtailment of tinned fish for breakfast that so aggrieved Watcyn-Williams. The level of detail in his description of the food is striking; Cook's mother must have been comforted by the knowledge her son was well provided for by the army. A conscientious mother would also note her son's own attention to his eating and be reassured that he was sufficiently aware of the need for a healthy diet to purchase essential items not forthcoming in the ration, such as fruit. Cook's letter announces both the army's success in fulfilling its obligations to the men and also his own ability to ensure proper eating for himself whilst away from the care of his family.

Complaints about the ration

If, unlike Cook, the men were unhappy with their rations they had the opportunity to communicate their dissatisfaction to the army hierarchy. In general, the army did not welcome criticism from its men, but food was an area in which grievances could legitimately be registered. Statistics record that between 1915 and 1918, 677 complaints were received 'from all sources regarding soldiers' messing'.[116] The complaints were collected from all of the army's establishments and outposts and not solely from the training camps in Great Britain, but it could be argued that the majority would have come from the home camps for two reasons. Firstly, soldiers on active service generally had more pressing concerns with which to occupy themselves and, secondly, the men were likely to be more critical of the army's efforts at the beginning of their service. During the rites of passage, meals were judged more closely against civilian eating standards, as family meals were still in recent memory. Army training and service were designed to desensitise the new soldiers and, as their military experience grew, the men became less resistant to both the actual food served in the mess hall and the shocks and discomforts of this strange new life.

Whilst the army's formal process for the collection of complaints gives the impression that grievances concerning food were if not welcomed at least tolerated, that was not the experience of the majority of soldiers. George Coppard recalled the daunting appearance of the Orderly Officer and Orderly Sergeant in the mess hall after a meal: 'the Sergeant would breathe fire, smack his cane on a table and yell out, "Any Complaints?"'[117] It took a brave, if not foolhardy, man to risk the wrath of the NCOs and officers and express dissatisfaction with the food. If a man were sufficiently courageous to voice his opinions, he knew he was unlikely to be offered a resolution. The response to grievances was generally unhelpful. A.E. Perriman recalled a man at his training camp complained to the Colour Sergeant that the breakfast tea was disgusting, as it was served with 'grease from the previous meal floating on top'. The NCO's response was: 'there's nothing wrong with that' and he then proceeded to stir the offending tea with his fingers, a final insult that provoked the complainant's pal to throw his own basin of tea into the Sergeant's face and thus precipitate a fist fight.[118]

Both Coppard and Perriman volunteered at the beginning of the conflict, when complaints regarding food were most numerous. A detailed breakdown of the statistics is not provided, other than by year, which demonstrates a steady decline over the war, from 359 in 1915 to 58 in 1918. The overall decrease in complaints may have been indicative of the steady improvement in army food from the initial, disorganised days at the outbreak of the war. New recruits in the training camps were more likely to complain than the experienced soldiers on active service, but perhaps the new recruits' expectations of army life were lowered as the war progressed. Certainly at the start of the conflict, volunteers may have had their expectations of living conditions in the army raised by the public acclaim that accompanied their exodus from civilian life. A.E. Perriman describes marching through Newport in August 1914, between crowds of cheering townspeople: they 'were being treated as national heroes'.[119] P.H. Jones, who volunteered at the same time in Hertfordshire, said that the men were showered with gifts of food by the local populace: 'A gentleman in Watford bought out a whole fruit stall as it stood, and told the lucky coster to give us the lot.'[120] Spontaneous demonstrations of enthusiasm and generosity such as these disappeared as the war dragged on and later recruits did not have their sense of importance, and possibly entitlement, inflated by such overt admiration and gratitude. In addition, the chains of command and complaint, which were pretty unreceptive to volunteers, were even less likely to tolerate grievances from the conscripts who arrived from January 1916 onwards. Helen McCartney recounts the story of a new conscript, who on one of his first visits to the mess hall complained that his bowl of tea was cold, to which the Sergeant Major replied that this was unsurprising as it had been waiting for him for two long years.[121] Whatever the differences between the expectations of the conditions of service held by volunteers and conscripts as discussed earlier in the chapter, the sharp decline in complaints over the war is perhaps an indication of the army's lack of interest in the criticisms of the latter.

In a similar manner to the higher level of complaints made at the start of the war, the majority of disturbances fuelled by shortages of rations, such as the 10th Essex's debacle on Shorncliffe Downs, occurred in 1914 and early 1915. However, they were not exclusively confined to this period and, in December 1915, W. Edwards recalled an incident at Euston Station, when three hundred soldiers in transit refused to board their train that evening until they had been fed, their anger roused by having been given nothing to eat at all that day.[122] Edwards's experience was not isolated, but the majority of protests after the first winter of the war differed from his in that they were concerned with the quality of food rather than its quantity. F.A.J. Taylor's description of an incident in his camp in Wiltshire was more typical. The men's bread ration had been cut once and biscuit substituted – a highly unpopular move. When a further reduction was instituted, the men rebelled and occupied the mess hall, shouting and banging on the tables until they forced a reversal.[123] Once the camps had been properly constructed and supply systems put in place, the recruits in the home camps did not starve. However, the availability of food did not necessarily equate to a satisfaction with the rations, as we shall see in Chapter 5.

A significant factor in managing the expectations of later recruits was their witnessing of the deterioration in domestic supplies. The difficulties with food prices and shortages on the home front would have ensured that the men became more closely attuned to privation, or at least lack of choice, when it came to their diet. It became increasingly apparent to the nation that food shortages were a troubling by-product of the conflict. The Board of Trade's figures show a 61 per cent increase in food prices between July 1914 and July 1916, and working-class diets in particular became increasingly restricted.[124] In March 1917, J. Hollister wrote to his father, 'things in London beginning to be serious, no potatoes to be had, sugar almost unobtainable, meat and cheese 1s 6d, butter 2s 4d, bread 11d'.[125] Later that year one-third of the three thousand shoppers who queued for several hours for margarine in Walworth Road, London, were sent away empty-handed.[126] Food shortages were a key factor in the outbreak of militancy in the British Army in the summer of 1917, although three long years of grinding warfare and the revolution in Russia no doubt also played their part. The dissatisfaction resulted in the first and last Soviet of the British Army meeting in Leeds on 3 June 1917. Its key purpose was to hail the overthrow of Tsarism and demand the creation of Soldiers' Councils throughout the army, based upon those in revolutionary Russia.[127] There was a general lack of enthusiasm for such an innovation amongst the ranks. The Home Counties and Training Reserve at Tunbridge Wells was exceptional in its establishment of such a Council and the drawing up a list of grievances.[128] The injustices they listed demonstrated little in the way of an over-developed political consciousness and concentrated on more prosaic issues, one of which was food. The men's key concern was the hunger of their dependants rather than their own. They demanded an increase in the Separation Allowances in order that their wives and children should not suffer, as retail food prices steadily increased.[129] Whatever the justification for the Soldiers' Council's demands, it was soon disbanded and its manifesto of wrongs ignored. The author, Lance Corporal Dudley, was promptly posted to France and, within two days, the Commanding Officer disciplined or dispersed the remaining members.[130]

Despite the failure of the soldiers' political efforts in the spring and early summer of 1917, an undercurrent of unrest persisted in the home camps and remained evident throughout the year. The vicar of Great Leighs in Essex recorded an incident at a local training camp in August. The men complained that their food was inadequate, refused to eat it, and sat for forty-five minutes drumming loudly on the mess tables in protest. They were then ordered to get back to their work but defied the Sergeant Major. Eventually, the Commanding Officer was called and he judged their complaint 'well-founded' and promised improvements.[131] In the autumn of 1917, the Bishop of Oxford wrote to the government requesting an investigation into the conditions at a camp in Shoreham. Apparently, food was short and the rankers registered their anger by refusing to work in the evening, following what they regarded as an insufficient tea at 4.30 pm. Worryingly they signalled their dissatisfaction by a refusal to sing 'God Save the King' on church parade and at the close of concerts.[132] In general, however, the lowering of expectations and the absence of acute privations resulted in the men's displeasure being manifested in a less extreme fashion: marches and loud protests gave way to complaining, or 'grousing', to give it its military title. Grousing was an integral part of army life. Grumbling was acceptable, if not *de rigueur*, amongst the rankers and became enshrined in many of the soldiers' songs:

> Grousing, grousing, grousing,
> Always bloody well grousing.
> Grousing at the rations,
> And grousing at the pay.[133]

The art of grumbling, the expression of dissatisfaction without any real attempt to make a significant fuss that would draw the attention of the authorities, was central to most rankers' war experience.

Records provide a wealth of evidence that food in both its civilian and military settings became a focus for concerns and disaffections that were not purely calorific or financial. By 1917, there were high prices and shortages but there was an additional element of resentment related to the seemingly interminable nature of the conflict and the disproportionate pressures its continuation brought to bear on soldiers and war workers. The duration of the war was not a financial or emotional negative for all, and as time progressed it became increasingly obvious that certain people were exploiting the situation to their advantage, and resentment towards profiteers fed such concerns. Whatever the individual strands that constituted the grievances, it was shortages or the high cost of food that became the focal point for protestors. Ease of access to supplies had come to represent the division between the possibly unjustly privileged and those who were forced to suffer far worse wartime privations. Bernard Waites acknowledges the significance, and describes food difficulties as 'the chief cause of a generalised discontent which amounted to a heightened "them/us" view of the world'.[134]

The rankers' accounts demonstrate their dissatisfaction with much army food, but also point to their rations as being a critical factor in their absorption into the military world. The link between food and identity is clear and, two hundred years later, David Bell and Gill Valentine echoed Brillat-Savarin with the phrase 'We are where we eat' in the title of their book on the impact of the physical location upon eating.[135] Food and the manner and the place of its consumption are all central to an individual's sense of identity and men constructed their new role as soldiers partly through the eating of military food. The bully beef and biscuit of the basic ration was as much a reinforcement of a man's new life as a soldier as his serial number or uniform.

Evidence suggests men were particularly resistant to army rations at the point of entry, as they struggled to acclimatise to the unfamiliarity and hardships of life as soldier. Active service, as will be seen later, had its own better documented stresses and horrors but the initial shock of military life was experienced by many men almost as profoundly as the sight of their first dead body. The training camp was a Rubicon, a moment of transition that, certainly in the first weeks, traumatised men in a manner that was an intimation of their first experience of trench life. In the same way that some of them would become used to battlefield scenes and think it humorous to shake the outstretched hand of a partially exposed corpse, so the recruits became accustomed to the military life into which circumstances had thrust them. After the initial shock of the barrack mess hall, repeated exposure and, of course, hunger forced an adjustment to the new. Army rations and dining became a routine aspect of the new soldiers' lives, in the same way as uniform and drill. As time progressed, complaints about the food became a lingering dissatisfaction rather than an outrage. The men's apparent acceptance, however, was not necessarily deep-rooted. There was an innate fragility in their relationship with their food: irregularities of supply, changes of environment, and political events could fracture the compliance. The shocking privations at Etaples, revolution in Russia or three days without bread could all trigger real anger or distress, at a pitch that rose above the day-to-day grumbling.

The British Army had little influence over Russian politics but it had, or should have had, complete control over the processes that supplied its soldiers with food. The war presented unprecedented logistical challenges, and feeding the new recruits was just the beginning of a food chain that extended over time and geography, across the Channel, through France and Belgium, to the millions of men who served on the Western Front throughout the four years of the war. In the following chapter, the manner in which the rations were delivered to the hungry men will be explored.

Notes

1 Stopher Family Correspondence, Ipswich Records Office, HD 825, letter dated 2.6.1915.
2 Burnett, *Plenty and Want*, p. 271.
3 Silbey, *British Working Class*, p. 72, and Barnett cited in David Englander and James Osborne, 'Jack, Tommy, and Henry Dubb: The Armed Forces and the Working Class' in *The Historical Journal*, 21: 3 (1978), p. 595.
4 Mintz, *Tasting Freedom*, p. 70.
5 Bet-El, *Conscripts*, chapter two, 'Basic Training', pp. 41–63.
6 Bet-El, *Conscripts*, p. 27.

7 Adrian Gregory, *The Last Great War* (Cambridge, 2008), p. 77.

8 Bet-El, *Conscripts*, pp. 173–174.

9 Eric Leed, *No Man's Land. Combat and Identity in World War I* (Cambridge, 1979), p. 2.

10 Douglas, 'Deciphering a Meal', p. 260.

11 Holmes, *Tommy*, p. 103.

12 Peter Simkins, *Kitchener's Army: The Raising of the New Armies 1914–16* (London, 1988), p. 75.

13 Sidney Allinson, *The Bantams: the Untold Story of World War I* (London, 1981), p. 41.

14 *Statistics of Military Effort*, p. 833.

15 S. Palmer and S. Wallis (eds), *A War in Words. The First World War in Diaries and Letters* (London, 2003), pp. 20–21.

16 Simkins, *Kitchener's Army*, p. 68 and p. 194.

17 Sgt Denis Willison, National Army Museum (hereafter NAM), 7001/2.

18 Frederick Gale, Essex Regimental Archive, diary entry dated 10.9.1914.

19 Gale, Essex Regimental Archive, diary entry dated 1.10.1914.

20 Eric Hiscock, *The Bells of Hell Go Ting-a-Ling-a-Ling* (London, 1976), p. 4.

21 M. Watcyn-Williams, *From Khaki to Cloth* (Cardiff, 1949), p. 51.

22 Peter Simkins, 'Soldiers and Civilians: Billeting in Britain and France', in Ian F.W. Beckett and Keith Simpson (eds), *A Nation in Arms. A Social Study of the British Army in the First World War* (Manchester, 1985), p. 173.

23 H. Cartmell, *For Remembrance. An Account of Some Fateful Years* (Preston, 1919), p. 32.

24 Simkins, *Kitchener's Army*, p. 247.

25 Simkins, 'Soldiers and Civilians', in *A Nation in Arms*, p. 174, and Messenger, *Call-to-Arms*, p. 114.

26 Michael MacDonagh, *In London During the Great War. The Diary of a Journalist* (London, 1935), entry dated 5.8.1914.

27 Cartmell, *For Remembrance*, p. 30.

28 Michael Young, *Army Service Corps*, p. 46.

29 See, for example, Ian F.W. Beckett, *Home Front 1914–1918. How Britain Survived the Great War* (Richmond, 2006), which describes disturbances in London and at Wrexham in 1917 as the hungry population was forced to queue for limited bread supplies, p. 116.

30 Lieutenant-Colonel T.M. Banks and Captain R.A. Chell, *With the 10th Essex in France* (London, 1924), p. 1.

31 Julian Putkowski, *British Army Mutineers 1914–1922* (London, 1998), p. 20.

32 Cartmell, *For Remembrance,* pp. 33–34.

33 Putowski, *British Army Mutineers,* p. 21.

34 E.P. Thompson, 'The Moral Economy of the English Crowd in the Eighteenth Century', *Past and Present*, 50 (1971), pp. 76–136.

35 Andrew Rawson, *The British Army Handbook 1914–1918* (Stroud, 2006), p. 29.
36 In the absence of proper weapons it was common for men to train with wooden rifles and machine-gun sections practised with dummy weapons or obsolete Maxim guns. Rawson, *British Army Handbook*, p. 29.
37 Ian F.W. Beckett, 'The Nation in Arms 1914–1918', in Beckett and Simpson (eds), *A Nation in Arms*, p. 20.
38 Simkins, *Kitchener's Army*, p. 241.
39 The drive to provide hutted accommodation for recruits was completed by the spring of 1915.
40 Simkins, *Kitchener's Army*, p. 244.
41 Robert Roberts, *Classic Slum*, p. 189.
42 In Max Arthur, *When This Bloody War Is Over. Soldiers' Songs of the First World War* (London, 2001), p. 3.
43 Silbey, *British Working Class*, p. 105.
44 Simkins, *Kitchener's Army*, p. 177.
45 Coppard, *With a Machine Gun*, p. 2.
46 Joanna Bourke (ed.), *The Misfit Soldier: Edward Casey's War Story, 1914–1918* (Cork, 1999), p. 31.
47 Robert Roberts, *Classic Slum*, p. 189.
48 H.T. Bolton, IWM P262, undated diary entry.
49 R. Clark, NAM 7606–45, diary entry dated 21.8.1914.
50 *Statistics of Military Effort*, p. 843.
51 *Statistics of Military Effort*, p. 586.
52 Lieutenant-Colonel J.H. Patterson, *With the Judæans in the Palestine Campaign* (London, 1922), p. 29. I am grateful to Henry Morris, curator of the Jewish Military Museum London, for directing me to this information. For an assessment of the experience of Jewish soldiers in the German Army, see Stephen Schouten, 'Fighting a Kosher War: German Jews and Kashrut in World War I, 1914–18', in Ina Zweiniger-Bargielowska and Rachel Duffett (eds), *Food and War in Twentieth Century Europe* (Farnham, 2011).
53 Colin Spencer, *The Heretic's Feast: A History of Vegetarianism* (London, 1993), p. 297.
54 *Manual of Military Cooking and Dietary Mobilization*, produced by HMSO in 1915 and reprinted in 1917 and 1918.
55 *Statistics of Military Effort*, p. 580.
56 Walter Holyfield, Essex Regimental Archive, letter dated 'August 1916'.
57 Sid Liddell, Essex Regimental Archive, letter dated 24.1.1915.
58 F.A.J. 'Tanky' Taylor, *The Bottom of the Barrel* (Bath, 1978), p. 65.
59 Don Cook (ed.) *1914 Letters from a Volunteer* (London, 1984), letter dated 25.10.1914.
60 John Jackson, *Private 12768: Memoir of a Tommy* (Stroud, 2005), p. 17.

61 R. Gwinnell, IWM 01/38/1, Memoir, pp. 68–69.

62 Joseph Murray, *Gallipoli 1915* (Bristol, 2004), p. 35.

63 *The Army from Within*, p. 30.

64 E. Townshend (ed.), *Keeling Letters & Recollections* (London, 1918), letter dated 1.10.1914.

65 Townshend, *Keeling Letters*, article dated 26.9.1914.

66 R.K.R. Thornton (ed.), *Ivor Gurney. War Letters* (London, 1984), letter dated 3.8.1915.

67 Victor Turner, *The Ritual Process* (London, 1969), p. 95.

68 Arnold van Gennep. *The Rites of Passage* (London, 1965), p. 29.

69 Tom Hickman, *The Call-Up. A History of National Service* (London, 2004), p. 38.

70 A.E. Perriman, IWM 80/43/1, Memoir, p. 1.

71 J. McCauley, IWM 97/10/1, p. 6.

72 Jackson, *Private 12768*, p. 18.

73 Coppard, *With a Machine Gun*, p. 2.

74 C. Jones, IWM Con Shelf, letter dated 8.9.1914.

75 Felipe Fernandez-Arnesto, *Food: A History* (London, 2001), p. 133.

76 Lévi-Strauss, *The Origin of Table Manners*, p. 507.

77 Norbert Elias, *The Civilizing Process. The History of Manners* (Oxford, 1978), p. 57.

78 Elias, *Civilizing Process*, p. 125.

79 Elias, *Civilizing Process*, p. 116.

80 F.E. Noakes, *The Distant Drum* (Tunbridge Wells, 1952), p. 18.

81 George Herbert Hill, *Retreat From Death: A Soldier on the Somme* (London, 2005), p. 18.

82 E. Norman Gladden, *The Somme, 1916-A Personal Account* (London, 1974), p. 64.

83 Hodges, *Men of 18*, p. 27.

84 Gray, *Confessions*, p. 48.

85 John Laffin, *World War I in Postcards* (Gloucester, 1988), p. 27.

86 Wyndham, *Queen's Service*, p. 23.

87 Ross, *Love and Toil*, p. 27.

88 Thompson, *Lark Rise*, p. 29.

89 Dayus, *Her People*, p. 109.

90 Paul Fieldhouse, *Food and Nutrition: Customs and Culture* (Beckenham, 1988), p. 86.

91 Gwinnell, IWM 01/38/1, memoir, pp. 68 and 75.

92 For example, John Bourne, 'The British Working Man in Arms', in Hugh Cecil and Peter Liddle (eds), *Facing Armageddon: The First World War Experienced* (London, 1996), p. 346.

93 In the latter part of the war, women were trained to act as camp cooks but they remained a very small minority.

94 Robertson cited in McGuffie, *Rank and File*, p. 34. In the Victorian army only a small percentage of the rankers were permitted to marry; couples in this group were eligible for the limited number of married quarters available. Such 'legitimate' army wives were determined as being 'on the strength', and their husbands also received extra provisions. However, many men married without the permission of their regiment and their wives were not included in accommodation or ration distribution, hence they had to make their own arrangements, which often meant camping out in the barrack rooms.

95 Herbert Hill, *Retreat from Death*, p. 17.

96 Quoted in William Ian Miller, *The Anatomy of Disgust* (Cambridge, MA, 1997), p. 1.

97 Paul Rozin, 'Why We Eat What We Eat, and Why We Worry about It', *Bulletin of the American Academy of Arts and Sciences*, 50:5 (1997), p. 41.

98 Tilsley, *Other Ranks*, p. 121.

99 Dayus, *Her People*, p. 10.

100 Roberts, *Classic Slum*, p. 116.

101 Burnett, *Plenty and Want*, p. 191.

102 Gerald Bennett, *Eating Matters. Why We Eat What We Eat* (London, 1988), p. 153. The recent trend to fast food reinforces Bennett's theory; the interiors of 'food stops' are invariably brightly lit, often with tables to stand rather than sit at. Such conditions discourage those eating from the primitive dangers of lingering or relaxing and ensure they remain alert and ready to move on should dangers, or more customers, present themselves.

103 Coveney, *Food, Morals and Meaning*, p. 11.

104 B. Britland, IWM 88/57/1, letter dated 22.12.1914.

105 Simkins, *Kitchener's Army*, p. 242.

106 Holyfield, Essex Regimental Archive, letter dated 'August 1916'.

107 Watcyn-Williams, *From Khaki to Cloth*, p. 50.

108 Susanne Freidberg, *Fresh: A Perishable History* (Cambridge, MA, 2009), p. 237.

109 Cited in Christina Hardyment, *From Mangle to Microwave: The Mechanization of Household Work* (Cambridge, 1988), p. 6.

110 Housman, *War Letters*, letter dated 27.3.1916, p. 201.

111 Visser, *The Rituals of Dinner*, p. 45.

112 Bennett, *Eating Matters*, p. 7.

113 See Michael Roper, 'Slipping Out of View: Subjectivity and Emotion in Gender History', *History Workshop Journal*, 59 (2005), pp. 57–72, and *The Secret Battle: Emotional Survival in the First World War* (Manchester, 2009).

114 Britland, IWM 88/57/1, letter dated 26.12.1914.

115 Cook, *Letters from a Volunteer*, letter dated 25.10.1914.

116 *Statistics of Military Effort*, p. 874.

117 Coppard, *With a Machine Gun*, p. 4.

118 Perriman, IWM 80/43/1, memoir, p. 2.

119 Perriman, IWM 80/43/1, memoir, p. 1.

120 P.H. Jones, IWM P246, memoir, p. 7.

121 McCartney, *Citizen Soldiers,* p. 130.

122 Jesse Short Collection, IWM 220 (3152), 1/20.

123 Jesse Short, IWM 220 (3152), 4/11.

124 Beckett, *Home Front,* p. 110.

125 J. Hollister, IWM 98/10/1, letter dated 19.3.1917.

126 Beveridge, *British Food Control,* p. 196.

127 Putkowski, *Mutineers,* p. 13.

128 Ian Beckett states that there were only two Soldiers' Councils, the second was in Birmingham but was equally short lived; 'The Nation in Arms', in *A Nation in Arms,* p. 24.

129 Englander and Osborne, 'Jack, Tommy, and Henry Dubb: The Armed Forces and the Working Class', p. 604.

130 Putkowski, *Mutineers,* p. 13.

131 Munson (ed.), *Echoes of the Great War,* entry dated 11.8.1917.

132 William Allison and John Fairley, *The Monocled Mutineer* (London, 1978), p. 131.

133 Arthur, *When This Bloody War Is Over,* p. 67.

134 Waites, *A Class Society at War,* p. 224.

135 David Bell and Gill Valentine, *Consuming Geographies: We Are Where We Eat* (London, 2003).

4

Feeding the men: army provisioning, the cooks and the ASC

The previous chapter illustrated the men's reaction to their first experience of army food–a response that was framed in a context of shock and revulsion, which sprang as much from their precipitate entry into a military world as it did from the meals placed in front of them. Whatever the difficulties inherent in the men's incorporation into their new existence, by 1914 the army's failures in earlier contexts had resulted in its acknowledgement of the importance of proper feeding to both the morale and the physical health of its soldiers. Delivering adequate food to the men in the home camps was in itself a challenge, as evidenced by the frequent shortages at the beginning of the war. However, the logistical efforts required in servicing the network of camps across Great Britain paled beside those necessary to feed the men scattered across the base camps, rest camps, reserve areas and front line trenches of the Western Front. In 1931, Colonel R.H. Beadon wrote a rather favourable analysis of the ASC's supply endeavours during the war, his positive views no doubt influenced by his own membership of the corps. In it he quotes an earlier German strategist and declares that 'the maxim of von Moltke that "no army food is too expensive" was faithfully observed throughout'.[1] Beadon asserts that the men's food was the military's top priority and therefore, no expense had been spared in ensuring the soldiers received regular, good-quality rations. The confidence Beadon displays in the army's achievements, and the performance of his own ASC, is evident; his enthusiasm supports his main aim which is to emphasise the importance of the service and supply units, roles that had received little attention, let alone praise, in the postwar analyses.

Beadon's assessment was not endorsed by large numbers of rankers, whose accounts of the war are often critical of the rations they received on active service. The men's unflinching appraisal of army food on the Western Front will be considered in the following chapter; the purpose here is to explore the army's provisioning processes: the systems put in place to supply the men and the type of rations delivered. In addition, the chapter considers the men's responses to groups in the lengthy food chain whose experience of eating was regarded by them as very different from that of the ordinary soldiers. Beadon's ASC was responsible for much of the supply process and the relative protection that their position afforded its men was a cause of much anger and scorn amongst the other rankers. The unit cooks, men whose proximity to the cookhouse normally ensured a safe distance from the firing line, were also much derided by the rankers. In a similar fashion, 'brass-hats' at the rear, were perceived to have an easier existence than the ordinary ranker, and even the junior officers who served in the front line were often resented for their priority access to any dug-outs available. The advantage that the men identified was not related purely to the increased physical safety of their leaders. Subalterns in the trenches were vulnerable too, given both the poor quality of many British dug-outs and the impossibility of even the most reluctant officer remaining under shelter for the whole of their tour of front line duty. Other issues fuelled the resentment in the ranks and one important factor was the different eating experiences of the groups: officers at the front might, dug-outs notwithstanding, share the risk of shelling, but they usually managed to maintain superior food supplies.

The new recruits had struggled through the strangeness and discomfort of the training camps and emerged acclimatised, at least to some degree, to life as a soldier. Once trained, uniformed and kitted out, the men took their next step into active service, and for most of them that meant the route across the English Channel to France. The Western Front had the largest concentration of British soldiers and was, fortunately, the closest to home. Catering for the soldiers based at a greater distance, such as Gallipoli or Mesopotamia, presented further complexities in terms of increased shipping tonnage for the longer journey and difficulties arising from the impact of climate on food storage. It was only a relatively few miles from the French coast to the front line trenches, but these miles had to be traversed with a vast tonnage of food and supplies. The sheer scale of the operation was astounding, dictated by the number of soldiers who served there: by November 1918, the ration strength on the Western Front had reached 2,360,400, while that at home stood at 1,514,993.[2]

The pre-First World War experiences had caused the army to place greater emphasis on the importance of food to its soldiers. The Colonel Beadon mentioned above was not alone in his interpretation of the significance of the provisioning aspects of the conflict. Other commentators appear to ascribe a special importance to the relationship between food and the British fighting man. In his reflections on the First World War, the military strategist Basil Liddell Hart claims that 'it is particularly true of the British Army that it only gives of its best on a well-filled stomach'. Liddell Hart does not provide evidence of why he believes this to be a peculiarly British racial characteristic, and, as it was the French Army that mutinied over rations, it would seem that such concerns transcended national boundaries. Liddell Hart also quotes what he describes as an old martial rhyme: "'Battles may be fought and won, but the British Army dines at one.'"[3] The lyric sounds as if it pertains more to the officers' mess than the mass catering for the rankers, although, given the nuances and class-divisions of the language, it is more likely that the officers would have 'lunched' rather than dined at one. Whatever the rank, the tenet was clear that mealtimes mattered in the British Army; eating had a fundamental importance, besides which even the waging of war might appear a transient occupation. Liddell Hart extends his argument on the importance of food to other nations and their armies; he asserts that the war was eventually won by the food blockade of Germany and their collapse was due 'more to emptiness of stomach [both soldiers and civilians] produced by economic pressure, than to loss of blood', a view shared by a number of modern historians.[4]

The enthusiasm in their postwar writing of individual military commentators for the successes of army provisioning is shared by the authors of *Statistics of the Military Effort of the British Empire*; a similar tone of uncritical assessment is present in the War Office's assessment of army feeding. Perhaps unsurprisingly for an official account, it appears that all went unequivocally well; the soldiers ate heartily and 'it was found possible in 1916 and onwards, to reduce the ration without detriment to the adequate feeding of the soldier'. Veterans reading those lines may not have recognised the generous appraisal of their provisioning, nor the notion that they may have overeaten before 1916. It is likely their attention would have been drawn to the next sentence, where the army congratulates itself upon the 'millions of pound per annum' saved by the reduction in the ration, money gained, as many soldiers' accounts would have it, at the expense of the men's well-being.[5]

Transporting food

Whatever the differing opinions of the army's success or failure, the hungriest soldier in a front line trench would have agreed with Liddell Hart's pronouncement: 'strategy depends on supply – without security of food the most dazzling manoeuvres may come to naught'.[6] 'Security of food' embraces a number of different and possibly conflicting pressures. The soldiers' dietary requirements had to be balanced with the need to supply other materiel, and food preferences had to be considered in the context of the type and cost of food available, together with its ease of transport and storage. Whatever the satisfaction of the subsequent commentaries, they do not explicitly acknowledge the fundamental reason that was at the root of much of the men's hunger: soldiers' food was not the highest priority on the army's transportation list. The supply of arms and ammunition, without which the army was impotent, was more important: men might function to some degree when empty, the guns would not. The men's rations were denied second position on the list of priorities by the quantities of forage required for the huge number of horses and mules used by the army. The animals formed a critical part of the weapon supply chain by pulling the ordnance wagons, so their food was inextricably linked to the successful achievement of the army's top priority.[7] The availability of mechanical transport, particularly at the start of the war, was limited. The use of vans and lorries expanded as the conflict progressed, but animals remained central to the army's distributions systems throughout. By late 1918, 404,000 horses and mules were in use on the Western Front and the provision of their food supply was a considerable task.[8] Unlike the motor vehicles' requirement for petrol, the animals needed to eat whether or not they were actually being used and, on average, they each ate 25 lb of food a day.[9] Indeed, the daily ration statistics for the supply of a division show that 120,000 lb of oats, hay and bran were required for their animals, a tonnage that considerably exceeded that of the soldiers' food.[10] It has been calculated that during the war, 5,438,602 tons of forage were shipped from Britain to the Western Front, a figure which slightly exceeded the weight of ammunition transported, but must have vastly outstripped it in volume.[11]

The demands of war influenced not only the question of whether there was space available to carry the men's rations but also the type of food that could be accommodated on the supply transports. T.E. Lawrence declared that 'the invention of bully beef has modified land-war more profoundly than the invention of gunpowder'. Lawrence's logic was based on the belief that range was more important to strategy than force and the highly calorific and easily transportable tinned meat facilitated rapid troop movement.[12] Bully beef may have excited the strategists, perhaps because those planning troop movements and battle orders at HQ rarely ate it, but it had the opposite effect on the men at the front. The limits of contemporary nutritional science militated against the ranker; the army's preoccupation was to deliver the requisite energy values to the troops: calories were all that mattered. The essential nature of vitamins and trace elements was unclear and there was little understanding of the 'omnivore's paradox': the struggle between the fear of the new and boredom with the old. Men wanted, and the official ration scale to some degree described, a varied diet, pleasing differences in taste and texture that were not too far distant from familiar foods. All too often, the army's quickest and easiest solution to rationing problems was bully beef and biscuit; the former delivered a large number of calories in a relatively small tin and biscuit, unappealing as it was, had similar energy values to the far more popular, but less easily stored and transported, bread.

Whatever provisions, whether bully or bacon, the army chose to deliver, the creation of sustainable supply lines was essential to military success. Failure to maintain proper procedures generally resulted in disaster. The Germans discovered this to their cost in the rapid advances of the Ludendorff Offensive later in the war, when in the spring of 1918 the men outran their supplies and what was a militarily successful manoeuvre ground to a hungry halt. Strategy and success in battle were undermined by the German Army's inability to maintain the delivery of rations, a problem that as Liddell Hart points out was founded upon national food shortages as well as the rapid advance of the troops. The distribution of food was an integral part of the military system, indivisible from the efforts of the other corps. In the British Army, much of this work was performed by the ASC; indeed, an account of the army's provisioning systems is in many ways the story of the ASC, which was responsible for the movement of other items such as ammunition, forage and the post, as well as food. It organised the supply and transport of the rations from the Channel ports to the points near the front line, where the Regimental Quartermasters took over their onward distribution. In addition, the ASC was responsible for the education and training of the unit cooks, the vast central storage depots and specialist sections such as the water tank companies, the butchery units and the bakeries in France and at home which produced great quantities of bread for the men at the front.

Nothing in the ASC's history had prepared it for the First World War; the lessons learned in the limited campaign of the Boer War had been assimilated but the years since its conclusion, with only a small peacetime force to supply, had offered no real challenges. It was a corps that lacked the cachet of the prominent regiments: a commission in the ASC hardly ranked with one in the Guards. The nature of its duties conspired against it attracting the cream of militarily ambitious and able men. Richard Holmes highlighted the lack of recognition the ASC has received, both at the time and subsequently, when he comments that in the indexes to the fourteen volumes of *The Official History of The Great War*, the ASC is listed on a mere four occasions.[13] At the beginning of 1914, the corps was small with a strength of 6,431 officers and men. Its main depots were at Aldershot and Woolwich and its responsibilities split, organisationally, between Supply and Transport. Most of the latter was still performed by the horses, whose appetites have already been noted. Consequently, the total number of mechanical vehicles in 1914 was a mere 115, of which 80 were lorries.[14] Indeed, the initial shortage of motor transport created some of the most striking images of the war when London buses and commercial vans, commandeered by the army to fill the gaps in their supply lines, traversed the French countryside in 1914, some still display-ing the livery of the businesses from which they had been requisitioned. It was apparent that the traditional organisational division was ineffective for the great task ahead, and a more integrated approach was required. In September 1914, the Supply and Transport arms of the ASC were united for the first time under the leadership of Brigadier General S.S. Long – a commander renowned for his somewhat irascible but wholly determined approach to the forcible securing of essential food supplies for the army noted in Chapter 2. As the conflict progressed, the ASC expanded in line with its task, and by November 1918 numbers had risen to 325,881 and its tally of motor transport to 121,702.[15]

The numbers of the ASC grew, but its prestige, certainly in the eyes of the ordinary soldier, did not. The ASC was perceived as being protected from the real dangers of warfare and the resentment that this engendered is significant as it no doubt influenced the assessment of its efforts. The low esteem in which the Corps was generally held is reflected in a letter that C.R. Jones, who served with the Civil Service Rifles, wrote to his family. In it he complains: 'When you meet people or soldiers at home in the RE or RTOs or the ASC, please remember that these regiments do not compare with the infantry which does all the donkey work holding trenches.'[16] It was easy for regular troops to dismiss the ASC's role and achievements, and popular infantry marching songs reflect the pervasive attitude:

> We are the ASC,
> We cannot fight, we cannot march,
> What ------- good are we?[17]

In the midst of the criticisms and ridicule, it is possible to forget that supply was an essential part of the war and the ASC had reason to be proud of its achievements, as one of its own songs made clear:

> They will see you get your dinner though the shells disturb your tea.
> It's a job that's not exciting,
> And they haven't time for fighting,
> Yet they do their bit! . . . So, hats off
> To the ASC.[18]

The ASC's rhyme acknowledges that its personnel were not fighting men. For many of them this would change when manpower shortages experienced towards the end of the war resulted in men who had not held a rifle since training camp being placed in the front line. The ASC song hints at their presence in forward areas where they too were at risk from the German snipers or shelling, and supply duties could carry a high degree of risk. The rhyme implies that a lack of excitement was a burden for the ASC, that its men in some way longed for the thrilling challenges of the front line soldiers; a view, it might be supposed, that could have come only from men who had little idea of the brutal nature of the fighting men's front line service.

Maintaining the supply lines

Whatever the shortage of martial stimulation, the challenge the army faced in supplying rations to so many men, in such diverse locations, was enormous. Early experience, in particular during the disorganised retreat from Mons where the supply lines had broken down completely, emphasised the necessity of a robust and effective chain of delivery. During the retreat, ASC supply points were forced to issue rations and ammunition at the roadside 'on an opportunity basis', which appears to have been an official euphemism for 'random'.[19] The accounts of soldiers caught up in the event indicated that the haphazard nature of delivery omitted many of them, who were certainly hungry for food, if not munitions. T.H. Cubbon's diary records the complete lack of consistency in supply and the vagaries of eating when in retreat. On 26 August 1914, Cubbon was jubilant when his unit stumbled upon 10 tons of rations left by the side of the road in the panic of the withdrawal, the hungry men 'feasted' and took away with them as much as they could carry. The other entries for this period are considerably less happy. On 5 September he had had nothing to eat for thirty-six hours, on 12 September he had half a tin of bully beef and two biscuits in the same period, and on the 30th of the month he and five other soldiers had to share a daily ration of a quarter of a loaf, a piece of cheese and 1 lb of jam between them.[20] Some men became accustomed to the repeated failures in supply and it became the subject of bitter humour. One group of stragglers, when offered food by an officer, initially declined, replying ironically 'rearguards ain't expected to eat. So we 'ave give it up, we 'ave. It's a bad habit, any'ow. Ain't it boys?'[21] At this point in the war, the supply systems of the British Army were in disarray and men often went hungry. Enterprising officers, such as Major H.A. Stewart, did their best to negotiate via the local mayor for provisions from farmers and shopkeepers, but success was limited.[22] The hunger during the retreat did not unduly concern the Quartermaster General Sir William Robertson, who wrote, 'I have no anxiety, and never have had any worth mentioning in regard to food supplies, but from the very first I have had a very great deal of anxiety with respect to ammunition.'[23] Robertson's letter makes the priorities discussed earlier explicit: feeding the guns was of far greater concern than feeding the men. There was always the possibility of obtaining food from alternative local sources; supplies of bullets or shells would not be so easily found.

The experience of Mons had a profound influence upon the army's planning and logistics strategists. It stimulated the development of supply systems and processes which demonstrated a more complex level of care and planning than had previously existed. The establishment and maintenance of the supply lines was facilitated by the mainly static nature of the remainder of the war, which permitted the construction of fixed lines of provisioning. The retreat by the British Army in the face of the German advance in the spring of 1918, however, precipitated events sadly reminiscent of Mons. As the Germans overran the lines, the British supply systems, carefully nurtured for over three years, collapsed and food was once again in short supply for many of the fleeing men. The diary of J. Sanderson describes the opportunistic approach forced upon his unit, including taking food from abandoned YMCA canteens, looting local shops and stealing chickens.[24] The experience of men like Sanderson was not acknowledged by the most senior echelons of the army, who viewed the rout as a 'controlled retreat', executed 'smoothly and successfully . . . there was never any lack of food or ammunition for the troops'.[25]

Later that year, in its own final rapid advances, the army was better prepared to respond innovatively to the supply challenges movement presented, it being easier to plan for forward rather than backward travel. S.L. Green, a military chaplain, who advanced with the troops in November 1918, recalled that the roads had been blown up 'and for one or two days the only possible way of getting our rations was for aeroplanes to drop sacks of food for the men'.[26] The airlift of supplies was relatively unusual, but proved highly effective in bridging what might, in earlier years, have been an impossibly long gap between the front line soldiers and their supply dumps.

Bookended between the periods of rapid movement in 1914 and 1918, the army operated a generally stable supply system. Over the course of the war, the bulk of the food eaten by the soldiers was shipped to the continent rather than purchased locally. The pressure on shipping resulted in strenuous efforts to save tonnage. For example, alternative, lighter packing materials were considered by the army including the issue of jam in papier mâché containers rather than tins and paper packets for the hardtack biscuit. The latter proved a failure as the biscuit quickly spoiled, and one might suppose that the jam and papier mâché combination would prove disastrous in the rain-soaked trenches of northern Europe. Indeed, the official record indicates that the experiments may have been less than successful as it states, 'it has not been found possible to obtain sufficiently accurate data to judge how far these lighter cases stood the tough handling in the field'.[27] Such small-scale measures were insufficient and officers were encouraged to do what they could to explore the possibility of sourcing essential supplies from the locale. The *Field Service Pocket Book* urges them to reconnoitre the butchers, bakers and grocers in their area, with particular emphasis on the availability of tea and sugar, the lifeblood of the British rankers.[28] In order to co-ordinate efforts, the Supplies Purchase Department was created in 1916, and from its headquarters in Paris it worked to increase the army's local supply contracts and hence relieve the pressure on shipping. Great quantities of essential items were bought from French and Belgian suppliers, ranging from brandy to pigeon food, the latter giving an insight into the intricacies of the military's communications network. The procedures required to transport the food to the men were defined with precision and a booklet held by the Imperial War Museum entitled *Supplies and Supply*

Transport in the 38th (Welsh Division) describes them in minute detail.[29] The book seems to have been privately printed, but its official appearance and recommendations suggest that it had the army's endorsement. Similar maps and accounts, but rather less detailed, can be found in other reviews of the supply systems, which add veracity to the 38th's experience. The book was written by a 'Senior Supply Officer' and he appears to have covered virtually every eventuality pertaining to the transport of supplies on the Western Front. A diagram from the book (Figure 4.1) provides an outline of the fundamentals of the system.

The Supply Officer's diagram allows us to track the movement of rations from the Base, or Base Supply Depot (BSD) to give it its full title, through the various modes of transport, to the soldiers in the trenches. A series of BSDs were constructed near the Channel Ports to store the unloaded cargo. Calais and Boulogne provided the BSDs for the Northern Line of Communication, and Dieppe, Le Havre and Rouen serviced the Southern Line. The quantity of food and other necessary items held at these depots was vast; in one hangar at Le Havre, eighty thousand tons of 'articles of supply' were stored at any one time, in a building more than half a mile long and over 600 ft wide.[31] Figure 4.2 showing the cheese store at the Calais BSD gives a good impression of the great size of the storage areas.

The scale of the storage requirements made it imperative to keep provisions moving forward, in order to avoid congestion at the BSDs, where the daily arrival of supply ships kept up a constant pressure on the available space. The sheer size of the operation is difficult to comprehend. The BSD statistics provided by Michael Young in his book on the ASC give an insight into the scale of the project. For example, in 1918, the Boulogne BSD's highest monthly issue of frozen meat was 21,658,847 lb, that of bread 15,875,667 lb and its highest daily feeding strength was 670,266 men.[32] The army's initial resistance to frozen meat had been overcome and supplies of Argentine beef, as well as meat from Australia, New Zealand, the United States, Canada, Brazil and South Africa, were used from 1914 onwards.[33] Originally the supplies were shipped to Great Britain and the quality of the meat inspected there before repacking and onward transport to France. It soon became apparent that the quantities were so large it made the consequent overhead of time for double-handling unsupportable, and it was decided to ship the meat directly from source to the BSDs. The use of relatively new technology was not without its problems. 'Experimental shipments' of frozen sausage were trialled from the sausage factories set up under War Office

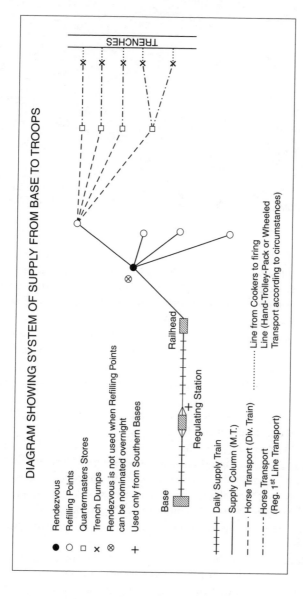

4.1 The system of supply from base to troops

4.2 Cheese store at a Base Supply Depot in Calais

control in London, Liverpool and Aldershot, but rather worryingly for
the men's digestions met with only 'partial success'. Tinned bully beef
presented fewer transportation problems and was shipped from around
the globe. In an effort to ensure the quality of the preserved meat, the
War Department sent two expert food inspectors to the Americas and
two to Australia, where they remained for the duration in order to
examine and report on the conditions in the canning industries.[34] Tins
of 'Pork and Beans' purchased in the United States and Canada and cans
of 'Meat and Vegetables' produced at home were also used to add variety
to the soldiers' rations.

The ASC had a number of specialist bakery units established at home,
at the BSDs and in the field, the latter expanding from six in 1914 to
thirty-one by the end of the war.[35] The soldiers' demand for bread was
consistently high: for almost all it was the familiar substance that had
figured most prominently in their prewar diets. The official records confidently state that the bakeries' efforts ensured that 'a regular supply of
bread to the troops was always maintained'.[36] Figure 4.3 shows a group of
ASC bakers standing beside mobile bread ovens displaying the products
of their efforts.

Unfortunately, as we shall see in the next chapter, the men at the front
were less convinced that the high levels of production extolled in the official records actually translated into a regular and edible supply of bread
for their consumption. Other ASC specialist units included water tank

4.3 British bakers and their travelling bread ovens (date unknown)

companies, which operated from the bases and carried large quantities of drinking water forward to the soldiers in bespoke containers. The *Field Service Pocket Book* suggests that one gallon per man per day is sufficient for 'drinking and cooking purposes', but in stationary camps five gallons per man was ideal and ten gallons for each horse.[37] Where tanks were not available or practicable, and this was the case in many of the narrow trenches nearer the front, petrol cans were used to transport drinking water to the front. The taint of gasoline the cans passed to their contents caused the men to be as unimpressed with the quality of the water as they were with the bread supply.

The mountains of supplies stored, and also baked, at the depots had to be rapidly pushed out to the men. One of the ASC's most important tasks was to load the supply trains that pulled up to the doors of the BSDs each day. It was essential that the trains were packed as efficiently as possible in order to maximise capacity and avoid spoilage, and a manual entitled *The Stacking and Storing of Supplies* was produced to assist the men in this task.[38] Under normal conditions, the army's supply systems aimed to send a daily supply train from the BSDs to each division. A train consisted of rations for around twenty thousand men and 5,400 horses and included other essentials, such as oil, disinfectant and petrol. In August 1914, there had been four divisions on the Western Front but by November 1918, the number had risen to sixty-four.[39] Figure 4.1 suggests a relatively straightforward process, in that it demonstrates a one-to-one relationship between a BSD and the division it supplied. The difficulty with such an arrangement was that it required each depot to hold the full range of stores required. Colonel R.H. Beadon's account of the process indicates the practical difficulties of all the BSDs holding a supply of each item, especially as many of the ships arriving at the individual ports carried only one type of cargo. Therefore, rather than redistribute a variety of supplies across the BSDs at the first opportunity when the ships docked, which would have necessitated the construction of specialised storage facilities such as freezer units at each site, it was simpler for some depots to specialise in particular items. The decision was made that the northern BSDs would hold a variety of commodities, but those in the south would be responsible for individual elements of supply: for example, one stored frozen meat, while another dealt only with petrol.[40] A train would be loaded at each BSD with its particular stocked item, or variety of items, in sufficient quantities to supply all the trains for the divisions running that day. The train then ran to a Regulating Station, where the supplies would be redistributed into the required amounts for each division and repacked on to one train for each, then taken on to the railhead nearest to the troops.

The railheads, built ten to fifteen miles behind the front line and out of range of most of the enemy artillery, were sites of constant activity. As the great volumes of supplies were offloaded, it must have seemed inconceivable that a soldier might ever go hungry, given the vast quantities of provisions pouring up from the depots. In his privately published memoir of 1931, Stanley Levy, who had served in an ASC Motor Transport company, questioned why none of the 'new war books' contained a description of a railhead. He believed that they were a 'most interesting and colourful spectacle' and warranted greater coverage in accounts of the war.[41] Levy was clearly unaware of Gilbert Waterhouse, a poet killed on the first day of the Battle of the Somme in 1916, whose volume of poetry *Rail-head and Other Poems* was published posthumously. The title poem, *Rail-head*, describes the scene at Someville:

'Dusty and dirty and full of noisy din,
"If 'e fights upon is stomach, this 'ere army oughter win!"
Someville is the Rail-head, full of noisy din,
Full of men and horses and mules and paraffin,
Frozen meat and apricots and peaches-a-la-tin . . .'[42]

Waterhouse's enthusiasm reflects the view of the official records that the stomachs of fighting soldiers were always well-filled. It is understandable that the sight of such riches would feed the conviction that all was well with the supply systems of the British Army. Whatever the quantities on display at the railhead or the BSDs, the rations still had some distance to travel. The end points of the railway supply system were often a considerable distance from the billets or camps in the reserve areas and, of course, even further from the front line trenches. The route the food took from the BSDs to the men at the front entailed its passing through many hands along the way. It seems that some items had less success in completing this journey than others, for example tins of apricots and peaches disappeared long before those of bully beef.

Once the supplies had been unloaded at the railhead, they were transported onward by the mechanical vehicles that made up the divisional supply column. The trucks took the appropriate quantities, determined by the exact strength numbers provided by the division's Senior Supply Officer, to the refilling points, where supplies for each brigade were dumped. At the refilling points, they were further divided by regiment and the divisional train would then haul them to the individual Regimental Quartermaster's Stores. This train was not a locomotive but a convoy of wagons and carts pulled by nearly four hundred horses and staffed by over four hundred officers and men. At the stores, the process of subdivision continued: the rations were split again and issued to the Company Quartermaster Sergeants, who would then put each platoon's supplies into sandbags marked with the platoon number. Transport for the last part of the journey, to those troops at the farthest points from the BSDs, was determined by conditions on the ground. Sometimes it was possible to use hand trolleys, but often the mud meant that men had no alternative but to carry the heavy bags on their shoulders. The army's procedures state that whenever possible men should carry sufficient rations for forty-eight hours when they went into the trenches, in order to save on the hazardous work of resupplying those at the front. The general principle was that ration parties were to be formed from the troops at the rear and sent forward, rather than compromise the line by taking men from there to track back for supplies.[43] Circumstances were such that this was not always possible and it was common for men to be sent from the front to the rear to collect the food, as the *Trench Standing Orders, 1915–1916, 124th Infantry Brigade* make clear.[44]

Challenges to delivery

An analysis of the supply chain on the Western Front reveals the considerable efforts and precise organisation dedicated to feeding the soldiers, demonstrating the complexity of the journey rations made from the BSDs at the ports to the men at the front. In order for the system to work effectively, it needed to be a ceaseless repetition of activity: each day, as one train was being loaded at base, another was off-loading at the railhead and the contents of a third were being distributed to units by the divisional train. These trains were manned by the ASC and permanently allocated to the supply of a particular division. The trains were split into sections to perform their various duties, as in addition to the transfer of supplies they were responsible for the conveyance of the officers' baggage and the delivery of letters and parcels.[45] The routes they followed to supply the division were, given the exigencies of war, prone to change; missing the rendezvous points, particularly in forward areas, was a constant concern. The 10th Essex's experience highlights the difficulties of finding secure routes for the supplies. On one occasion, the head of the train stopped just in time as he was about to 'deliver the Essex rum and rissoles to a German commander at Renard Farm.'[46] The capture of a supply train would have been a coup for the enemy, and the British Army's instructions were clear on the procedure to be followed should one come under threat. The officer in charge was expected to ensure that all the horses were shot and the supplies burned prior to surrender, although one does wonder whether there would have been sufficient time to kill hundreds of horses before the Germans were upon them. ASC officers responsible for the trains were acutely conscious of their responsibility. One man caught up in the retreat from Mons recalled how worried he was of enemy attack as he knew how much 'Les Allemands would like to get their hands on the Train'.[47]

Aside from the possibility of ambush, which was relatively unlikely, life as part of the divisional train presented its own dangers, chiefly from shelling. The level of peril was dependent upon the general enemy activity in the sector and the proximity of the supply lines to the front. While wagons, horses and their drivers could be injured in the barrage, it was the last stage of the rations' journey up to the front line that was particularly hazardous. The need to feed the men at the front was common to all armies and it was not unheard of for the opposing sides to reach an accommodation. Captain H. Wilberforce-Bell served in a sector where there was a tacit understanding that each side did its best not to fire upon the other's ration parties.[48] His memoir describes service in the early part of the war, when such shared courtesies may have been more common, before four years of fighting had eroded feelings of mutuality. It is perhaps more likely that Wilberforce-Bell's experience was a function of geography rather than chronology. Tony Ashworth's research highlights the disparity between the sectors in the front line. In some areas, shelling and sniping continued relentlessly, while in others an understanding was reached which resulted in a token show of aggression each day – the 'morning hate'. In these quieter sections, truces at mealtimes were common, and one soldier recalled that safety was guaranteed, to the extent that the carrying of rations across open ground was unexceptional.[49] The descriptions of the truces in Ashworth's account are not as widely evident in the soldiers' accounts researched for this book. It is likely that the independent suspensions of hostilities were not regarded as suitable subject matter for the letters likely to be censored by potentially unsympathetic officers, or for the diaries in which men were forbidden to record any matters of a sensitive nature. A number of memoirs do make reference to the 'morning hates', but even there the tone tends toward pained endurance, rather than any manifestation of a comforting reassertion of control that the existence of such truces suggests to Ashworth.

For the majority of soldiers, ration party work was regarded as a deeply hazardous duty. E. Brunsdon remembered the fear he felt at having to leave the camp and walk in the pitch dark, through trenches nearly waist deep in water, carrying unwieldy and bone-achingly heavy sacks of provisions. It was a service he professed to be happy to provide, believing as he did that it was absolutely essential that the soldiers at the front received their food and the comfort of a hot drink.[50] P.H. Jones wrote that 'our greatest bugbear' was the delivery of rations under sniper fire and discusses the dangers at some length. Indeed, he devotes a considerable chunk of his memoir to the process, giving the section its own title: 'How the Rations Came in at La Chappelle d'Armentieres', and providing a detailed description of how the supplies were carried forward and at what cost. The space that Jones allocated to the matter indicates the importance of food deliveries and the traumatic nature of the ration parties. There is also a sense of his admiration for the complexity of the procedure; the way in which all the discrete parts, the trains, lorries, horses, handcarts and sacks, come together to meet the men's needs. Jones, throughout his lengthy account of his army service, is quick to identify the military's failings, but in the minutiae of his description of the rations' journey there is a sense of purpose and well-being. His writing suggests that, whatever the dangers of ration party duty, he was in some way comforted by the intricacies of army provisioning systems; that the details of supply indicated a level of concern and a determination to service the troops that was all too frequently absent in other areas.[51]

The conditions in the trenches created their own casualties, without the assistance of German barrage. Men who stumbled into deep, water-filled shell holes found it hard to extricate themselves, especially when weighed down with packs of rations. The routes in many places were only wide enough to accommodate men walking in single file, not two men struggling to carry a 56 lb box of meat tins. In fact P.H. Jones describes just such a challenge and its resolution by the dangerous manoeuvre of breaking cover and carrying it across the top of the narrow trenches.[52] In the darkness it was difficult to navigate the complex web of paths, and disoriented soldiers could easily wander into German territory. When the front line troops were required to move back to collect the food, it might be assumed that escape from the front, even for a short period, would be a much sought after opportunity. However, men were not always keen to participate; any movement in the trenches was a hazardous occupation, and soldiers generally felt safer when they were securely dug in, preferring to remain as static as possible. Whilst some men experienced truces during ration delivery in the trenches, others state that they were aware that the Germans paid particular attention at mealtimes and were on the lookout for men carrying supplies up the line. A.P. Burke shared his dislike of ration party duty under enemy surveillance in a letter home to his family: 'Fritz is wide awake to the fact & strafes like H---.'[53] Sidney Rogerson recalled that on the Somme in 1916 it was rare for ration carriers to complete a journey without casualties and, on some occasions, the whole party was wiped out.[54] The rations were brought forward at considerable cost to their bearers, a fact that Patrick MacGill describes most viscerally in *The Great Push*, when he writes of hungry soldiers eating bread that had been stained red with the blood of one unfortunate carrier.[55] As a professional author, MacGill would be forgiven for exercising his imagination but blood-spattered bread was not just a literary image, it could be a reality for the ordinary Tommy at the front. Fred Wood describes receiving such a loaf, but as he and his pals were very hungry 'we scraped the worst off and ate it'.[56]

The provisions the men carried forward were supposed to be a reflection of the official ration scales of the British Army: an issue of 4,193 calories per day for men at the front, reduced to 3,472 calories for those in the lines of communication.[57] The army had calculated that soldiers needed a minimum of 3,000 calories a day, lower than this and their effectiveness deteriorated rapidly.[58] Of course, the figures in the statistics represented the official line, and the food men actually received frequently bore little resemblance to that which the army's scales and recommendations had led them to expect. The army often struggled to produce amounts anywhere near the published scale. In January 1918, Captain J.C. Dunn noted in his diary: 'fresh meat, 12 oz – in practice it has fallen sometimes to 200 lb among eight hundred men [4 oz]'.[59] The emphasis on meat in the ration, which reflected both its traditional prestige in the British diet and also perhaps the notion that red meat was the most appropriate diet for the red-blooded fighting man, placed great strain on butchery supplies. By mid-1915, the War Office had realised that 'the meat resources of the world were becoming increasingly restricted'. In response to this, army records state that there was an attempt to switch to cheaper meat products, such as the rabbit referred to in the previous chapter, and the issues of sausages and brawn were also increased. The army also achieved further savings in its meat supply by reducing the meat portion of the men's diet and increasing the vegetable allowance to compensate. Official statistics categorically state that this did not affect the dietary value of the ration, which seems unlikely given the quite different properties of the foodstuffs. However, the annual saving of 7,000 tons of meat made the adjustment most welcome at the War Office.[60] Evidence, particularly from soldiers' accounts, indicates that the real meat alternative offered by the army was usually bully beef, an item that was generally met with approval only by the hungriest of soldiers.

Growing their own

The army was aware of the regular shortfalls in the rations provided from the BSDs and the fact that the losses were not fully compensated for by additional purchases from local suppliers. One item that appears to have been in particularly short supply was vegetables; central provisioning frequently failed and the restrictions on large-scale agriculture around the front meant that the availability of local produce was limited. Although the ration scale remained unchanged at 8 oz of vegetables a day for each man throughout the war, this generous figure had a tenuous relationship with the actual amount provided. Enterprising officers made their own arrangements, and Captain A.O. Temple Clark obtained the use of a one, and a-half-acre field, spent £5 of his own money on an order of seed potatoes from London and tasked two of his men, who had been agricultural labourers in civilian life, to plant and tend the crop. This worked especially well as a fellow officer undertook a similar project with cabbages and the swapping that ensued resulted in a better diet for a large number of men.[61] Potatoes were a particular problem during the winter of 1916–17 following a poor harvest, when even this great mainstay of the soldiers' diet was unavailable or much restricted for many months. The shortages were commented upon at home as well: the diarist Michael MacDonagh noted in mid-April 1917 that he had not eaten a potato for weeks.[62] It is difficult to locate references to food shortages in the army's contemporaneous records; no doubt this would have been a subject unhelpful to morale both at home and abroad. It does seem significant that Army Order No. 154 for 1917 states that the potato ration for prisoners in military gaols was to be reduced from 8 oz daily to 6 oz five times a week, which almost halves their entitlement and gives an indication of the struggle to maintain supplies.[63]

In the spring of 1917, a series of vegetable gardens in the back areas were instituted by the army in an attempt to grow its own produce.[64] The ASC's Director of Supplies and Transport had initially organised the work, but the gardens were taken over by the Army Agricultural Committee following its formation in January 1918. The official records confidently state that, by the end of the war, the army in France was 'practically self-supporting in vegetables and had . . . saved large quantities of forage'.[65] However, as the soldiers' accounts indicate that they appear to have been offered very few vegetables, the army's self-sufficiency may not have been hard to achieve.

The effort required to work the gardens was not always forthcoming. It was yet another task for the hard-pressed ranker, and, because the gardens were sited at rest and base camps, the requirement for labour came at a point in his service when a soldier might have hoped to be 'at rest'. In addition, the cyclical nature of life on the Western Front meant that soldiers had no guarantee that they would be able to reap what they had sown or weeded. In their camp near Elverdinghe, the men of the 10th Essex were exhorted to dig over two acres of land, in order to grow vegetables, but were reluctant to expend the energy required for cultivation in order that other soldiers camped there at harvest time might enjoy the fresh food. This account also records that, even worse, such efforts could sometimes benefit the enemy, as they had done in the Somme area when German troops had overrun British territory and inherited the carefully tended gardens.[66] If cultivated vegetables were unavailable, an imaginative approach to wild sources in the hedgerows was occasionally employed. Eric Hiscock recounts his experience in a convalescent camp in France, where the MO, concerned by the lack of vegetables in the men's diet and keen to utilise the wild greens available, ordered that the abundant nettles surrounding the camp should be picked and cooked. Sadly, the uninterested fatigue parties charged with the task were careless in their harvesting and picked any green plant that they found, and were equally careless in their washing of the 'vegetables'. Hiscock reports that it did not take long for food poisoning accompanied by sickness and diarrhoea to break out, and within a week 'the whole camp was running to the latrines'.[67]

Gardens in camps were only one aspect of the army's venture into the world of agriculture; its main area of activity was attempting to provide the ever-increasing quantities of forage required for the horses and mules. By 1916, the pressures on the shipping required to transport the enormous volume across the Channel had become unsustainable, and efforts were made to grow hay on the abandoned agricultural land near the front.[68] As the army could not grow either all the forage or the vegetables needed, a possible alternative was the purchase of supplies for both horses and men from local farmers. All such transactions were supposed to be negotiated through the Mission Militaire Française, set up by the French Army in an attempt to secure fair prices and avoid the highly unpopular requisition orders invoked by the military authorities. A key difficulty for French agriculture was the absence of fit men to work the fields, but in order to avert the manpower crisis the British Army was willing to offer its own rankers as temporary farmhands at harvest time. The rankers employed in the fields increased in number as the war progressed, the numbers of the soldiers stationed on the Western Front grew and food supplies became more restricted. Craig Gibson, in his analysis of the British Army's relationship with the farmers, comments that the rankers were generally unwilling to help for a number of reasons. The men detailed to work on the farms were often officially 'resting' and felt disinclined to engage in heavy agricultural work, just as they had in the gardens in the rest camps. Even if they did have sufficient energy, labouring was not perceived to be a suitably military occupation by many men, who felt that toiling in the fields was a degrading step too far away from a soldier's duties. In addition, there was a feeling that, as the French farmers owed their continued presence on their land to the British soldiers' sacrifices in the line, any further expectations of help were excessive.[69] Despite the general lack of enthusiasm, farm work was not universally despised and some soldiers viewed a period of digging and reaping as a pleasant interlude in their war service; it also had the added possibility of socialising with the women who had remained on the farms after their men had been called up. A *Daily Mail* postcard of the period shows a casually dressed soldier, leaning on his spade, as he chats to a French girl whose face is becomingly tilted upwards in an attitude of rapt attention as her hands fill a basket with the vegetables he has uncovered. The caption 'Are they only discussing potatoes' makes it clear that shared agricultural duties had interesting possibilities, and the investment of hard labour might well pay dividends in the romantic arena.

Even with the supplements available from local supplies, the provision of fresh and also dried vegetables was an area in which the army struggled. Indeed 'vegetables' implies a variety that was generally absent, and in most instances the word was synonymous with 'potatoes'. In the detailed breakdown of supplies sent to a division, the only vegetables specified are 7,500 lb of potatoes daily and 2,500 lb of onions four times a week.'[70] There is an annotation to the entry which states that if fresh supplies were not available 'dried vegetables or dried fruits or vegetables locally purchased are issued in lieu'. It appears overly optimistic, as we have seen, to assume that either fresh local supplies or reserves of the dried items would be available on such a scale. Fresh fruit was an even rarer ingredient than vegetables in the rankers' rations. Any fruit they did consume was usually in the form of jam, a substance that, with potatoes, stood between the rankers and scurvy. The varieties provided by the army were the subject of much comment and, as a number of popular marching songs assert, the rankers always seemed to get the least appealing:

> Plum and Apple,
> Apple and Plum,
> Plum and Apple,
> Apple and Plum,
> There is always some.
> The ASC get strawberry jam
> And lashings of rum.
> But we poor blokes
> We only get –
> Apple and Plum.[71]

It was not only the tins of jam that provided a welcome variation from the standard protein and carbohydrate diet that prevailed in the army.

Cans of 'Pork and Beans' offered a legume choice, but the mixture was generally regarded as too greasy to be appealing, the pork used being of the fat belly variety. A limited quantity of vegetables was provided in the cans known as 'M & V' (meat and vegetables), most commonly referred to as 'Maconochie', after one of the main manufacturers of the product. Cans had the advantage of being easily transported and stored, and for the men, a good tin of 'M & V', that is, one with a low fat and gristle content, represented a reasonably enjoyable meal, eaten hot or cold. It was more interesting than pure bully beef, easily accessible and did not require the interventions of a cook to make it edible.

The cooks

Ironically, the lack of involvement of the unit cooks in the preparation of food often added to its edibility since, much as in the home camps, they were not renowned for their culinary skills. In addition to its supply and transport responsibilities, the ASC was responsible for the training of army cooks, men who had been nominated by their unit to staff the cookhouse. In his 1918 study of the New Armies, Captain Basil Williams wrote that many of the complaints regarding food related to its preparation rather than the ingredients; it was felt by many that the cooks took the rations and rendered them inedible.[72] Williams noted that army cooks were held in the same low regard as the ASC. He believed this was perpetuated by the tendency to appoint lacklustre rankers to the kitchen, despite the fact that 'on the efforts of the regimental cook depends in a large measure the fighting efficiency of the whole unit'. Williams recognised that it was an 'exceedingly arduous' role and that 'the man who is indifferent in other duties is hardly likely, under any circumstances, to prove useful in the regimental cook house'.[73]

As described in Chapter 2, the army had long realised that well-trained cooks were essential for the provision of good food and from late 1915 onwards it had markedly increased the number of cooks it educated. Over the duration of the war, 67,350 men were instructed at Aldershot and the additional Schools of Cookery set up in Great Britain after 1914; another 25,277 cooks were trained at the Schools of Cookery established in France.[74] In most instances, the cookhouse was staffed by soldiers with no previous culinary expertise, something which appeared to be a badge of honour for active service units. The 3rd Battalion of the Suffolk Regiment reported in 1916 that it had received a consignment of professional cooks but had, it wrote rather disdainfully, rejected them as 'the good soldier cook has wrestled with the rations from that day to this without professional assistance beyond classes of cookery at various places'.[75] The implication was that trained chefs were inappropriate: their skills were regarded with suspicion rather than admiration. Perhaps the feeling was that professional chefs might impart a degree of culinary finesse to the proceedings which would somehow unman the soldiers, who were best served by enthusiastic amateurs 'wrestling with' rather than cooking the rations. The equation of wrestling with cooking also seems significant, imparting as it does a martial quality to the cookhouse that it might otherwise have lacked.

Motivational efforts were undertaken to improve the cooks' performance, often in the form of contests between units in an attempt to increase the pride taken in their work. J. Sanderson recorded in his diary a divisional competition that offered a prize for the cleanest, tidiest cookhouse, and R. York Rickard proudly noted that his travelling cooker was 'the only one reported clean', in an inspection by a visiting dignitary.[76] As an MO, Captain J.C. Dunn had a professional interest in ensuring that the men were fed properly and he expressed concern regarding the wide variation in the cooks' abilities across different units. Dunn believed that this resulted from the practice of companies being allowed to manage their own cooking arrangements, with a consequent lack of control over the standard of their products.[77]

While the skills of some of the cooks may have been lacking, the challenges they faced were great, given the limited ingredients and facilities available. The army did what it could to support them and its key textbook for cooks, the *Manual of Military Cooking and Dietary Mobilization*, was revised to include greater information on food preparation in cookhouses set up on active service. The original manual provided extensive details of how to prepare and cook food for men who were stationary in camps, but it paid less attention to the demands placed upon catering by the movement of troops. In the subsequent issues of the manual, increasing attention was given to the challenges of preparing food in the field, whether supporting the men on marches or setting up kitchens in temporary billets and forward areas. In these later editions, there was a greater explanation of cooking terms and more detailed instructions on the most basic tasks, such as making tea, which, the cooks were advised, should never be made in a vessel that had contained broth or soup without first washing the container.[78] The brewing of tea in an unwashed soup cauldron was – according to the unhappy rankers – an all too common occurrence. There is additional substantiation of their repeated complaints from the journalist Michael MacDonagh. In late 1914, as part of his research for an article, he sampled the skills of army cooks and subsequently wrote in his diary 'I can vouch for it that the tea has a meaty flavour!'[79] MacDonagh was appalled by the food produced on his visit to the army camp, declaring it 'execrable'. Despite the quality of the food, he echoed the view of the *Suffolk Regimental Gazette* in his stated preference for amateur cooks, concluding that the War Office would be dismissive of any suggestion that professionals should be provided. It is clear from the level of detail in the army's cookery guidelines that it had realised that most of the men it was training had no previous cooking experience and required explicit guidance on the simplest of duties. The manual's range is broad, and it includes intricate descriptions of how to butcher animals should the opportunity arise, and provides recipes for all parts of the carcass, from nose to tail. It does seem somewhat optimistic that a cook who needed to be told how to brew tea would metamorphose into a master butcher and confident chef when circumstances demanded. The butchery details provided were for cows and sheep, but opportunities for general cooks to put the detail into practice appeared to be scarce, although the subject's general unsuitability for inclusion in the men's accounts may be a reason for the lack of references. The ASC provided specialist field butchery units and it is likely that they would have dealt with any planned slaughtering. The cooks may not have had many chances to butcher cows and sheep, but the abundance of dead horses on the Western Front, regular victims of the shelling, frequently presented them with ad hoc supplements to the meat ration.

A number of cooks were diligent and worked hard to master the skills required. A.J. Simmons attended a cookery school in Colchester in September 1915 and filled two notebooks with painstaking lists of recipes and tips to improve the rations.[80] C.R. Keller recalled his enthusiasm for his temporary posting as a cook and viewed it as an excellent opportunity to improve the men's diet, making nourishing soups and creating porridge from ground biscuit. Unfortunately, he soon found himself back on the other side of the serving table when a permanent cook arrived. The new man did not live up to Keller's standards; instead he proved to be lazy and uninterested, and the diet swiftly returned to meals of minimum preparation and maximum monotony.[81] It was tempting for cooks, regardless of their training, to revert to the easiest options – bully and biscuit – which was of course the least appetising for the men they were supposed to support.

The preparation of hot meals was especially difficult away from the permanent kitchens. In addition to the standard manual, the

Quartermaster-General's Branch issued a booklet, *Cooking in the Field*, in November 1917, specifically to address such problems.[82] The publication describes in detail the construction of alternative ovens less demanding of fuel, such as hay box cookers, which could be used to prepare meals for smaller groups of men. The booklet served to remind cooks that shortages of fuel could be overcome and were no excuse for reverting to a cold diet. In addition there were a number of new recipes, although 'new' is not strictly accurate. The names of the dishes may have been novel, but the ingredients must have induced a sense of *déjà vu* in the men. Bully beef remained the chief constituent, whether in 'Bread Soup' (bully with bread and stock), 'Spring Soup' (bully with vegetables and stock) or 'Potted Meat' (minced bully with pepper).[83] Even allowing for different tastes and expectations, it is hard to believe that some of the recipes were palatable, for example the suggestion for Fish Cakes:

FISH CAKES[84]

Ingredients	Method
10 tins Bully Beef	Pass the meat and herrings through the
10 tins Herrings	mincer. Add breadcrumbs, pepper and
4 lbs Breadcrumbs	mashed potatoes and mix with a little
4 lbs Potatoes	stock.
2 ozs Pepper	Shape into cakes, roll in breadcrumbs or
A little stock	flour and fry in hot fat.

The booklet is indicative of the army's awareness that soldiers were not always fed as well as they should have been. It is emphatic on the importance of varying their diet: 'to serve the same dishes day after day shows lack of initiative and interest on the part of the cook, besides making the meals dull and monotonous for the men'. This is certainly true, but it seems that the men's well-being was not the sole concern of the author. The preface of *Cooking in the Field* explains how critical it is that the men are fed properly for their morale and health, but it also emphasises the good housekeeping aspects of the process. The importance of the cooks' awareness of possible economies is stressed, because as the publication states 'where men mess together in comparatively large numbers great savings can be effected without in any way stinting the meals'. The pressure on food supplies at home and abroad had increased considerably by 1917 and the emphasis on economy in the cookhouse is a reflection of these shortages. The dual role of the cook is reiterated throughout the booklet, with ideas for new dishes accompanied by reminders about the importance of the careful management of supplies. Thrift was reinforced by the inclusion of balance sheets in which the smallest amounts of rations issued had to be recorded. The significance of fats, in particular, is evident with the introduction of an innovation named the 'Dripping Account'.[85] Fats were an expensive foodstuff and cooks were required to keep close control of them. This included the suet from butchered animals, which could be rendered down into dripping, or the grease they were supposed to skim off the top of cold washing-up water, from which glycerine could be extracted for use in the manufacture of explosives.[86] The official statistics highlight the success of this operation and record that the glycerine obtained amounted to approximately 2,800 tons, a sufficient quantity to produce propellant charges for 28,000,000 shells for the 18-pounder guns which formed the backbone of the Royal Artillery's operations.[87]

Positions of privilege

The army's published requirements make it clear that the role of an army cook, if all the designated functions were performed properly, was a demanding one. The cooks' burdens and responsibilities were widely unacknowledged by other soldiers. A.Stuart Dolden comments in his memoir that, before he became a cook: 'I used always to pull their legs unmercifully, telling them that they had a "cushy job", and that it was not soldiering at all.'[88] Unsurprisingly, Dolden writes that he revised his opinion once he realised the hard work involved. Dolden's published account of life as an army cook is relatively unusual, suggesting that most of his compeers were not motivated to describe their war service in the kitchen. The response 'I cooked', to the question 'What did you do in the war, Daddy?' was not one that many men wanted to articulate publicly. The chief function of a soldier was to bear arms, to fight the enemy to be engaged in support tasks; whether driving for the ASC or preparing meals, was to be an accessory to the main event. The skills of the support workers were 'civilian' skills that were perceived to be outside the essence of soldiering, which was the ability to fire a gun or twist a bayonet, not drive horses or fry bacon. Perhaps too, there was a degree of resentment that many in the ASC were practising skills which would stand them in good stead in the postwar world; a driver or a cook would have skills transferable to the civilian job market, unlike the more rarefied competencies infantrymen acquired.

For the majority of the rankers, cookery was regarded as a feminine enterprise; an aspect which compounded the cooks' position on the periphery of 'proper' soldiering. A number of soldiers used the traditionally feminine nature of the cook's role to pour scorn upon the men that undertook it. A hardened soldier in F.A. Voigt's novel-memoir sneers 'why, tain't a man's job, it's only old women what goes inter the cook-'ouse'.[89] Yet the cooks themselves sometimes revelled in their introduction to a world from which they had generally been excluded in civilian life. Some used their new experiences as a point of shared interest in their communications with their mothers. The tyro cook A.P. Burke was proud of his efforts for his officers' latest meal and wrote to his family: 'it was top hole especially the [rice] pudding – that's where I specialize. I remember how I used to break the skin for Ma on Sunday Morning – Ma you will have to watch your laurels.'[90]

The cook's life was not necessarily one of unmitigated ease and safety; in some circumstances they could find themselves under greater pressure than the men they fed. For example, when the troops were on the move, sometimes for days at a time, the cooks had to march behind the travelling kitchens. Instead of spending the allotted ten minutes in each hour's march at rest, they had to tend the ovens and their contents. It was not easy to prepare food in such circumstances, where the fifty minutes of marching was time enough to allow the stew to either burn or prove to be irretrievably under-cooked, both outcomes which would result in hungry and disappointed soldiers. In addition, there was the sense of responsibility that many felt towards the men they fed. R. York Rickard served as a cook in the Civil Service Rifles and wrote in his diary on 18 October 1915, 'They [ordinary soldiers] are having a rougher time than we cooks are and I am willing to do anything for their comfort. Thank God I am a cook'.[91] Rickard's comments read as both an admission of guilt, a recognition that others were risking far more than he, and an acknowledgement of his relief that he was able to enjoy the relative security of the cook's role. Whatever the burdensome nature of his duties on long marches, they did not compare to the regular life-threatening danger of service as an ordinary infantryman.

Discomfort on long marches was bearable, but the cooks' physical safety was not always guaranteed and there were occasions when they were as exposed as any front line soldier. Indeed, in January 1917 Rickard himself had lost confidence in the safety of his position and no longer felt the relief he had earlier expressed. He found himself cooking under continuous shelling on the Ypres Salient, a bombardment so severe that his assistant went 'temporarily mad . . . the worst case of "wind-up" I have seen'.[92] In well-led units, with conscientious officers to ensure the proper levels of support for the men, cooks were less protected from the realities of war, whatever their regular colleagues might have suggested. Cooks were not permitted to lurk in the safety of the back areas but were expected to take the travelling cookers close enough to the front line to provide the soldiers with a hot meal. Proximity to the enemy often meant that the cooks were as vulnerable as any other soldier. Major H.A. Stewart appears to have had a rather optimistic view of the operation of the mobile cookers. He observed that, in the manner of unofficial truces regarding ration parties referred to earlier, as the Germans used the same kind of cookers, 'there seemed a tacit understanding between the combatants to refrain from shooting at these vehicles'.[93] At times of unplanned retreat the cooks may well have been slowed by the responsibility for their equipment, the abandonment of which would no doubt have resulted in some form of inquiry. During the Ludendorff Offensive of spring 1918, E.S. Styles recalled that the cooks had no option but to flee, causing disappointment amongst the men who were 'hoping to have something hot for ration, [until] Jerry came along and captured the field cooker full of stew, the cooks had to run for it.'[94].

Whatever the realities, the perceived relative safety of the unit cooks was a frequent grouse of front line troops, but it was the ASC that became the main target for their bitterness. Soldiers' songs and jokes are full of scathing references to the less than valorous conduct of the support staff, or the 'Anglais Sans Courage', as some called them.[95] The addition of 'Royal' to their name in 1918 did nothing to improve perceptions, and the new acronym, RASC, was given the translation 'Run Away Somebody's Coming'. Sergeant Major Ernest Shephard wrote indignantly in his diary of an ASC baker who had been awarded the Distinguished Conduct Medal for 'producing the maximum amount of *bread*. Ye Gods, what an insult to a *fighting soldier*, who risks life daily.'[96] There is an editorial note against the entry explaining that the story of the baker's DCM 'was almost certainly apocryphal'. This was not the case and records show that in 1916 ASC Acting Staff Sergeant-Major T. Martin did in fact receive this honour, 'for continuous good services throughout the campaign as Master Baker in charge of a bakery. He displayed conspicuous ability and resource'.[97]

Admittedly, bakers at the BSDs were in no physical danger from the enemy, stationed as they were well beyond the reach of shelling, but just as cooks might find themselves under threat, so those in the ASC transport units worked in dangerous situations as they ferried supplies forward from the railheads. Indeed, they could be even more exposed than those in the trenches, as other soldiers sometimes acknowledged. ASC motor vehicles were also used to transport working parties forward and it was common for the men to ask the driver to stop before the lorries reached dangerously exposed junctions and crossroads, in order that they might get out and walk. They felt that the motor columns presented too visible a target for enemy gunners and would resume their position in the trucks only once they had passed through the risky areas.[98] Those of the ASC working with the horses and mules on the trains delivering the rations had the additional problem of dealing with frightened animals. Christopher Stone hints at the difficulties that entailed when he wrote home of one transport party: 'Five mules killed, and the rest not liking the dark and the mud and the shelling one little bit.'[99] When shelling started, the men had to try and hold on to the pack animals and were therefore not at liberty to dive for the nearest available cover, as any other soldier would have done. As noted earlier in the chapter, movement was a dangerous activity near the front line where being upright could make soldiers vulnerable. Santanu Das has identified 'a regression to the clumsy horizontality of beasts' in the trenches, where men preferred to 'creep, crawl, worm and burrow', in order to avoid exposure to the violence that surrounded them.[100] Whilst service in a front line trench was deeply disturbing, it at least afforded the opportunity to 'dig-in', to use the physical geography as a shield against the onslaught. In addition, men could take comfort from each other's presence. A number of photographs from the trenches show soldiers huddled together against trench walls or in dug-outs, rather like cornered beasts, but there was some small sense of security in the proximity of the earth and other men. The ASC men were often denied this meagre comfort; the nature of their work was movement and in exposed areas they were as much at risk as a front line soldier.

Extra food

It was not just physical safety that ordinary soldiers used as a determinant of privilege: control over food supplies was real power in a world where men could at worst go hungry, or at best longed for relief from the monotony of much of their diet. W.M. Floyd recorded in his diary that he made it a point of principle never to argue with a cook, as it was invariably 'bad for the stomach'.[101] It was widely accepted that, in terms of food, 'the ASC took the best and the officers' batmen the pick after that'.[102] The next in line were the unit cooks. The ASC had access not just to food, but to other important items such as beer, whisky and coal. I.T. Rees's diary describes his life as an ASC driver, and throughout the whole of 1918 there is not one reference to a lack of food. During 1918, a year when the British Army experienced both retreat and advance, a high proportion of the soldiers' accounts make reference to food shortages, but it appears that Rees was able to eat well and his attentions were focused on scrounging alcohol and fuel rather than rations. He is delighted when, on a trip to the coal dump, he manages to smuggle a couple of hundredweights back in the wagon box for use in his billet.[103] Rees was seeking to warm his own room, but some soldiers in privileged positions sought to sell their gains on the open market. Ordinary soldiers were resentful of not only the inequality in food supply but also the fact that the cooks and the ASC profiteered at the expense of the men. David Englander and James Osborne recognised the corruption surrounding food supplies. They calculate that the actual food the ordinary soldier received was equal in value to only a small percentage of the money spent on its procurement: as little as half in the camps at home.[104] There was prewar evidence of the bribery surrounding the award of army supply contracts, and no doubt many soldiers would have been aware of a recent scandalous court case. In January 1914, eight staff from the grocery firm of Lipton's were prosecuted, together with eight army officers, over the payment of large sums to the latter as 'sweeteners' in an effort to gain lucrative supply contracts for army canteens. The proceedings made it clear that the army quartermasters and cooks were routinely involved in such schemes and received generous Christmas presents as inducements.[105]

The taint of corruption lingered and there are references in numerous soldiers' accounts to the cooks exploiting army supplies, and consequently the men, for their own gain. The abuse of their position that some of the ASC men displayed was not particular to the First World War. A.F. Corbett recalled his service in the Boer War: when he was ill with enteric fever and given an eighth of a tin of condensed milk to aid his recovery, he saw the NCO in charge of supplies 'having no illness at all . . . enjoying a tin all to himself'.[106] The privileges access to food supplies brought were considerable and very lucrative. P.H. Jones's unpublished memoir refers to a café which 'seems to have an unlimited stock of English Army jam, about which the ASC could probably unfold a tale', and R. Gwinnell asserted that a large portion of the rations was sold to local people by the cook.[107] The latter soldier also thanked God that, unlike others, he had never stooped so low as to steal food when on ration party duty.[108] Whist stealing from one's peers was a crime to which few soldiers or veterans were likely to have admitted, their vehemence in its condemnation demonstrates the revulsion the misappropriation of food provoked. The cooks and the ASC had access to supplies and the opportunity to commit such offences, and some did. The possibility of systematic theft was open as well to the quartermasters, who in the confusion of the supply dumps might easily pick up items that had been overlooked. Captain A.O. Temple Clark recalled one such opportunist who always had a spare limber (a horse-drawn cart) standing by for such extras, and Temple Clark notes that this man's activities worked 'to his considerable benefit'.[109] There is no mention of the officer taking the man to task, although Army Order No. 346 issued in September 1915 addressed the problem of the 'improper disposal of rations and forage' and states that: 'Commanding officers will take effective measures to ensure that no portion of the ration which is capable of being used as human food is illegally sold or otherwise made away with. They will deal severely with soldiers under their command found to be implicated in such illicit traffic.'[110] *The Manual of Military Law* is equally categorical on such matters and Section 18 of the Army Act specifically provides for the prosecution of embezzlers.[111] The desirability of pursuing such charges is considered in the context of the widespread issue of scrounging in Chapter 6, as clearly theft was not a problem confined to those in the support services. Whatever the lapses amongst the rankers, the men regarded those with direct access to food supplies with suspicion. The diary of F.W. Sutcliffe provides an example of such concern and also evidence of the way in which an officer responded to the problem. Sutcliffe's diary is packed with references to food shortages and the resultant hunger amongst the men. Matters come to a head in August 1918 when the grumblings became sufficiently loud to reach the ear of the commanding officer. Sutcliffe and his pals believed the cooks were misappropriating their rations, or, as he describes it, 'we had an idea that there was some twisting going on with our grub'. The major resolved the matter by relieving the cooks of their position and installing a trusted and respected soldier to run the cookhouse.[112] Sutcliffe makes no mention of any official inquiry or court martial having taken place, and it might be supposed that his commander's response in keeping the matter on an informal footing was not uncommon.

The tasks that the unit cooks and the ASC performed were of organisational necessity, but men whose primary role was to hold a steering wheel or a saucepan rather than a rifle would always be resented by the rankers. A position of relative safety must have appealed to many of the ordinary soldiers, but perhaps they were equally repelled by it: to avoid the ultimate demand of masculinity, the responsibility of killing or being killed for one's country, carried with it a certain sense of embarrassment. Cooks and members of the ASC were relieved of some of the shame associated with their privileged position, as men were at least officially, allocated to such posts at random. Pragmatism suggests a place in the ASC, or as a batman or cook, could be given as a reward or perhaps in response to family connections or financial inducement, but for the majority the unit in which they served was determined by the army's need not the individual's preference. George Herbert Hill who volunteered in July 1915, did try. After the Recruiting Sergeant had vetoed his first ambition of a place in a cavalry regiment, Hill wondered whether a posting to the ASC might be forthcoming. The Sergeant dismissed him with a grimace: 'That's not a regiment . . . Besides there hasn't been a vacancy in that bleeding crowd since 1914.'[113] Hill, like most new recruits, found himself in the infantry.

Officers' eating

The rankers' resentment regarding superior food was also directed at another group within the military: their officers, whose eating arrangements were generally quite separate from their own. The system of messes for officers, both commissioned and non-commissioned, continued on the Western Front as it had in peacetime and the elaborate rituals, particularly of the former, were preserved as far as possible. John Baynes describes the conventions of the 2nd Scottish Rifles' officers' mess which included: Turkish cigarettes only in the ante-room; no smoking at all between 7.30 pm and the start of dinner; after-dinner smoking only after the port had circulated twice, and new officers were compelled to wait three years before they could stand on the hearth rug.[114] Strict regulations were a common feature, and Captain A.O. Temple Clark, who served with the ASC, recalled the junior officers' early morning rush to breakfast, a result of the mess rule that forbade a subaltern from entering the dining room after 8.30 am.[115] The demands of the conflict appear to have had only a limited impact on such arcane formalities in the theatre of war, where to maintain standards of dining was regarded as a point of honour and essential to proper officer conduct and morale.

Gary Sheffield asserts that 'a limited meritocracy emerged in the British Army during the Great War' and it is certainly the case that casualty rates amongst junior officers forced a widening of the recruitment criteria.[116] The broadening of the officer intake was not warmly embraced by the army's hierarchy. When William Carr, a Scottish farmer, applied for a commission in 1916, he knew that he had failed because of the look of incredulity on the panel's faces when, in answer to their enquiry, he told them that games had not been played at his school.[117] The necessity of commissioning men who deviated from the traditional requirements of the British Army did not result in an associated widening of the acceptable comportment and attributes of the officers. The new style of officers, despite lacking a private income or an education from the best public schools, were still expected to adopt the established values and behaviours of the rank. Their challenge was not only to lead their men but to 'pass' amongst their more socially illustrious peers as acceptable members of the mess. Those unprepared by their background for the officer's world had to learn fast, and Sheffield notes that non-public-school officers soaked up 'public-school values' through education, training and socialisation.[118] Commissioned rank had, throughout the history of the British Army, been a confirmation of social status – an officer *was* a gentleman – but the influx of officers from wider social strata threw the equivalence into doubt. In order to present a convincing 'officer persona', an understanding of the complex eating rituals of the mess was essential. Martin Petter quotes Stuart Cloete, a public-school-educated son of a financier who was appalled by the type of officers he served with in a reserve battalion in 1917: 'Many of them came from the lower middle class and had no manners, including table manners, of any kind.'[119] The non-officer-class recruit was expected to assume the appropriate persona through the consumption of 'officers' food' and the absorption of 'officers' manners'.

Whatever the trials in the officers' messes, food was an area where the contrast between life in and out of the ranks was highlighted. The differences between the officers' eating and that of their men were more visible on active service than they had been in the training camps. The geographical separation between the two groups was often less demar-cated, for example, in village billets where they could find themselves as next door neighbours. The hierarchy of culture and customs amongst the British was not a feature of every army. Australian soldiers, in particular, were appalled by what they perceived as its injustices and unnecessary rigidity. In his analysis of troop morale, J.G. Fuller comments that R.C. Sherriff's play *Journey's End* was met with bemusement by postwar audiences of Australian veterans. The theatregoers could not comprehend a world where the officers lived and ate in the relative safety of a dug-out, while their men endured the exposure of the trenches.[120] The Anzac experience may have been the exception to the rule as there is evidence of a sharp division between officers' and men's eating in other militaries. For example, the German Army, where a chant popular amongst the rankers and frequently inscribed on the toilet walls of the leave trains ran as follows: 'den Offizieren Mannschaftsbrot und Mannschaftsessen, / dann ware der Krieg schon lang vergessen' ('If officers got men's bread and men's food, / The war would already be long forgotten').[121] Many British officers acknowledged the superiority of their circumstances to those of the men and echoed Julian Bickersteth who wrote home, 'These [infantry rankers] are the men who are always treated worst . . . they live in the greater hardships'.[122]

Key to the comfort of the officers were their batmen: a servant's role many rankers were happy to assume, as it afforded a degree of protection from the usual hardships. On the Western Front, it required time and effort to eat well; the batman was dedicated to obtaining the best rations available, scrounging possible additions, and, when there was no mess cook, preparing the food as tastily as possible. Captain Henry Ogle confirmed this advantage, even in the line where, although his servant ' could never be sure when he would catch me, nor where . . . he never failed to be there on time with food, drink or some oddment'.[123]

Regardless of the presence of batmen, the broadening of the officer base and the conditions of the conflict, have prompted a number of historians to argue that the conflict brought the officers and their men into a close and equitable relationship. George Robb states that 'trench warfare provided exceptionally favourable circumstances for the development of close inter-rank relationships'.[124] Belief in the relative democracy of the trenches emanates more strongly from the officers' accounts than those of their men. Eric Leed quotes a postwar group 'Comrades of the Great War', a name which admittedly gives a clue as to their political sympathies, where one veteran declared 'there was no comradeship in the trenches. It was simply a case of members of the working classes held down by brutal and iron discipline. Different rations, different pay and different risk. The class line was as clear in France as it is at home.'[125] For this ranker as for so many others, food was a key point of differentiation between the two groups within the army. The view expressed here was extreme, and in circumstances where good junior officers shared fully their men's front line experience and when they too were reduced to a reliance on the most basic of army rations, a degree of empathy and camaraderie did develop. In the trenches, the men's resentment often shifted away from those officers who shared service at the front towards the brass-hats and HQ personnel, privileged in the safety and relative comfort of the rear areas. Food provided a focal point for comparison between these different lifestyles. Frederick Hodges remembered the resentment and anger caused by the staff officer who curtailed a brief, and all too rare, visit to the men at the front with the words 'Keep up the good work. I must be off! We've got roast pork for dinner tonight.'[126]

The view of a community bonded together in the face of a common enemy, whether it was the Germans or the brass-hats, was one subscribed to by the young front line officer Sidney Rogerson, who wrote: 'In spite of all the differences in rank, we were comrades, brothers dwelling together in unity.'[127] However, this perceived unity did not extend to the central aspects of day-to-day living; Rogerson, for all his talk of equality, did not eat with his men when in the line. The sharing of food can be regarded as an egalitarian act; Elizabeth Gaskell writes that there is 'Nothing like the act of eating for equalising men. Dying is nothing to it.'[128] She asserts that, in the context of an industrialist setting up a canteen for his workers, the common act of eating had the potential to equalise men, regardless of education, rank and class, to a greater degree than any other bodily function or experience. Whatever the truth of such an assertion, the British Army was not an environment in which it was put to the test.

Even when in the line, officers usually had a cook to prepare their meals, a privileged position for a ranker. Jack Sweeney, who spent much of his war filling such a position, was well aware of his good fortune: 'My luck is in . . . it is better than doing sentry duty.' The price that Sweeney paid was the frustration caused by the struggle to produce acceptable meals, in terms of both the number of courses and their quality, on an old pail filled with coke.[129] Not all men were as obliging as Sweeney, and the letters Canon J.O. Coop wrote home to his wife contain numerous references to his cook, the recalcitrant Murphy, whose culinary skills appeared to have left everything to be desired. Murphy undercooked the pork, omitted sugar from the apple sauce and then produced a dish of bread sauce which Coop described as being ' the most senseless cooking mess I ever saw and it tasted worse than it looked'.[130]

Despite the occasional hopeless cook, officers' food was generally of a higher quality than their men's. Possibly the only occasion, in terms of army provisioning, when the men may have eaten better than their officers was on long marches where travelling kitchens were used. The cooks' efforts throughout the morning would hopefully result in a hot meal at the men's dinnertime. Sidney Rogerson thought the stews produced, which he tasted in his capacity as supervisor of the rankers' welfare, were pretty good 'even if, as sometimes happened, a kipper or two had found their way among the meat, vegetables and biscuits, "maconochies" and beans'.[131] In his praise of what sounds an unappetising mixture, Rogerson is dismissive of what he regarded as the unsophisticated palates of the rankers. He believed that these were men who would find it hard to differentiate between kippers and beef, and, even if they could, the combination would not be of concern to them. The making of stews and soups for the men was popular with officers for reasons other than the boost to morale that hot food could provide. *Cooking in the Field* comments favourably on the digestibility and wholesomeness of such dishes, but then goes on to hint rather ominously: 'nor does any other method of preparing food afford as many opportunities of utilizing material which would otherwise be wasted'.[132] Rogerson believed that, whatever the combinations, it was a tastier option than the cold luncheon that the officers had, there being insufficient time for their cook to unpack the mess equipment and prepare a hot meal in the hour's break.

The provisioning of the rankers on the Western Front presented the army with a logistical challenge on an unprecedented scale, and its official records are self-congratulatory in the description of their achievements. The complexity of the supply systems, the detailed cookery manuals and the sheer volume of provisions transported are evidence of the effort expended in the attempts to ensure the men were properly fed. The groups responsible for the supply and delivery of the rations such as the ASC and the cooks attracted criticism from the ordinary soldier, as did the officers with their much resented food privileges. The rankers' dismissal of the ASC was not echoed by other commentators, a number of whom were more enthusiastic about their achievements. An ardent *Daily Mail* journalist, despite his recognition that the ASC lacked the obvious glamour of the fighting men, still managed to compose an overwhelmingly heroic article on the movements of a ration supply train: 'There is none of the stimulant of speed, no dashing forward, no heartstirring plunge through the barrage – just the steady plod-plod of the slow, strong old horses and the rock and bump of wagons on the rutted, broken roads.'[133] Similarly, *Punch* printed a poem in February 1918 celebrating those unsung heroes 'the plucky old Cookers', who risked their lives preparing food in the 'shell-swept wastes'.[134] The men at the front were considerably less generous in their estimation of both the pluck of the ASC and the cooks, and were frequently disappointed by the army's attempts to feed them, as we shall see in the following chapter.

Notes

1 Colonel R.H. Beadon, *The Royal Army Service Corps. A History of Transport and Supply in the British Army* (Cambridge, 1931), p. 95.
2 *Statistics of Military Effort*, p. 877.
3 B.H. Liddell Hart, *Thoughts on War* (Staplehurst, 1999), p. 75.
4 Liddell Hart, *Thoughts on War*, p. 45.
5 *Statistics of Military Effort*, p. 580.
6 Liddell Hart, *Thoughts on War*, p. 75.
7 Major General Julian Thompson, *The Lifeblood of War. Logistics in Armed Conflict* (London, 1991), p. 41.
8 *Statistics of Military Effort*, p. 877.
9 Beadon, *The Royal Army Service Corps*, p. 96.
10 Senior Supply Officer, *Supplies and Supply Transport in the 38th (Welsh Division)* (London, date unknown), pp. 25–26.
11 John Keegan, Richard Holmes, with John Gau, *Soldiers. A History of Men in Battle* (London, 1985), p. 235.
12 Lieutenant-Colonel G.C. Shaw, *Supply in Modern War* (London, 1938), p. 10.
13 Richard Holmes' Introduction to Young, *Army Service Corps*, p. 3.
14 Young, *Army Service Corps*, pp. 383 and 385.
15 Young, *Army Service Corps*, pp. 383 and 385.
16 C.R. Jones, IWM 05/9/1, letter dated 1.1.1916. 'RE' = Royal Engineers and 'RTO' = Railway Transport Officer.
17 Coppard, *With a Machine Gun*, p. 51.
18 Young, *Army Service Corps*, p. 99.
19 Young, *Army Service Corps*, p. 57.
20 T.H. Cubbon, IWM 78/4/1, diary.
21 John Laffin, *On the Western Front. Soldiers' Stories from France and Flanders 1914–1918* (Gloucester, 1985), p. 16.
22 Major H.A. Stewart, *From Mons to Loos. Being the Diary of a Supply Officer* (London, 1916), p. 13.
23 Ian Malcolm Brown, *British Logistics on the Western Front 1914–1919* (Westport, 1998), p. 63.
24 J. Sanderson, IWM 87/33/1, diary entry dated 10.4.1918.
25 Letter from Haig, cited in Ian Brown, *British Logistics*, p. 185.
26 S.J. McClaren (ed.), *Somewhere in Flanders. Letters of a Norfolk Padre in the Great War* (Dereham, 2005), letter dated 4.12.1918.
27 *Statistics of Military Effort*, p. 848.
28 *Field Service Pocket Book 1916*, p. 72.
29 A Senior Supply Officer, *Supplies and Supply Transport in the 38th (Welsh Division) by a Senior Supply Offices (London, n.d.).*
30 A Senior Supply Officer, *Supplies and Supply Transport*, p. 4.
31 Beadon, *The Royal Army Service Corps*, p. 98.

32 Young, *Army Service Corps,* p. 390

33 See reference in Chapter 2 to the army's *1899 Supply Handbook,* which stated that frozen meat lacked nutrition.

34 *Statistics of Military Effort,* p. 842.

35 *Statistics of Military Effort,* p. 859.

36 *Statistics of Military Effort,* p. 842.

37 *Field Service Pocket Book 1916,* p. 52.

38 Beadon, *The Royal Army Service Corps,* p. 98.

39 Tony Ashworth, *Trench Warfare 1914–1918. The Live and Let Live System* (London, 2000), p. 9.

40 Beadon, *The Royal Army Service Corps,* p. 101.

41 Stanley J. Levy, *Memories of the 71st and 83rd Companies RASC MT 1914–1918* (private publication, 1931), p. 37.

42 Lines from *Rail-head* found in Essex Regimental Archive; Waterhouse served with the Essex Regiment.

43 *Notes for Infantry Officers on Trench Warfare* (London, 1916), p. 39.

44 Cited in Stephen Bull, *An Officer's Manual of the Western Front 1914–1918* (London, 2008), p. 81.

45 *On the Road from Mons with an Army Service Corps Train. By Its Commander* (London, 1916), p. 8.

46 Banks and Chell, *With the 10th Essex,* p. 237.

47 *On the Road from Mons,* pp. 11 and 62.

48 Captain H. Wilberforce-Bell, *War Vignettes: Being the Experiences of an Officer in France and England during the Great War* (Bombay, 1916), p. 31.

49 Ashworth, *Trench Warfare,* p. 25.

50 E. Brunsdon, IWM 85/15/1, memoir, p. 39.

51 P.H. Jones, IWM P246, memoir, pp. 94–7.

52 P.H. Jones, IWM P246, memoir, pp. 71.

53 A.P. Burke, IWM Con Shelf, letter dated 11.5.1916.

54 Rogerson, *Twelve Days on the Somme,* p. 52.

55 Patrick MacGill, *The Great Push* (Edinburgh, 2000), p. 110.

56 Martin Pegler, *British Tommy 1914–18* (Oxford, 1996), p. 26

57 *Statistics of Military Effort,* p. 586.

58 Richard Holmes, 'Battle, the Experience of Modern Combat' in Townshend (ed.), *The Oxford Illustrated History of Modern War,* p. 204.

59 Dunn, *The War the Infantry Knew,* p. 434.

60 *Statistics of Military Effort,* p. 850.

61 Captain A.O. Temple Clark, *Transport and Sport in the Great War Period* (London, 1938), p. 108.

62 MacDonagh, *In London During the Great War,* diary entry for 15.4.1917.

63 *Army Orders 1917,* No. 154.

64 A. Smith, *Four Years on the Western Front* (London, 1922), p. 226 and p. 281.

65 *Statistics of Military Effort,* p. 583.

66 Banks and Chell, *With the 10th Essex*, p. 246.
67 Hiscock, *The Bells of Hell*, p. 106.
68 Craig Gibson, 'The British Army, French Farmers and the War on the Western Front 1914–1918', *Past and Present*, 180 (2003), p. 179.
69 Gibson, 'The British Army, French Farmers and the War', pp. 217–218.
70 A Senior Supply Officer, *Supplies and Supply Transport*, pp. 25–26.
71 Arthur, *When This Bloody War Is Over: Soldiers' Songs of the First World War*, p. 84.
72 Captain Basil Williams, *Raising and Training the New Armies* (London, 1918), p. 47.
73 Williams, *Raising and Training*, p. 49.
74 *Statistics of Military Effort*, p. 580.
75 *Suffolk Regimental Gazette 1916*, West Suffolk Records Office, Bury St Edmunds.
76 J. Sanderson, IWM 87/33/1, diary entry dated 3.2.1917, and Jill Knight, *'All Bloody Gentlemen': The Civil Service Rifles in the Great War:* (Barnsley, 2005), p. 74.
77 Dunn, *The War the Infantry Knew*, p. 264.
78 *Manual of Military Cooking* (1917), p. 65.
79 MacDonagh, *In London During the Great War*, diary entry dated 25.9.1914.
80 A.J. Simmons, IWM Misc. 163 (2503).
81 C.R. Keller, IWM 02/55/1, memoir, p. 69.
82 *Cooking in the Field*, S.S.615 (London, 1917).
83 *Cooking in the Field*, pp. 17–20.
84 *Cooking in the Field*, p. 29.
85 *Cooking in the Field*, pp. 32–33.
86 *Cooking in the Field*, pp. 34–35.
87 *Statistics of Military Effort*, p. 873.
88 Dolden, *Cannon Fodder*, p. 64.
89 F.A. Voigt, *Combed Out* (London, 1929), p. 55.
90 A.P. Burke, IWM Con Shelf, letter dated 2.4.1916.
91 Knight, *'All Bloody Gentlemen'*, p. 61.
92 Knight, *'All Bloody Gentlemen'*, p. 101.
93 Stewart, *From Mons to Loos*, p. 181.
94 E.S. Styles, memoir, Essex Regimental Archive.
95 Alan Wilkinson (ed.), *Destiny. The War Letters of Captain Jack Oughtred M.C. 1915–1918* (Beverley, 1996), letter dated 25.9.1917.
96 Bruce Rosser (ed.), *A Sergeant-Major's War: From Hill 60 to the Somme. Ernest Shephard* (Marlborough, 1987), p. 57.
97 Young, *Army Service Corps*, p. 374.
98 Young, *Army Service Corps*, p. 111.
99 G. Sheffield and G. Inglis (eds), *From Vimy Ridge to the Rhine. The Great War Letters of Christopher Stone DSO MC* (Marlborough, 1989), letter dated 19.11.1916.

100 Santanu Das, *Touch and Intimacy in First World War Literature* (Cambridge, 2005), pp. 43–44.

101 W.M. Floyd, IWM 87/33/1, diary entry dated 24.9.1914.

102 Denis Winter, *Death's Men*, p. 147.

103 I.T. Rees, IWM 87/55/1, diary entry dated 5.2.1918.

104 Englander and Osborne, 'Jack, Tommy and Henry Dubb', p. 600.

105 Alec Waugh, *The Lipton Story* (London, 1952), pp. 167–169.

106 Cited in McGuffie, *Rank and File*, p. 373.

107 P.H. Jones, IWM P246, memoir, p. 187.

108 Gwinnell, IWM 01/38/1, memoir, pp. 76 and 109.

109 Clark, *Transport and Sport in the Great War Period*, p. 149.

110 *Army Orders 1915*, No. 346.

111 *The Manual of Military Law* (London, 1918), p. 397.

112 F.W. Sutcliffe, IWM 97/26/1 diary entry 18.8.1918.

113 Herbert Hill, *Retreat from Death*, p. 15.

114 Baynes, *Morale*, p. 28.

115 Clark, *Transport and Sport in the Great War Period*, p. 34.

116 Sheffield, *Leadership in the Trenches*, p. 33.

117 William Carr, *A Time to Leave the Ploughshares. A Gunner Remembers 1917–18* (London, 1985), p. 13.

118 Sheffield, *Leadership in the Trenches*, p. 44.

119 Petter, 'Temporary Gentlemen', p. 141.

120 Fuller, *Troop Morale*, p. 53.

121 Alexander Watson, *Enduring the Great War. Combat, Morale and Collapse in the German and British Armies, 1914–1918* (Cambridge, 2008), p. 138.

122 John Bickersteth (ed.), *The Bickersteth Diaries 1914–1918* (London, 1995), p. 234.

123 Michael Glover (ed.), *The Fateful Battle Line. The Great War Journals and Sketches of Captain Henry Ogle, M.C.* (London, 1993), p. 168.

124 George Robb, *British Culture and the First World War* (Basingstoke, 2002), p. 87.

125 Eric J. Leed, 'Class and Disillusionment in World War I', *The Journal of Modern History*, 50:4 (1978), p. 681.

126 Hodges, *Men of 18*, p. 178.

127 Rogerson, *Twelve Days on the Somme*, p. 60.

128 Elizabeth Gaskell, *North and South* (London, 1994), p. 433.

129 D.J. Sweeney, IWM 76/226/1 & 1A & Con Shelf, letter dated 17.12.1915.

130 Canon J.O. Coop, IWM 87/56/1, letters dated 18.10.1915 and 28.10.1915.

131 Rogerson, *Twelve Days on the Somme*, p. 116.

132 *Cooking in the Field*, p. 11.

133 'The Food Must get There', *Daily Mail* 14.9.1918 cited in Young, *Army Service Corps*, p. 129.

134 *Mr Punch's History of the Great War* (Stroud, 2007), p. 204.

5

Eating: the men and their rations

The food provided for the men reflected the fundamental nutritional understanding of the period: calories were critical and the only dietary items that mattered were protein, fats and carbohydrates. The calories were frequently delivered without regard to their form, as taste was always secondary to energy values. It is apparent that even the relative variety of meals and foodstuffs described in the ration scales and the official cookery books was difficult to deliver under the conditions of the conflict. Warfare was not conducive to fine dining for the ranks. Of course it is probable that, if the soldiers had been served delicious food daily, it would not have had the same savour as it did in peacetime consumption, but would have been tainted by the general misery of their position. There was little that institutional feeding could do to comfort men who had to endure the conditions of the First World War, but there was much it could offer as a magnet for the men's dissatisfactions both the specifically dietary and the more general.

The soldiers' songs, diaries, letters and memoirs are full of complaints about the rations they received from the army. Expectations could be very high and it is difficult to see how those of Private S.T. Eachus, who arrived in France in June 1916, could reasonably have been met in a theatre of war. Eachus was vehemently critical of army food and wrote in his diary, 'have heard a good deal about German atrocities, but certainly in some respect the British are quite as bad and cruel, for weeks together we have not had a second vegetable, often none at all'.[1] Most people, soldiers or civilians, were unlikely to rank the lack of a second vegetable on a par with the 'Rape of Belgium', but the bitterness of the grievance indicates the anger, indignation and sense of injustice that inadequacies in the ration could trigger in the rankers. Eachus was critical of army provisioning on the Western Front, but his complaints are interspersed with memorable meals. After one dinner, Eachus recorded his satisfaction: 'boiled mutton, desiccated vegetables and cauliflower with bread to mix with the gravy, it was both good and liberally supplied'.[2] The disparity in Eachus's diary entries demonstrates the variability of one soldier's experience, a variability that can be extrapolated by the 5,704,416 men who served in the British Army during the conflict.[3]

Central to the diversity of the rankers' personal responses to the ration was the complexity of their relationship with food. The army's provisioning systems were founded upon the need to fuel the soldiers, whilst, for the men, eating was experienced as a social and emotional act not merely as a nutritional event. The men's consumption was more broadly framed than the criteria of those responsible for provisioning, and the high calorie count of a foodstuff did not necessarily make it palatable. As the men's initial experience of the training camps indicated, influences affecting responses to food were often unrelated to its taste or content: a delicious meal could taste vile if consumed in difficult circumstances. Eachus, who was so exercised by the lack of a second vegetable on 16 August 1916, may not have cared half so much on the 17th, or indeed, may have been twice as angry on the 18th. External influences undermined normal logic, and the soldiers themselves could be surprised by the seemingly random nature of their own responses. Joseph Murray exclaimed: 'War is a queer pastime! It plays havoc with all reasoning. What is essential one minute is of no importance the next.'[4]

The recruits who had undergone the rites of passage in the home training camps of the army had to absorb the new shocks of life on active service. They had to be incorporated into the rest camps, the camps in the line, the trenches and, ultimately, the battlefield. The environment was frequently deeply unsettling and the distress engendered by these new settings seeped into the evaluations. Of course, the complaints voiced about food did not all arise from disturbances to the soldiers' emotional equilibrium. There were shortfalls in the ration, corroborated by officers' notes and accounts, and its quality frequently fell short of the advertised menu plans. In Chapter 4, the official army view of provisioning was considered, together with those of the ASC, the cooks and the officers, who, because of their vested interest in its success, had a relatively high opinion of the rationing process. Here the rankers' experience of food on the Western Front will be explored, a narrative of eating which will demonstrate that their experiences and perceptions were often very different from the official records.

Once the initial transition into the military had been completed, it might be presumed that the men would have become inured to the idiosyncrasies of army catering; that they would have developed, if not a liking for the rations, at least an acceptance of them. To some degree this was the case: necessity compelled the recruits to accept army rations as one of the burdens of life as a soldier. In the same way that most of them became used to the uniform or the 'army language' they had found so disturbing, army food lost much of its initial power to shock. However, the soldiers still found plenty to complain about in a less energetic but quietly persistent fashion. The men's complaints had moved from the initial acute phase, fuelled by the shock of military life, to the chronic stage, where the shortcomings of army food generated a low-level ache rather than a stabbing pain.

For most of the men, food on the Western Front differed significantly from that which they had received before. If, in France and Flanders, they had received a diet that bore a closer resemblance to either the official ration scales or even the food they had been given in the camps at home, then their dissatisfaction might well have been reduced. Disappointingly, the holding camps in France, which given that they were static might have been expected to deliver reasonable food, often failed to do so. Lawrence Attwell wrote home from the base camp at Le Havre: 'If we stay here much longer I shall be in a position to appreciate almost anything in the edible line that you could send me. The food here has been rougher than anything I have ever had before.'[5] Attwell's choice of adjective is interesting: 'rougher' implies worse, although not necessarily less. It conveys the crude harshness of army life in contrast to the comforts of home, and in this instance 'home' appeared to include the training camps. The problem with the vast French base camps was the relatively rapid turnover of men. They did not stay there for the long months of training as they had in the camps at home, but often passed through in a matter of days or weeks before they were pushed out into the line. The transient population meant that there was no long-term relationship between the cooks and the men. Greater permanence might have resulted in decent meals whether from the pressure of complaints or from a sense of responsibility for the men's well-being, nurtured by familiarity and camaraderie.

Attwell was adamant in his condemnation of the food, but the variability of both the rations and the men's emotional states means that the assessment of the food delivered was neither an exact nor an objective science. The rankers were prone to oscillate between anger and enthusiasm in their feelings on army rations. Sergeant A. Reeve wrote in his diary: 'we have no cause to grumble at the food'[6] and five weeks later 'at present I can't grumble [about the food]',[7] and yet he *does* grumble at some length in a number of the other entries in this period. The repetition of the need not to grumble rather implies the opposite, that the food frequently gave him cause for complaint. Reeve was a regular soldier, although it is not clear of how many years, standing. He did comment that the rations were an improvement on those he had eaten in earlier years: the biscuit was better and the jam was 'really first class, made by leading firms'.[8] It was unusual for jam to be singled out for praise by the soldiers; rather it was frequently criticised, as the song bemoaning 'plum and apple' quoted in the previous chapter makes clear. Reeve was writing at the start of the war and it was probable the military had purchased and issued whatever commercial supplies were available. Later on in the conflict, when the lower-grade army issue of 'plum and apple' was standard fare, jam became a subject of derision. Reeve was emphatic in his dislike of the first sausages he ate in France, which he insisted were made from 'garlic and frogs' legs'.[9] It sounds a highly improbable sausage recipe: garlic perhaps, but frogs' legs were no doubt an imaginative embellishment, an indication, perhaps, of the apprehension foreign parts inspired in the men. Reeve's experience as a regular soldier may have left him inured to army catering in a way that the 'civilian soldiers' were not, and only something as startling as garlic in his sausages would provoke an acute response.

The diary of T.H. Cubbon, who served with the King's Hussars from the outset of the war and experienced the chaotic Retreat from Mons in the summer of 1914, is full of references to the army's failure to provide for its men. His comments regarding the collapse of the supply lines were considered in the previous chapter. Yet, for all the frustration that the uncertainty of supply and real hunger generated, Cubbon's diary was at its most miserable subsequently, when the food situation had in fact stabilised. On 4 October 1914 he wrote, 'Fried some bacon in canteen lid in end of dug out with paper, so as to have something respectable for Sunday's Dinner . . . Sunday is the worst day of the lot to me, everything seems so miserable as the comparison seems to strike me more.'[10] On this occasion, Cubbon did not even have to eat the despised tinned bully: he had bacon, the rankers' favourite item in the ration. Cubbon tried to use this food as both a salve for his distress and a commemorative marker for past Sundays. Nevertheless, his tone indicates that the food was incapable of lifting the general gloom he felt, and a meal that was, objectively, sound in both calories and taste failed to console him. The rations supplied by the army had not just to satisfy physical hunger but to negotiate the myriad of other attributes associated with meals and mealtimes. In Chapter 1, Ilana Bet-El's assertion that rankers' concerns about food were a matter of either insufficient quantity or, where rations *were* freely available, disappointment in their quality was explored.[11] The men's accounts, however, demonstrate that meals functioned in a more complex fashion: as emotional litmus paper, a medium through which other feelings, not obviously related to food, were gauged and articulated.

For Cubbon, the army's inability to provide a decent Sunday dinner triggered a range of feelings that informed a wider disaffection than one related solely to his diet. He wanted something 'respectable', a food that signified a special meal, an item not served every day. This was an eating experience that echoed the working-class custom of Sunday respectability, when even the poorest made an effort to differentiate that day from others. In addition, it was unlikely that Cubbon would have cooked his civilian Sunday dinner himself; food preparation, certainly for noteworthy meals, was a woman's task in the working-class families described in Chapter 2. It was perhaps when forced to cook for themselves that soldiers felt the lack of wives and mothers most deeply. Cubbon's diary does not indicate if he was a religious man, a factor for some in determining the significance of Sundays. The diary of J. Williams, a keen lay preacher, includes marked references to 'my first Sunday in the army', 'the dawn of my first Sunday in France' and 'my first Easter Sunday in France'.[12] Cubbon's comments indicate that one did not have to be a practising Christian to have felt the lack of a Sabbath deeply. The grinding monotony interspersed with enervating fear that typified active service was unpunctuated by the familiar days of rest and celebratory meals that had relieved their civilian existence. The traditional Sunday dinner, so important to the men, was absent from front line service. As Private Fenn wrote rather dispiritedly in his diary on (Sunday) 14 October 1917, 'Hardly know Sunday from any other day.'[13] The small piece of bacon that Cubbon fried on his makeshift stove carried a weight of expectations, memories, fears and resentment that were disproportionate to its size and nutritional importance.

The assumption underlying Ilana Bet-El's assertion above is that lack of food was always the most critical problem, or in the words of an old proverb: 'man has many problems but a hungry man has only one'. The belief is founded on the conviction that when food is available people will eat it. Admittedly this hardly seems an unreasonable premise, but evidence indicates that it is not quite as simple and, in extreme cases, people are prepared to go hungry in the presence of food. Gerald Bennett cites the citizens of Naples who in 1770 starved rather than eat the alien potatoes shipped to them as a substitute for the failed wheat harvest. In Bengal in 1943, after the failure of the rice crop, deaths resulted from the local population's resistance to the unfamiliar wheat that humanitarian agencies provided to relieve the problem.[14] More recently, in the Korean War American POWs died of malnutrition because they refused to eat the rations provided for them, which, although nutritious, 'seemed to them repulsive'.[15] There are no records of First World War rankers starving themselves to death rather than eat bully beef and biscuits, but it is important to acknowledge that complaints regarding diet should not be dismissed as insignificant grumbles over the irritating absence of a favourite food. The anger that arose from being compelled to eat substances they despised and could sometimes barely stomach was traumatic for many men: eating 'takes in the world', and it was a world that often repulsed the ranker.[16]

Difficulties with the rations

In contrast to the complexity of the men's responses, the military's provisioning processes were based upon the assumption that each soldier received the same, standard ration, dependent upon his position in the line. The military regulations permitted substitutions, and when the specified item was unavailable a replacement was offered. Commonly, the army's criteria of what constituted a suitable alternative were not those of the rankers. Cavalryman Ben Clouting was less than pleased when he and seven others received a two-day ration consisting of a 56 lb cheese, a tin of biscuit and several tins of plum jam.[17] Officers, too, were occasionally bemused; Captain J.C. Dunn recorded in his diary in March 1917, 'a battalion issue of sardines instead of meat is odd'.[18] A reading of the official statistics sheds some light on the army's fondness for sardines, which was not shared by the men, as a number of their accounts make clear. Britain's policy of blockading the enemy's economy sometimes required it to provide an alternative market for goods which had previously been exported to Germany, and Norway's sardine exports were one such item. The purchase of fish that was once designated for German consumption was regarded as a coup by the

War Office; its substitution for 'a small portion of the meat ration' had the pleasing effects of 'affording variation in the diet' for the fortunate soldiers at the same time as it restricted the enemy's food supply.[19] Such variations in the diet were seldom welcomed, and even George Hewins, whose poor prewar eating experiences had probably made him more accepting than many, was later moved to reflect on his own experience with fish: 'funny mixture . . . jam and herrings! How about that for a diet? I thought: It's better'n *nothing!*'[20] The army's failures to deliver recognisable or proper meals were translated by the rankers as a lack of care. The disregard for their palates emphasised to them the salutary fact that they were regarded as bodies that needed to be stoked with calories rather than human beings who were entitled to civilised meals. The men might not always have liked the army food as specified in the ration scales, but they liked it a good deal better than the random mixtures which were all too frequently distributed.

The importance of geography in provisioning has already been noted, and it was a factor of which the rankers were keenly conscious. Frank Gray commented that the diet at HQ was vastly better than that which he ate in the line: 'In theory every British soldier gets the same or equivalent daily ration on active service, but I ever found that in practice the nearer one got to the front lines the shorter the rations became. The difficulty of transport had some effect, and the number of hands through which the food had to pass had even more effect.'[21] The rankers did have access to other food, sources which will be explored in the following chapter, but it was the official ration that provided the bulk of nutrition for the majority of the men, particularly in the forward positions, where alternative supplies were difficult to obtain.

For many soldiers, their first experience of the difficulty of eating on the move was the boat trip across the Channel, which could hint at the deprivations to follow. S.T. Eachus wrote of his troop ship to France in June 1916, 'There was nothing to eat or drink, except what we could manage to buy and a poor cup of tea cost 3d.'[22] Rations were not always in such short supply, and Lawrence Attwell wrote home that bully beef and biscuits were available on his troop ship, although 'the biscuits can only be broken with difficulty'.[23] When it was not an irritant, biscuit was something of a standing joke for many of the rankers. A Bruce Bairnsfather cartoon in the popular 'Old Bill' series shows two soldiers crouched round a rather feeble-looking fire; the character's pal urges him to 'chuck us the biscuits, Bill. The fire wants mendin'.'[24] There were more artistic uses for biscuit, as Nicholas J. Saunders's book on the artefacts

5.1 Sergeant Herring's biscuit picture frame

produced in the trenches makes clear. It includes an image of one biscuit on which a seascape has been rather beautifully painted and subsequently framed.[25] Biscuit as decoration was not unusual, and Lieutenant R. Skeggs was amused to visit a dug-out decorated with cigarette pictures mounted upon them.[26] Figure 5.1 is taken from the Imperial War Museum's collection and demonstrates how Sergeant M. Herring, through some judicious carving, created a rather fetching picture frame in which to display a memento of his wife and twin children.

The problem of biscuit consumption was one that concerned many rankers. F.E. Noakes thought that the biscuits resembled those given to dogs but were 'not unpalatable to hungry men with good teeth'.[27] Unfortunately, hungry men far outnumbered those with good teeth and at points in the soldiers' service, when in transit or in lines distant from more varied sources of supply, tins of bully beef and hardtack biscuit were the only food available. Hardtack could be converted into palatable dishes, but it required considerable time, effort and additional ingredients, and all of these, unlike the biscuit, were in short supply.

Bully beef and biscuit formed the core of the iron rations that all soldiers carried with them, a development of the first British Army pack introduced at the end of the nineteenth century, as noted earlier.[28] The food was intended for emergency use only and, like the contents of their water bottles, could be touched only with the permission of an officer. There was a widespread and sobering myth that a Corporal had been executed for eating his iron rations without permission. The events were in fact more complicated than this, and the man had been shot for taking the decision to evacuate a forward position after spending three days under continuous bombardment with no fresh supplies. In the circumstances, the soldiers had eaten their emergency rations without an officer's permission, but this was secondary to their retreat.[29] Whatever fears some might have had about the consequences, hungry men tended to take matters into their own hands. T. Dalziel recorded in his diary 'Issued with emergency rations and warned not to open them until ordered but owing to the QMS [Quarter Master Sergeant] failing to issue any rations . . . we all broke into the emergency rations.'[30] On occasion, newer and younger recruits were more anxious regarding the contravention of regulations, and an officer in the 10th Essex was surprised to be asked by a seventeen-year-old 'diminutive soldier', at the end of a long, hot day's fighting, whether he could now have a drink.[31]

Eating in the camps in France

Once they had crossed the Channel, the first destination for many men was one of the large holding camps at Calais, Rouen, Le Havre and Etaples, where soldiers received further drill as they waited for the call to move up into the line. These were disorienting and unwelcoming places; aside from the lack of physical comforts, the men endured the uncertainty of knowing neither when they would be called to the front nor with which unit they would serve. New recruits or wounded soldiers returning from convalescence were used to fill the gaps in the line, regardless of the regiment to which they might originally have been assigned. Frederick Hodges arrived with the Bedfords but left as a Lancashire Fusilier: he remembered his unhappiness as 'friends who stood in line next to one another were parted by a hand and an order, and marched off to different Regimental Base HQs'.[32] The conditions at Etaples were particularly miserable. The enormous camp was notorious for failures in accommodation and the savagery of the discipline enforced by the NCOs, but also for the poor quality and quantity of its food. Aubrey Smith passed through in July 1917 and recalled that breakfast was at 5.45 am, prior to a day of infantry drill where 'two biscuits and a piece of cheese were carried by each man, this being the sole nourishment afforded him until 5.30 or 6 o'clock at night'.[33] After a day on the infamous Bull Ring, the dinner the men returned to was inadequate. For many soldiers, the main meal of the day consisted of two slices of bully beef, two biscuits and an onion.[34] Etaples was described by Wilfred Owen as a 'kind of paddock where beasts are kept a few days before the shambles'.[35] Owen's slaughterhouse analogy is pertinent; condemned men were traditionally entitled to choose their last supper. The rankers waiting at Etaples were aware that, for some, there would not be many meals remaining and their poor quality was an added insult to the sacrifice that awaited them. The anger and resentment mounted and the men mutinied in September 1917: poor food, whilst not the main grievance, was a contributory factor. However unpleasant their stay, the length of time that men spent at the bases was limited, usually only a few weeks, and once they were assigned to a unit they were unlikely to return.

Allocation to a regiment fixed the men's military identity, but did not confer a geographical stability, unless they were posted to a unit at a permanent HQ away from the fighting. On the Western Front, the majority of troops were in a state of perpetual rotation and it was unusual to remain in the same location for more than a few weeks. The movement was dictated by the policy that, wherever possible, units should serve only one week at a time in the front line. The policy was not rigidly adhered to, and in quieter sections companies lingered as conditions were relatively good. Equally, in dangerously exposed areas men might endure a prolonged stay, as the difficulty of moving men in and out inhibited earlier release. The regular pattern of activity ensured a continual shift from the trenches, back to the reserve lines and then further back still to the rest and training camps, before the cycle was repeated. Food was more plentiful and better prepared in the regimental camps, although often monotonous. B. Britland wrote home to his mother: 'We get plenty of good food but not much variety',[36] and A.P. Burke told his family, 'Am getting fed up with army rations, bread & jam for breakfast & tea and stew for dinner.'[37] Monotony was preferable to hunger, and there were references to the scarcity of rations, even whilst in the camp. An officer on a carrying party recalled an exhausted ranker collapsing before him with the words 'You know, sir . . . we don't get enough to eat'.[38] The official ration was often stretched very thin, as evidenced by F.A. Voigt, who describes the rasher of bacon a soldier received as 'a fragile wisp' and was concerned that 'the wind might blow [it] away'.[39] Hungry rankers were reduced to "working the double", which meant getting in to the mess hall as soon as the bugle sounded in order to have a hurried meal, exit by the rear door and go back to join the tail-end of the queue for a second dinner.[40]

Occasionally, extra rations were offered by the army as an incentive for difficult and dangerous tasks. In October 1916, volunteers were required from amongst the ex-miners in the Leeds Bantams for a 'hush-hush job', which it later transpired was the digging of the tunnels to be used in the Battle of Arras. Volunteering was an activity that rankers quickly learned to avoid and, as the unit had just come out of the front line, no one was inclined to step forward. The Commanding Officer then promised double rations as an incentive. Charles Rowland recalled that the whole company volunteered, and pay books had to be produced in order to identify those who really had been miners in civilian life.[41] It is not clear whether the men were aware of the level of risk involved before they made their decision, but it raises the question: how hungry does a man have to be to risk his life for extra food? These rankers were clearly sufficiently hungry to accept an added level of risk if extra food were available.

The quantity and quality of food served in the camps was important to the rankers, but, as in similar establishments at home, the manner in which the food was consumed was also significant. The lack of adequate cutlery, crockery and even seating in the mess halls reinforced the degradations of military life. Although the home training camps had allowed the volunteers and conscripts to gain a degree of experience in army eating before they arrived in France, dining on the Western Front proved to be a different military environment. The rankers' sense of unease was further fuelled by their increased distance from home and decreased remoteness from the front line. Opportunities did arise for the men to allay their uncertainties. The billeting of troops in a farm or house, rather than tents or temporary huts, afforded them a chance to recreate a more familiar and comforting domestic environment. Barns and outbuildings did not offer quite the same possibility. Men could feel like herded beasts in such agricultural settings, but a farmhouse or cottage could transport the soldiers a reassuring emotional, if not geographical, distance from the war. A. Sambrook recalled that the familiar size and layout of the dwellings was made even more homely through the addition of drying clothing and towels: 'there's nothing like a few shirts and socks hanging up to remind us of home'.[42] For most men, it was not the presence of laundry in billet living that conjured up home life, rather it was the opportunity for more civilised dining.

Cloths and cutlery

Despite the exhausting nature of active service, the men often found sufficient energy to improve the comfort of their billet, and much of this effort was directed to the dining arrangements. A. Reeve noted in his diary that, on arrival, his new billet was 'like a pig-sty', but the men got to work and 'took down a door for a table and made chairs from empty tins. Got a fire going and generally made things more cheerful.'[43] Rankers' accounts contain numerous references to the contrast between meals eaten in such accommodation and those taken in the mess hall. R.S. Ashley recorded a billet where 'we always laid the cloth for our meals' and, if not all the men were needed on working parties, they would cut cards 'and the lucky one would stay behind and have a hot drink ready for the others on their return'.[44] P.H. Jones was fortunate to be billeted in a farmhouse where the fleeing occupants had left a sack of potatoes in the attic. On occasion, additional provisions *were* found but commonly the food available was the same as that eaten in a camp. It was the surroundings and the manner in which they were consumed that was significant. Jones himself was less enthused by the extra potatoes than he was by the fact that it was ' the first time we have eaten off china plates at a decent table since the war broke out'.[45] In S.T. Eachus's billet, the men procured further trappings of civilisation: 'We have even flowers in neat little glasses upon the table, which little feature is most pleasing and probably encourages a poor appetite and increases a good one.'[46] In environments such as these, men were able to recreate something of their civilian eating pasts, an impossibility in the barrack mess hall. China, a tablecloth, posies of flowers were all civilising reminders of the world from which the men had been removed; a reassertion of the dignity consonant with the proper dining conduct that was denied them in the mess halls.

There was an additional aspect to civilised meals that had a special significance for the rankers, as illustrated by Eachus, who, like Jones, was delighted with the discovery of crockery: 'We eat our food upon china plates, just like the officers.'[47] In this last comment, Eachus articulates a point of considerable bitterness for many of the rankers that was identified in the preceding chapter. Charles Messenger suggests that the resentment was not universal, and that some rankers felt that it was appropriate for their superiors to have better food and dining conditions. Messenger cites an officer who overheard his batman explain to another soldier, that officers were entitled to better food as they were 'used to better grub at home than us . . . it's hard for them to miss what they have always had'.[48] Unsurprisingly, the view came second-hand via an officer whose batman was hardly likely to agree with another's criticism when his master was in earshot and the prospect of a return to trench life loomed. On the contrary, the majority of men's accounts express considerable resentment at the superior nature of officer's food. F.A.J. Taylor's actions were far more representative of the rankers' attitude; recalling his stint as a waiter, he said he made a point of serving the most unpleasant officers cold soup. It was an action he himself described as 'petty' but 'it was our only way of hitting back at those types who . . . treated us like dirt'.[49] The logical conclusion of Messenger's argument would be that any man who came from a home where meals were taken on proper plates, at a table with a cloth, warranted similar treatment in the army. This was not a distinction that home life had conferred upon officers alone. The ranks held a high proportion of men, like A. Reeve and S.T. Eachus, who had higher expectations of mealtimes than those the military offered. The writing of the two men, in its fluency and references, indicates a sound education, a lower-middle-class rather than working-class background. In any case, membership of the working classes did not preclude men from an appreciation of decent dining: as earlier chapters have indicated, the serving and eating of food in a proper and civilised fashion was a key tenet in many such homes.

The British Army understood that proper feeding was important, not just physically but also for the men's morale. The demands of the war meant that the need to concentrate on providing energy superseded other niceties. The role of the officers in supervising their men's diet is clearly defined in army training manuals and many discharged their duty of care with enthusiasm and a degree of empathy.[50] Other officers displayed a kindly but insensitive patronage that indicated a lack of awareness of the hardships the rankers endured. W. Clarke remembered an occasion when he and seventeen other men had been issued with a loaf and three tins of bully as their food for the next two days. They were so hungry they immediately ate it all at once and a passing officer stopped to comment, 'That looks like a grand meal you're having, no complaints about the quantity, eh?' Clarke said they had not dared risk the officer's anger by telling him it would be some time before they received more rations, but recalled that the resentful men 'surmised what *he'd* had for *his* meal that day'.[51]

Gary Sheffield has explored the bond that he believes developed between men and their officers in the front line. He illustrates the basis upon which the subalterns' duty of care was founded through the example of two pictures which hung in the officers' mess at Sandhurst. The first painting shows a squire and groom standing beside a horse, with the former enquiring 'Well, Jim, has he fed all right?' The second depicts soldiers crouched around a campfire with the same squire, now an officer, asking 'Dinners all right, men?'[52] The title of the pair was *Noblesse Oblige*, and they were intended to be representative of the care and concern officers carried from their civilian to their military lives. They also hint at a possible parity between animal and human feeding in the army's psychology. In terms of supply, of course, forage ranked above men's rations, but in their delivery the rankers and the horses were often regarded with a similar rather practical paternalism. It was an attitude that was acceptable in the stables, but not to those in the ranks. Men did not want to feel that they were being fed and watered and that the civilised, human aspects of eating were unimportant; as Brillat-Savarin asserted, 'animals feed; man eats'.[53]

The customs that denoted proper dining were virtually impossible to recreate once the ranker had reached the trenches. In addition to the tensions inherent in the front line, where, even if the trenches were quiet, a man had to deal with 'the mental strain of there being no one else between him and the enemy', there was the logistical problem of supplying sufficient rations.[54] As with many instances of army food, the situation was variable and, at its worst, rankers could be very hungry indeed. W.A. Quinton remembered that, when he was on duty in the inaccessible 'toe' of the Ypres Salient, he lived on a couple of biscuits a day.[55] When the cooks were able to bring the field kitchens up to the front line and provide hot food for the troops, access and enemy action permitting, the soldiers ate better. Lawrence Attwell wrote home very cheerfully, 'We are having excellent food and plenty of it. Our cooks are in the line with us, so we get bacon or porridge for breakfast, hot stew for dinner, tea and a hot supper, when we have porridge, soup or tea and hot rissoles. Not bad, is it?'[56]

However, even in circumstances where kitchens were functioning at the front, the sheer numbers of the soldiers to be fed could cause the system to falter. In the preparations for the Battle of Arras 1917, General Allenby recognised the importance of food to the morale of his tunnellers. He ordered that the kitchens should be positioned in the tunnels to feed the hungry men as quickly and effectively as possible. Unfortunately, the numbers were so great that the kitchens were regularly overwhelmed by the demand and failed to provide the regular and satisfying meals that Allenby had ordered.[57] Commanding Officers tried to give their men a good breakfast on the morning of an attack, and rum, with its courage-enhancing properties, was often a key ingredient. The officers were not wholly enthusiastic regarding the provision of a rum ration, and one set of *Trench Standing Orders* states that 'the issue of rum in the trenches is as a rule undesirable'. The concern was that the difficulties in supervising its distribution meant that all too often it resulted in a few men becoming very drunk, rather than all the men receiving the egg-cupful to which they were entitled. The author of the orders, Major E.B. North, also notes that the issue of rum to sentries was inadvisable as it made them sleepy and 'unfit for the alert duties of a sentry'. Nevertheless, the orders do grudgingly acknowledge that if it was considered necessary, and it could be assumed that the hour before an advance would fall into such a category, a morning issue immediately after 'stand to' was best.[58] From the men's accounts, it seems that bacon was almost as popular as rum in terms of what constituted a cheering breakfast. Unfortunately, shortages probably resulting from the same less than equitable distribution that afflicted the rum ration meant that it was common for soldiers to miss out on the meat. A.W. Green remembered ruefully that, on the morning of the attack in which he was subsequently captured, 'The bacon didn't get as far as our platoon.'[59]

In the fashion of Green's missing bacon, it was not unusual for all manner of supplies to fail to reach the men at the front. The dangers ration parties faced have been considered in the previous chapter, but balanced against the hazards, and despite many men's protestations to the contrary, was the possibility of obtaining extra food. Rankers' accounts of their war experience are circumspect on the subject of pilfering from front line soldiers; it was not an act that warranted wide acknowledgement. It is evident that thefts did occur and instances of scrounging will be explored in the next chapter. Regardless of the opportunities for extra food, perhaps many men shared George Herbert Hill's view when he wrote that he was glad not to have been chosen for a dangerous ration party because his fear outweighed his hunger. This was despite the fact that the members of the party 'could easily sneak a couple of loaves buckshee on the way back, or a wedge of cheese, without anyone being a bit the wiser'.[60] Herbert Hill's ration party appear to have been carrying more interesting provisions than was generally the case, the standard fare being bully and biscuit. These items did at least have transportability on their side, and alternatives could be even less appetising after a long journey forward in the rough hessian sacks used to transport cold rations. Norman Gladden was revolted by the sacking fibres that formed an unpleasant coating on less resilient foodstuffs such as bread or raisins.[61]

In an effort to deliver hot food to men in those exposed areas that the travelling kitchens were unable to reach, the ASC developed pan-packs, large rucksack-like carriers which were strapped to the backs of the ration parties. They contained sealed dixies of stew packed tightly in straw or hay in an effort to preserve the heat of the food. Although they were unwieldy and relatively hard to manoeuvre through the narrow communications trenches, they had the advantage of at least keeping the men's hands free to balance themselves during the journey. Earlier attempts had been made to deliver hot food through the simple system of giving the ration parties the hot dixies to carry. This proved unpopular on two counts: firstly, without any attempt at insulation, the food was cold by the time it reached the front line; and, secondly, the men carrying the dixies found it extremely difficult to negotiate the often treacherous routes with a heavy canister in each hand. Sadly, the introduction of the pan-packs did not guarantee hot stew, and the food still sometimes arrived cold and congealed when journeys were particularly long or the packing inadequate. In addition, Gladden complained that, if the lid of the pack was not fastened properly, its carrier arrived with more stew on his clothes than remained in the container.[62] The cans of bully beef might not have been the most appetising of foods, but at least rankers could have some confidence in their provenance. Eating is problematic and insecure when the history and, hence, the wholesomeness of a foodstuff cannot be established. The arrival of untinned, unspecified meat stew could be a matter of concern, frequently met with disparaging comments regarding its suspect origins: 'the fucking stuff's mule, and I don't care who hears me', complained one of Eric Hiscock's pals.[63]

Food and digestion

Hiscock reserved most of his criticism for bully beef, which he describes as 'constipating provender'.[64] Its high fat and protein but low fibre content had unpleasant digestive consequences for many men. A few years before the war, this had been a problem of which Amundsen was aware when preparing the food for his expedition to the South Pole. He ensured that his meat supplies were mixed with both vegetables and oatmeal to provide a more fibrous and a less rich diet for the men.[65] Constipation was something of an occupational hazard for the rankers in the trenches, and the limited sanitary facilities at the front may have been as much to blame as the restricted diet. Men who found sleeping and eating in close proximity to other men inhibiting were likely to find defecating in a tin in an open trench even more of a challenge. David Bell and Gill Valentine point out that one of the key rules of consumption adults learn is that 'defecation must be separated in time and space from cooking and eating'.[66] The division of these activities was not easy when men were crowded together in the cramped and exposed conditions found in many front line areas. All stages of ingestion and digestion had to be shared with other men, and what would in civilian life have been confined to the 'privy', or private place, was now made public. Soldiers did not generally make reference to their toilet arrangements. O.I. Dickson was unusual in that he raised the subject in an oral history interview: 'the only thing that was disturbing was the latrines. That was the difficulty, great difficulty . . . That was bad.'[67] Jonathan Swift described the horrors of defecation: the stench that is the one thing whose power no other thoughts can resist, and in the close confines of the trenches it can be imagined that there was no escape from its reach.[68] Dickson's comments were made in an aside during his conversation with his interviewer, but it was hardly a subject for letters or for the memoirs of valiant veterans. Rather like VD, which was rampant but rarely acknowledged, the soldiers drew a veil over such unsavoury matters.[69] However, the army's manuals make numerous specific references to the matter of latrines, unlike VD. The provision of proper toilet arrangements was easier in the camps where a sanitary policeman was supposed to be appointed to each latrine to ensure that every man covered his excreta with earth.[70] A similar specificity is evident in *Notes for Infantry Officers on Trench Warfare*, which make it quite clear that the maintenance of the men's good health was dependent upon the cleanliness of their sanitary amenities.[71] The detailed requirements included the provision of trench latrines on a scale of at least two for every hundred troops, but such less than plentiful facilities resulted in the men's dark hints of their parlous state and stories of improvised toilet arrangements involving entrenching tools and a forceful hurling of the contents into no man's land.

The inability to assert the boundaries of normal behaviour may have facilitated the bonding between men. Intimate bodily functions were no longer hidden behind the facades of normal life and soldiers were stripped bare of the artifices of civilised behaviour, perhaps making them more open and receptive to forming the intense relationships that many veterans remembered. More recently, Brian Keenan recalled that an important moment in the forging of the profound bond he developed with fellow hostage John McCarthy was a dreadful night when McCarthy helped him cope with a prolonged attack of severe sickness and diarrhoea in the small, lavatory-free cell they shared.[72] Men, whether in close captivity or in the trenches, were exposed to the fundamentals of life in a way that, for all its horror and disgust, offered the possibility of a deeper connection between them than was usual in the civilian world.

Records indicate that the high-fat diet was a matter of self-congratulation for the military, as it was regarded as beneficial in the fight against disease. One MO wrote in 1919, 'splendid feeding with plenty of meat and fat [protected the men against] pneumonia and consumption'.[73] The prewar diet of most of the rankers was, as we have seen in Chapter 2, generally deficient in meat and fat, and a surfeit of it was not necessarily welcomed. Sidney Mintz writes that the American soldiers of the Second World War had 'never before had so much meat . . . thrust before them'.[74] The same could be said of these earlier British rankers, and they too were ambivalent regarding its pleasures. If the meat ration had been presented as the more familiar bacon, sausages or steak it would have been considerably more welcome. F.B. Smith, in his study of the prewar poor, references a *British Medical Journal* article from 1888 which describes how large portions of meat were rejected by severely under-nourished children, who much preferred 'light soup', that is one made from peas and lentils.[75] Similarly, for many of the rankers the sudden increase in fat and meat in their diet was not palatable; it was too rich, too distant from the food to which they had been accustomed. It was also served in tins, which, as the discussion of prewar eating indicated, were still regarded with suspicion by many of the working class who perceived them, regardless of their contents, as potential sources of contamination.

Subsequent knowledge has determined a physiological explanation for the impact the fatty ration had on the men's gut. Fat is not an easily digested food and the presence of high levels of dietary fat cause the secretion of a hormone which inhibits gastric emptying, in order to allow the prolonged time required for absorption.[76] The soldiers' high fat intake resulted in a slowing of peristalsis, making constipation commonplace. Conversely, the fried foods the rankers seemed to most enjoy, the bacon and the eggs and chips, may have had the opposite but equally deleterious effect on their digestive systems. Fried food contains acrolein, a substance which acts as an irritant to the stomach and intestines. The body's response is to speed up peristalsis in order to excrete it as quickly as possible, therefore diarrhoea can result from a diet excessively high in fried foods. For the rankers, who could indulge in their favourite foods only in relatively small quantities and at irregular intervals, an acute upset stomach triggered by acrolein may not have been that common. However, there was a less obvious but insidiously damaging side-effect: even a small increase in the rate of peristalsis results in the malabsorption of nutrients, as the food passes too quickly through the gut. It is likely that the fry-ups the rankers so enjoyed did little to improve their health, particularly in a diet that was generally short of the necessary vitamins and trace elements.

Whilst diarrhoea caused solely by too many fry-ups may have been unusual, it was like constipation, common in the trenches, generally as a result of dysentery or gastroenteritis. Food poisoning from badly pre-pared or poor-quality ingredients was frequently the cause of the men's suffering and the army's exhortations that meals should be prepared in hygienic conditions do not always appear to have been heeded. The *Field Service Pocket Book 1914* stresses that camp kitchens should be kept clean, food protected from dust and flies, and refuse disposed of properly.[77] The challenges of cooking on the move suggest it was likely that the practice was far more difficult than the theory suggests, and failures in cleanliness were no doubt commonplace. Whatever efforts may have been made in matters of food hygiene, these were frequently undermined by the lack of pure drinking water. An inability to quench the men's thirst was a problem of which the army was well aware but unable to resolve effec-tively. Regulations state that all drinking water should be boiled, filtered or treated with chloride of lime in order to avoid outbreaks of cholera, dysentery and enteric fever.[78] Chloride of lime, a bleaching substance, may have purified the water but it also made it undrinkable, 'even in the hottest weather', according to Jack Halstead.[79] The army also suggests that men needed to be trained to exercise restraint in the consumption of the limited water available: it was best to moisten the lips and mouth and drink only small quantities as large draughts could be injurious to the men's health.[80] One suspects that this concern had its origins in a desire to preserve limited water supplies as much as it did in a determination to ensure the fitness of the soldiers.

It is evident that men at the front were often very short of water; Joseph Murray who served in Gallipoli, where the heat made this an even greater problem, remembered men sucking stones to assuage their thirst.[81] W.V.

Tilsley's account of his experiences claims that on one especially hot day, when the water supplies had been exhausted, men were reduced to drinking their own urine, or at least wetting their dry lips with it.[82] The regular front line diet of bully and biscuit exacerbated the problems as the dry and fatty ration relied upon a good supply of water with which to wash it down. Additionally, the high salt content of bully beef added to the men's thirst. It is also known as corned beef, and it was the large salt crystals in which the meat was originally cured that gave it its name – corns being any kind of small pieces in seventeenth-century English.[83] Although the producers of the First World War product had since switched to using a brine solution, the degree of saltiness remained unchanged. Thirst drove the soldiers to drink from the puddles that formed in the shell-holes around the trenches. Unfortunately, a drop in the water level often revealed that the depressions contained corpses or body parts, and the gastric consequences could prove serious.

Soldiers' accounts make numerous references to bouts of sickness or diarrhoea resulting from what they believed to be 'ptomaine poisoning', the contemporary term for what we would call food poisoning. J. Williams noted in his diary the results of the previous day's dinner: 'stew, my word it nearly killed me, was awake all night had awful pains inside'.[84] The consumption of tainted food was common, given the general lack of food hygiene, the virtual absence of washing facilities and the propensity of the cooks to use up all food, regardless of its age or condition. Deborah Lupton notes the particular horror associated with acts of poisoning: how the contamination of food and of being compelled or tricked into eating a poisonous substance is particularly disgusting or defiling to the person.[85] It might be supposed that to be made ill by army food carried a special bitterness for the ranker. Whether volunteer or conscript, he hardly expected to be poisoned by the institution to which he had entrusted himself. At least death on the battlefield, or from festering wounds, was a terrifying but somehow proper end for a fighting man; expiring in the throes of gastroenteritis or salmonella poisoning was not. Poisoning was for the soldiers a fear usually associated with an enemy whom they believed to be sufficiently unsporting to engage in such despicable acts. On the occasions that the front line did advance, it was often accompanied by rumours of the local wells having been poisoned by the fleeing Germans as a final act of revenge. It was not only water supplies that were at risk: W.A. Quinton swapped food with German rankers during the 1914 Christmas Truce, but was warned by one of his pals that the chocolate he had received might be poisoned.[86]

Whatever their source, digestive problems brought a particular type of misery to the men in the trenches. Santanu Das describes the distress caused by the men's inability to police the 'boundaries of the body'. The membrane between bodily fluids and trench mud was felt to become permeable, feeding the fear that it was no longer possible to separate inside and outside, the self and the world. It is likely that concerns regarding food and digestion played a key part in such a feeling as under pressure, whether from poor quality rations or the impact of fear, the likelihood of involuntary spilling bodily fluids through defecation or vomiting was high.[87] The routines of active service are likely to have compounded intestinal upsets. Research indicates that shift workers, who like the rankers have to eat at times when, their bodies are urging them to sleep, suffer from far more stomach disorders than other workers, as a result of the strain that a lack of routine inflicts upon their digestive systems.[88] Despite their suffering, the men on the Western Front generally had fewer problems than those who served in hotter climates, where food hygiene was even more difficult to maintain. E.H. Cameron, an MO in the Mesopotamian campaign, wrote that it was virtually impossible to prevent contamination as 'a couple of seconds of exposure was sufficient time to allow numbers of flies to alight on the piece of food'.[89] A.P. Herbert's semi-biographical novel, *The Secret Battle*, illuminates the dreadful conditions at Gallipoli, where dysentery was widespread. He describes the horror of the men as they watched the ever-present flies moving ceaselessly between corpses and food.[90] In these locations, stomach problems are cited in a number of accounts of courts martial which resulted in military executions. Private Thomas Davis defended his absence from sentry duty on the grounds that stomach cramps had forced him to the latrine; he said that he was there for almost two hours and he was about to return to his post when he had a further attack.[91] Robert Browning was executed for sleeping whilst on sentry duty; in his defence he claimed he had 'recently been much troubled with indigestion and pains in my head'.[92] In these cases, defences of diarrhoea and indigestion were unsuccessful, perhaps because the army, and all of its members, had come to accept intermittent low-level stomach disorders as part of military life.

It was not only food and water that affected the digestion; the results of high-velocity shelling could turn the strongest stomach. William Ian Miller writes in his study of disgust, 'there are few things that are more unnerving and disgust-evoking than our partibility'.[93] The connection between the psyche and the stomach is well documented: 'stomach disturbances – sometimes called "emotional diarrhoea" . . . were, and still are, noted as among the most common symptoms of anxiety in combat'.[94] In 'Re-remembering the Soldier Hero', Michael Roper notes the fascination the stomach and its workings exercised over the men, both during and after the war. It is a fascination founded upon the ability of food and the digestive process to provide a physical basis for the manifestation of emotional states. Fear and terror in the trenches could be converted into vomiting and diarrhoea without the assistance of gastroenteritis. Similarly, distress, as well as boredom and monotony, could provoke a hunger that far exceeded the body's physiological need for food. F.E. Noakes wrote of heading for the camp canteen 'where I would wolf any sort of food that was available'.[95] Similarly, W.V. Tilsley describes a response to the contents of food parcels that bordered on the compulsive: 'for half an hour Bradshaw and his chum wolfed grub'.[96] The circumstances in which they found themselves could cause the rankers to eat for comfort, in a manner recognisable to our twenty-first-century understanding of eating disorders. The consumption of food represented one of the few areas of physical control which remained to some degree within the men's own determination.

Problems with teeth

In addition to gastric illnesses, the rankers experienced a number of other food-related health problems. A key difficulty for many of the working- and lower-middle-class recruits was that of poor teeth. Dental problems had a long history in Britain. Paul Hentzner, a Dutch visitor to the country in 1598, commented on the black teeth of its people, which he ascribed to the population's 'too great use of sugar'.[97] This was a weakness that could be tracked in the nation's military experience: in 1678 a recruitment standard was introduced which required grenadiers to have sufficient teeth to bite open the fuses of their grenades.[98] The British Army had a history of resistance to the recruitment of dentists, mainly because army surgeons felt that they were capable of dealing with such matters, a view vigorously endorsed at the start of the twentieth century in the medical journal *The Lancet*.[99] Problems during the Boer War, where a large number of men were invalided home because of dental caries, led to Newland Pedley travelling to South Africa at his own expense to become the British Army's first dentist. A handful of dental surgeons were engaged by the army after the war, but their impact was restricted by the regulations governing treatment. Limited funding meant that the military was less than generous in its dental care: for example, 'dentures necessary for mastication' could be supplied only to those sergeants who were regarded as being of good character. The army's first attempt at dental provision was disbanded in 1908 and care was provided by civilian dental surgeons on a part-time contract basis. When the BEF travelled to France in 1914 not one dentist accompanied them. It was only when General Haig developed excruciating toothache at height of the Battle of Aisne in October of that year that the cost of their absence was realised. No one was able to treat Haig and he was forced to await the arrival of a French dental surgeon from Paris. Haig's experience caused him to contact the War Office and request the recruitment of army dentists for the BEF. Following his intervention, twelve dentists arrived in November and a further eight by the end of 1914.[100] While this was better than nothing and the British Army's dental service continued to grow throughout the war, it always remained at an unsatisfactory level. At its peak there was one dentist for every ten thousand men, comparing unfavourably with the Canadians and Americans where the ratio was one for every one thousand.[101]

The matter of teeth was of great significance in an army where so many of the men suffered from the consequences of a lifetime of poor diet and little or no dental attention. Jokes about the state of the nation's teeth reached the pages of *Punch*. In August 1914 it published a cartoon of a disgruntled man at a recruiting office protesting to the MO who has just rejected him because of his rotten teeth: 'Man, ye're making a gran' mistake. I'm no wanting to bite the Germans, I'm wanting to shoot 'em.'[102] In the first months of the war, defective teeth were a major cause of unsuitability for service amongst the men who volunteered for the army. Patriotic dentists across the country stepped forward and offered to treat men for free in order to get them to the standard required by the army. C.J. McCarthy of Grimsby took out an advertisement in the local paper promising gratis treatment to the first twenty-five volunteers rejected because of their teeth who presented themselves at his surgery.[103] The extent of tooth decay throughout the working classes caused the army to review its recruitment dental policy and make it less stringent. Whereas previously a minimum number of teeth had been required, this was dropped as grounds for rejection, and, from February 1915 onwards, men could be passed 'fit, subject to dental treatment'.[104] Nevertheless, the issue of teeth and fitness for military service was one that continued to cause problems throughout the war. In 1917, the Reverend Andrew Clark noted in his diary the derision that James Humpfreys, a house painter, was subjected to by the village of Great Leighs. Humpfreys had applied for exemption from military service on the grounds that he had lost twenty-six teeth and his gums were not suitable for false teeth.[105] Clark does not record the outcome of the appeal, but some soldiers found that the need for dental care could be a positive advantage. George Watts writes in his memoir that he had good cause to be grateful for his own poor teeth as they kept him in Portsmouth with a series of dentist's appointments through the summer and autumn of 1916, while those with whom he had joined up made their way out to the First Battle of the Somme.[106]

If a man's teeth were in a sufficiently good state to pass the recruitment process, they were still not necessarily sound enough to deal with the density of army biscuit. As discussed earlier, even men with good teeth found it a challenge, and for men with bad teeth it could verge on the torturous. Many soldiers preferred to struggle on and some endured considerable pain rather than seek help; it was widely accepted that a visit to the army dentist could make matters worse rather than better. The pressure of time on dentists, who often saw forty to fifty men in a morning, meant that time-consuming remedial dentistry was rarely employed. Filling teeth was usually rejected in favour of the speedy but drastic option of extraction. Rankers who could no longer bear the pain of rotten teeth often found themselves equally uncomfortable *after* a dental appointment. C.R. Keller had most of his back teeth pulled to no avail and felt that the pain his teeth subjected him to was quite as bad as those who got a 'Blighty' wound in their arm or leg.[107]

Dentures were commonplace amongst the men, no doubt as a result of a treatment strategy that relied upon extractions. F.W. Sutcliffe describes in detail the numerous trips to the army dentist required to remove his remaining teeth, take an impression for his dentures, have them fitted and then altered on several further occasions.[108] False teeth presented an additional problem in that the loss of a set effectively rendered the soldier useless: the conditions at the front did not permit the creation of a soft diet for toothless men. The consequences of the loss of false teeth were recognised by those in command. Lord Moyne, who served both in Gallipoli and on the Western Front, noted in his diary that a fellow officer had mislaid his dentures: 'It really was very serious, as he would certainly starve before he could reach a dentist capable of producing a new set'.[109] Fortunately, the dentures were found, but others were less scrupulous. Canon J.O. Coop, who served as chaplain with the 4th West Lancashire Brigade of the Royal Field Artillery, wrote home to his wife that one of the men had a self-inflicted wound and 'to make more certain [his escape from the front line] he had thrown away his false teeth because he knew that men who lost their teeth were sent to base'.[110] Of course, dentures made the biscuit even harder to eat and action was required to make it more easily edible. The favourite concoction involved adding biscuit to a tin of boiling water and then pounding and stirring it to a porridge-like consistency; a tin of jam was added just before serving and the result was more or less palatable. Different cultures offered different alternatives and W.V. Tilsey drew attention to what he regarded as a novelty, the manner in which Indian troops ground theirs up to produce 'tasty pancakes, cleverly made from "dog" biscuits, they called chupattees [*sic*].'[111] In fact the British connection with Indian breads is specified in the cookery section of the *Field Service Pocket Book*, which provides a recipe for 'chupatties'. The chief ingredient is ordinary flour not ground biscuit, but one suspects that the instruction to flatten the mixture to the still very thick ¼ inch before frying would have resulted in a rather stodgy result.[112]

Difficulties with teeth were exacerbated by the men's poor rations, specifically the impact of low levels of ascorbic acid; a substance the body does not store in any great quantity and thus needs to consume regularly. Scurvy as a manifestation of a lack of ascorbic acid was widely understood, as discussed earlier, but scurvy is the third stage of a progressive illness caused by the deficiency. The preceding stages, unrecognised by contemporary medicine, appear to have had a particular relevance for the poorly nourished First World War rankers. Stage two, which generally occurs when ascorbic acid has been deficient in the diet for around six months, results in tissues, especially gums, becoming swollen. Small haemorrhages occur within the swollen tissue and infection frequently sets in; this causes the teeth to loosen and the mouth becomes extremely sore.[113] The frequent references to bad teeth and gums were likely to have been a reflection of the poor army diet, as well as deficient nutrition in civilian life. The lack of understanding of stage two ascorbic acid deficiency meant that it was only when matters worsened into full-blown scurvy, as they did amongst the Indian troops in Mesopotamia in 1915, that the medical services intervened. In a diet where fruit other than jam was virtually unheard of and vegetables other than potatoes, and even those lacking in the latter years of the war, were rare, it is likely that many men were suffering from this intermediate, sub-medical stage of the disease.[114]

The shortfall in ascorbic acid was exacerbated by the nature of army provisioning. Meat is another important source of vitamin C, but the level available is reduced by the canning process. In addition, subsequent storage depletes the level further as quantities of ascorbic acid are oxidised by the oxygen remaining in the headspace of the tin. Perhaps even more significantly, ascorbic acid is lost when food is kept hot for long periods: experiments indicate that a loss of 25 per cent occurs in 15 minutes and 75 per cent in 90 minutes.[115] Therefore it is likely that the stews that were kept warm for hours in the camp kitchens, travelling cookers and pan-packs would have lost much of their vitamin C content.

In addition to the difficulties with teeth and gums, a lack of ascorbic acid also impairs wound healing. This may have had serious implications for the boils that seemed to fester interminably and the flesh wounds that obstinately refused to scar, even in the absence of gangrene. Many men complain repeatedly of boils, recording fresh outbreaks in their diaries.[116] Soldiers were clear as to their cause: as one categorically stated, they resulted from 'blood trouble as a result of the poor diet'.[117] A further symptom of stage two deficiency is that the central nervous system becomes compromised; this can result in nervous fatigue and irritability, to the extent that the sufferer may lose control over reactions to events.[118] This was a condition that would have no doubt been recognised by many rankers during the course of life in the front line. Nervous fatigue was a symptom recognised by contemporary medical authorities in the case of full-blown scurvy. Dr Edward Atkinson, naval surgeon on Scott's final Antarctic expedition, noted in 1911 that 'mental depression' was present in sufferers.[119] It would, of course, be difficult to determine whether the cases of nervous fatigue demonstrated by the rankers were caused by a vitamin-poor diet or were the result of standing for days in a flooded trench, under heavy shellfire.

Eating in the front line

Hot food provided a limited antidote to the discomfort of life in the front line and, when the army's efforts were not successful, the men took matters into their own hands. Cookery was, of course, possible only in those sections of the trenches where a fire would not result in unwelcome enemy attention. The palatability of the rations could be improved enormously by heating them: 'Pork and Beans' or Maconochie were much more appetising hot than cold. One advantage of heating tinned meat on the more temporary trench fires may well have been that the stews spent less time simmering, and so retained greater levels of ascorbic acid. Despite the official enthusiasm for stews, *The Field Service Pocket Book* acknowledges that over-cooking bully beef was inadvisable. It states that 'the secret of making palatable dishes with preserved meat is only to heat it through, as cooking spoils it'.[120] Soldiers wrote home asking their relatives to send them small camping stoves and, if these were not available, they improvised and used an empty tin filled with whatever fuel they could find. Sometimes all that was available was the stub of a candle, which generated just enough heat to fry a rasher of bacon or warm a mug of tea. Cooking facilities were important; Frank Gray recalled an occasion when bacon made its way to the front but, as fires were forbidden, men had to eat it raw, and if they were not so inclined, they 'threw it away or oiled their boots with it'.[121] Gray also noted that men regularly lit fires in defiance of orders, an activity which could carry a high level of risk. Army manuals warned soldiers of the dangers of attracting enemy attention. Fires were outlawed in front areas and caution was even urged when digging new trenches, where the sparks caused by picks striking stones had reportedly been spotted at a distance of 600 yards.[122] Regardless of regulations, the men persisted, although attempts were made to minimise the smoke. F.J. Prew spent considerable time cutting the wood into tiny pieces that he reckoned were almost as small as matchsticks, as he believed this reduced the smoke emitted.[123] Lieutenant-Colonel T.M. Banks and Captain R.A. Chell, in their account of the 10th Essex, comment upon the perils of fire-making in the context of what they perceived as an indication of the openness and lack of subterfuge in the character of the British ranker. They write that 'Tommy doesn't like to skulk' and describe how men would determinedly disregard the presence of the enemy and fry their bacon over 'copiously smoking trench fires'.[124] The tone of the authors is one of admiration, as if this were a vindication of masculinity, an act of courage reminiscent of the Edwardian ideal of war as an extension of the 'play up and play the game' ethos of the English public school. The accounts of the soldiers indicate that it was their longing for hot food that motivated their recklessness, rather than a sense of defiance towards the enemy.

The impact of a front line position on a man's appetite varied; much depended upon the section of the line in which they were based and, of course, the man's personal reaction to battle conditions. Christopher Haworth remembered that the bombardment had a physical impact on him, but it was not hunger: 'shelling makes me frightfully thirsty: it always does'.[125] A biochemical explanation of the impact of fear on digestion indicates its repressive impact on gastric and intestinal secretions.[126] An accompanying lack of oral secretions would explain Howarth's dry mouth and, hence, thirst. Fear could often overwhelm hunger, and one soldier described how he had managed to carry hot food up to a trench being shelled on the Somme, but 'most of the men were so exhausted by the relentless firing that they couldn't be bothered to eat it'.[127] G.L. Raphael's diary entry for 12 April 1915 reads intriguingly: 'Hell on earth and rations 1 small loaf between 5 men'.[128] The juxtaposition of terror and food is striking. Raphael was enduring heavy shelling in a front line trench and, one would suppose, in fear of his life, yet the shortfall in rations is still worthy of an entry in his diary. Raphael's impetus may have come not so much from the desire for more bread but from an indignation that his suffering was unacknowledged, as evidenced by the army's inability to provide him with a decent meal.

In general, a quieter sector, without the appetite suppressant of high-velocity shells made men hungrier than the more dangerous positions. Norman Gladden recalled, 'It is surprising how much and how frequently one can eat when there is nothing to do.'[129] One officer noticed the rankers' interest in food and wrote home that 'the terrible monotony of the trenches concentrates all the men's thoughts and desires on food and drink'.[130] The tedium was exacerbated by the lack of variety in the rations, the day-to-day monotony of tinned meat and biscuit. Popular representations of trench warfare do not generally include 'boredom', a state that it is a world away from the incommensurable horror more conventionally associated with the conflict. The men's accounts do not provide a consensus on trench experience. W.H.A. Groom's response was 'Boredom, my foot'; he recalled that he was in a state of fear for 80 per cent of the time.[131] However, Groom's fear did not diminish his appetite and he later wrote that he was always hungry in the line and spent much of his pay on extra food.[132] It is hard to believe that Gladden's sense of ennui was to the fore on the occasion he ate a meal under bombardment, in a shallow shell-hole surrounded by corpses. Despite the conditions, his appetite remained keen, although he wrote: 'in retrospect I am surprised at my callousness in thus being able to enjoy a snack in the presence of horrifying death'.[133]

For many men, fear suppressed hunger and food was of little concern when their chief objective was to stay alive. Sidney Rogerson, an experienced officer, wrote of his enjoyment of a hearty breakfast before he led his troops up the line, but noted that a man on his first tour of duty 'ate practically nothing . . . It was no new thing for a youngster to be nervous when called on for the first time.'[134] H.R. Butt wrote in his diary that, like Gladden, he had become used to the results of shelling: 'we don't take any more notice of a dead person now than we do of a rat'.[135] The 'now' implies that he had been shocked in the past, but no longer; he does not explicitly say so, but it could be inferred that the ordinariness of such sights would no longer have an impact upon his appetite.

There was, of course, a telling difference between living with the horrors of the aftermath of fighting and the endurance of actual fighting or a barrage. The former may intimate a man's mortality but the latter presents it as a tangible outcome. The authors of *With the 10th Essex in France* believed that, in the midst of a critical battle, 'one's stomach revolted from food'.[136] The tradition of the army to provide men with a good breakfast before going over the top suggests men were prepared to eat heartily at such a critical point despite what lay ahead. Whether the men were actually hungry or not, shortages of food were particularly unacceptable at this point, and not purely on the grounds of the desire for rum and bacon considered earlier. After one very poor pre-push breakfast, a disgruntled ranker commented, 'the buggers don't intend us to die on a full stomach, do they?'[137] Lack of food was almost always interpreted as lack of care, and poor rations just before an attack carried an additional, frightening message: food was not to be wasted on men who were unlikely to return. There was an additional concern that, whatever the rankers' hunger, the threat of imminent death or injury added a powerful practical consideration. Abdominal injuries had a particularly high mortality rate because, once partly digested food had escaped into the body cavity, infection usually followed which in the absence of antibiotics was often fatal. The military strategist J.F.C. Fuller, who saw active service in the war, noted that 'in many cases, men deliberately avoided eating before battle, for fear of being shot through a full stomach'.[138] The men were torn between a desire to see tangible dietary evidence of the army's care, associated as it was with a possible future after the attack, and their concerns regarding wounds which might lead to a painful death.

In less terrifying circumstances, food could become central to celebrations. However, for the rankers such memorable meals were generally created from alternative sources of supply, as army rations rarely provided a cause for revelry. Officers had greater opportunities to feast and recreate joyful scenes from their past. The fourth of June is the Eton College Gala Day, and was a popular occasion for such festivities, so as the conflict carried on around them old Etonians gathered together to celebrate their schooldays. Brigadier-General F.P. Crozier was a hard taskmaster, but was happy to allow a subaltern leave from a busy part of the line to attend such a banquet, and C.P. Blacker recalled an event in S. Omer in 1917 which had three hundred guests.[139] At the latter celebration, the diners drank to excess and progressed through food fights to the destruction of the venue, smashing all the furniture, including the chandelier. Blacker believed that the criminal damage went unpunished by the military authorities as it was regarded as a reasonable outlet for the pressures of life on the Western Front. Food fights were not the sole prerogative of officers, Ernest Shephard's diary recorded an occasion in his NCO mess when 'to break the monotony we had a ramsammy with sawdust and jam. We all agreed after that it was the best laugh we have had for ages. We were smothered in sawdust and jam all over.'[140]

Christmas dinners

Food games and banquets were uncommon in the ranks, but the exception to this was at Christmas, when the army and its officers made every effort to provide the men with an excellent dinner. December the twenty-fifth was a day on which all rankers hoped to eat a special meal, and, as the Bairnsfather cartoon (Figure 5.2) illustrates, men were prepared to make their own arrangements if nothing else was forthcoming.

A celebratory meal was dependent upon the ranker's position in the line, and for those at the front on Christmas Day the rations were unchanged. John Jackson ruefully recalled his experience on the Somme in 1916: 'there was no Xmas fare for us at that time, none of the good things to be had usually associated with the festive season'.[141] In these circumstances, units deferred their festivities and celebrated when they were released from the trenches. Once a year, army catering excelled itself and men received a meal very different from the normal ration: 'Beef, Pork, Christmas Pudding, Oranges, Nuts and French Beer' as one participant remembered.[142] In some areas, preparations were particularly elaborate, and W.M. Floyd, who worked as an orderly at a hospital in Rouen, had a 'spanking Xmas' 1914, when a special tent was erected for an elaborate four-course dinner.[143] Some officers went to considerable lengths to obtain supplies for the special meal. Beer was the most important ingredient, although home-prepared food was also much enjoyed. F.E. Noakes was delighted with an excellent Christmas dinner in 1917 and commented that the mince pies 'were reported to have come from the Captain's Sevenoaks home'.[144] The purchase of supplies for the men was always appreciated but the homemade items were even better, providing as they did a taste of domestic solicitude.

His Christmas Goose

"You wait till I comes off dooty!"

5.2 'His Christmas Goose' from Bruce Bairnsfather, *Fragments from France.*

Christmas was an occasion when the officers were expected to do all in their power to make the meal festive for their rankers; traditionally, the normal order was inverted and officers served their men. The reversal of the rigid hierarchy of the army appears to have amused both parties. This carnivalesque act resonates with the behaviour of the 'sans culottes' of the French Revolution, who would occupy a château and force its once illustrious owners to cook a banquet and then serve it to the revolution-aries and local artisans. James C. Scott calls these incidents 'passion plays in food egalitarianism'.[145] Egalitarianism was not a feature of First World War military protocol, but Christmas Day was one occasion when the possibility of its existence was hinted at. It is notable, but unsurprising, that it was the specific act of eating rather than the general festival that provided the locus for this reversal of fortunes. With its associations of a freer world, the pleasure of eating was universal, an experience all men could share regardless of background or rank.

Christmas provided an opportunity for men to synchronise their actions with those of their families. Men and their loved ones did their best to build emotional connections between the two fronts, attempts to sustain the bonds of love and affection in the face of geographical dis-tance. In *The Secret Battle*, Michael Roper includes a prewar letter from Theresa Cripps to her son, who had just started boarding school. In it she writes, 'tell me what time you go to bed and that's when I'll always think of you'.[146] Soldiers in France, unlike public schoolboys, did not have the regular routine that made such fixity possible; their duties and locations were in a constant state of transition up, down and behind the line. If a man arranged with his wife or mother for her to think of him at a certain time, he was unlikely to have wanted her to picture him in a sodden trench or filthy billet. Problematically, everyday scenes on the Western Front were not conducive to sharing with loved ones. In their letters home, men tended to focus on natural symbols such as the rising and setting of the sun, birdsong or wildflowers as points or references that could be shared with those far from the scenes of battle.[147] The best known example of this desire is the Bruce Bairnsfather 'full moon' cartoon. The picture is split: on one side the bright moonlight is admired by the lovesick girl from her cottage window as it triggers memories of romantic assignations conducted in its glow. On the other side, her sweetheart, crawling across no man's land is exposed in its glare, and shakes his fist at the very same moon: a failed, or misconceived, notion of synchrony. Food, as will be explored in detail in the following chapter, provided a potentially unthreatening source of synchrony. It was a medium through which a series of experiences and memories could be conjured up by the men and their families, whether through the actual taste or the mere reference to foods that had once been enjoyed together.

Christmas dinner was the ultimate focal point for a connection with home. It was fixed chronologically and was the foremost celebration for the vast majority of the rankers; even the poorest amongst them would have experienced attempts to make the meal special in their prewar lives. The soldier knew exactly what, when and where his family would be eating; unlike other meals, and even other celebrations such as Easter or Sundays, Christmas dinner was fixed in every aspect. A.P. Burke's letter of 30 December 1916 poignantly captures the longing the men felt at Christmas: 'Never had I pictured home so much before – I could see you all, & although I was having a rotten time it was more than comforting to think you would be so happy at home.'[148] It is evident from the soldiers' accounts that many of them had made arrangements with their families to synchronise their thoughts in an attempt to bridge the distance between home and trench. Francis Brockett-Coward wrote home in a post-Christmas letter, 'I thought of you at 9.30pm [on the 25th] especially as I said I would & uttered a silent toast to you all.'[149] Similarly, W.H. Petty noted in his diary entry for Christmas Day that he had thought of his wife, Ella, at 9 am and then again at 12, when he envisaged her telling their daughter Biddy 'about Daddy'.[150] The importance of the day was the nature of its exact annual replication. Changes at home could destroy the image, creating a different picture, one that could not be recreated because it had never been imprinted upon the soldier's consciousness. Concerns were not nationally confined and Werner Liebert, a German ranker, wrote: 'I thought much about home and was sorry you were not having a Christmas tree, because I wasn't able to picture what you were doing.'[151] The longing for home at Christmas was a feeling that transcended rank and officers were just as likely to yearn for their families and past celebrations. Major H.A. Stewart was saddened by the memories prompted by his Christmas Pudding: it was 'something to remind us all of the day which in normal times we spend with so much happiness at home.'[152] Christmas rations were an annual treat and other significant civilian celebrations passed by unmarked; as Sergeant A.G. Beer commented, 'Pancake Tuesday and no pancakes'.[153]

The men's accounts are packed with criticism of army rations and they were clearly disappointed in much of what they received. When supply procedures broke down completely, the level of complaints appears to have had a degree of dependency on the men's direction of travel. Lack of food when advancing rapidly did not generate the same level of concern as it did when in retreat. Perhaps, psychologically, hunger was easier to bear in circumstances where the soldiers were not also oppressed by the prospect of being overrun by the enemy. In addition, the excitement of a successful attack served to mitigate the problem of ration shortages. Complaints about military food were framed in the context of high expectations, based upon the men's forfeiture of their civilian lives. Meals were very different from those in prewar days, sometimes nutritionally superior in both quantity and quality. Nevertheless, their calorific value rarely compensated for the surroundings in which they were consumed. Institutional feeding could never replicate the comforting domestic dining experiences many men had enjoyed at home. If soldiers wanted to recreate the pleasures of more intimate eating, then they would have to do this in the informal meals they shared with particular groups of friends. Soldiers' expectations were not determined by the need for the mess hall to look, sound or taste like home as they recognised that this was an impossibility. Regardless of the degree of realism in the standards they constructed for army food, it is interesting that the rankers relatively rarely slipped into drawing direct parallels with earlier and better civilian meals. The men preferred not to gaze back in such explicit detail on their pre-army lives; the comparisons between the past and their current situation would have been unbearably painful. Adjustment to life as a soldier could be made only by an acceptance, at least to some degree, of the conditions in which a man found himself. Rather like Lot's wife, to look back would be fatal, lest a man be turned into a figurative pillar of salt in the misery of the trenches. Pining for a civilian past just made the military present intolerable. In his memoir, Henry Williamson describes the difficulty in adjusting to life in the military and how too specific memories of, and comparison with, home made the process more difficult. Williamson writes that it was 'fatal to take your mother with you to war,' and taking her cooking could be equally dangerous.[154]

The quantity and quality of rations the men received were affected by external circumstances and the judgements the rankers passed on their food were influenced by an additional internal context. Supply varied but was especially intermittent and inadequate in the front line trenches. The rankers' understanding was frequently tested and they were critical of the army's inability to distribute food in a proper fashion to a front line that was static for much of the time. Edward Roe complained of the short rations: 'We did not mind in the early stages of the war when everything was at sixes and sevens, but now we have settled down in a permanent

trench, why should it run three men to a 1 lb loaf of bread?'[155] Roe identified a change in the perception of food supply in the duration of the
war, and many of the men's memoirs indicate that their views on the
subject continued to shift in the years following the conflict. In the main,
the most vehement condemnation of the army's provisioning failures
occurs in the soldiers' memoirs, rather than their diaries and letters. As
noted in Chapter 1, men's letters were censored twice: first by themselves
to avoid unnecessary distress to the families at home and secondly by
their officers. Opportunities for diary-writing were limited and, as complaints about food were deemed detrimental to morale, their inclusion
was against regulations. No such restrictions existed after the return to
civilian life, when bitterness and resentment could be freely expressed.

The nature of veterans' memoirs has itself become a field of extensive
historical enquiry; the shift in tone from patriotic pride to the more
cynical 'lions led by donkeys' post-Vietnam sensibility has been well
documented. For many veterans, food served as a mediator for their
war careers; the universality of its meaning allowed them to frame their
experiences in a manner that could be understood by any audience. The
memoirs of the 1960s and 1970s may reflect an increased emphasis on
the men's hunger, in contrast to the officers' plenty, compared to those
written in earlier years. What is most interesting, however, is the consistently plentiful references to food in so many of the autobiographies
throughout the whole post-1918 period. Dan Todman suggests that the
central struggle for veterans was to convey not only what war was *like*
but what it *meant*.[156] Perhaps because food is an area where the physiological and the psychological are closely intertwined, it is possible for it
to be used as a vehicle for both physical and emotional experience. When
a soldier describes the inedible rations he received, whilst the officers ate
roast pork, we understand both his desire for calories but also his pow-
erlessness in a world of oppression. Food became a metaphor for wider
injustices in an environment where the ranker's life, not just his diet, lay
in the hands of others.

It was not only the rankers for whom food was so important. Officers
too, were conscious of the particular significance that war service gave
to eating, where it assumed an absorbing quality that would have been
unacceptable in peacetime codes of conduct. Captain Jack Oughtred
wrote rather shamefacedly to his fiancée Phyllis, 'I am afraid you will
think I am becoming rather a glutton. But food and warmth are the two
most important things of life out here.'[157] His chagrin was echoed in
the letters of Lieutenant C.J. Hapfield, who apologised for 'the appar-

ent importance of meals' and explained that it was 'just human nature, nothing else'.[158] It is not clear what Hapfield's 'else' was, probably the descent into unacceptable piggishness. The rankers were equally aware of the comfort of food, and W. Clarke acknowledged that he had become inured to the death and suffering around him; 'Your feelings only came to the fore when it was a special mate who had been killed or wounded and then it would quickly go away. Because what you really wanted to do was to go to sleep, get warm, get clean and have a good hot meal.'[159] The rigours of the conflict, both physical and emotional, caused rankers to become preoccupied with their own basic needs, a preoccupation that was intensified by the failures and inadequacies in the army's rations. Clarke's comment underlines the importance of those 'special mates', and the next chapter will explore the significance of food in the bonding of these groups of pals.

Notes

1 S.T. Eachus, IWM 01/51/1, diary entry dated 16.8.1916.
2 Eachus, IWM 01/51/1, diary entry dated 2.5.1917.
3 Field Marshal Lord Carver, *Britain's Army in the Twentieth Century* (London, 1998), p. 41.
4 Murray, *Gallipoli 1915*, diary entry dated 7.5.1915.
5 W.A. Attwell (ed.), *Lawrence Attwell's Letters from the Front* (Barnsley, 2005), letter dated 20.3.1915.
6 A. Reeve, IWM 90/20/1, diary entry dated 3.9.1914.
7 Reeve, IWM 90/20/1, diary entry dated 11.10.1914.
8 Reeve, IWM 90/20/1, diary entry dated 3.9.1914.
9 Reeve, IWM 90/20/1, diary entry dated 18.8.1914.
10 Cubbon, IWM 78/4/1, diary entry dated 4.10.1914.
11 Bet-El, *Conscripts*, p. 114.
12 J. Williams, IWM 83/14/1 diary, undated diary entries March–April 1917.
13 Private Fenn, Suffolk Regimental Archive, GB554/Y1/109, diary entry 14.10.1917.
14 Bennett, *Eating Matters*, p. 8.
15 Fernadez-Armesto, *Food*, p. 154.
16 Bakhtin cited in Bell and Valentine, *Consuming Geographies*, p. 48.
17 Richard van Emden (ed.), *Tickled to Death to Go: Memoirs of a Cavalryman in the First World War* (Staplehurst, 1996), p. 133.
18 Dunn, *The War the Infantry Knew*, p. 302.
19 *Statistics of Military Effort*, p. 850.
20 Angela Hewins (ed.), *The Dillen. Memories of a Man of Stratford-upon-Avon* (London, 1981), p. 84.

21 Gray, *Confessions*, p. 181.
22 Eachus, IWM 01/51/1, diary entry dated 4.6.1916.
23 *Lawrence Attwell's Letters*, letter dated 18.3.1915.
24 Mark Marsay (ed.), *The Bairnsfather Omnibus* (Scarborough, 2000), p. 34.
25 Nicholas J. Saunders, *Trench Art* (Princes Risborough, 2002), p. 40.
26 P. Barton, P. Doyle and J. Vandewalle, *Beneath Flanders Field. The Tunnellers' War 1914–18* (Staplehurst, 2004), p. 207.
27 Noakes, *The Distant Drum*, p. 50.
28 The full iron ration in the First World War consisted of water, 1 lb preserved meat, 12 oz biscuit, ⅝ oz tea, 2 oz sugar, ½ oz salt, 3 oz cheese and two cubes of meat extract. See Cole, *The Story of the Army Catering Corps*, p. 59.
29 Julian Putkowski and Julian Sykes, *Shot at Dawn* (London, 1992), p. 102.
30 T. Dalziel, IWM 85/5/1, diary entry dated 21.12.1914.
31 Banks and Chell, *With the 10th Essex*, p. 200.
32 Hodges, *Men of 18*, p. 40.
33 Smith, *Four Year on the Western Front*, p. 255.
34 Douglas Gill and Gloden Dallas, 'Mutiny at Etaples Base in 1917', *Past and Present*, 69 (1975), p. 90.
35 *Wilfred Owen's Letters*, letter dated 31.12.1917, p. 306.
36 Britland, IWM 88/57/1, letter dated 28.6.1915.
37 Burke, IWM Con Shelf, letter dated 16.12.1915.
38 Mark VII, *A Subaltern on the Somme in 1916* (London, 1927), p. 158.
39 Voigt, *Combed Out*, p. 27.
40 Herbert Hill, *Retreat from Death*, p. 50.
41 Jonathan Nicholls, *Cheerful Sacrifice. The Battle of Arras 1917* (London, 1995), p. 28.
42 A. Sambrook, IWM 95/16/1, memoir, p. 50.
43 Reeve, IWM 90/20/1, diary, entry dated 18.1.1915.
44 Philippa Stone (ed.), *War Diary of Private R.S. Ashley 2472, 7th London Regiment 1914–1918* (South Woodford, 1982), entry dated 29.7.1915.
45 P.H. Jones, IWM P246, memoir, p. 46.
46 Eachus, IWM 01/51/1, diary entry dated 11.5.1917.
47 Eachus, IWM 01/51/1, diary entry dated 11.5.1917.
48 Messenger, *Call-to-Arms*, p. 448.
49 Taylor, *Bottom of the Barrel*, p. 219.
50 See Roper, *The Secret Battle*, chapter 4, 'Learning to care'.
51 W. Clarke, IWM 87/18/1, memoir, p. 9.
52 Gary Sheffield, 'Officer–Man Relations, Discipline and Morale in the British Army of the Great War', in Cecil and Liddle (eds), *Facing Armageddon*, p. 413.
53 Cited in Jeffrey M. Pilcher, *Food in World History* (Abingdon, 2006), p. 64.
54 W.H.A. Groom, *Poor Bloody Infantry. A Memoir of the First World War* (London, 1976), p. 17.

55 W.A. Quinton, IWM 79/35/1, memoir, p. 53.

56 *Lawrence Attwell's Letters*, letter dated 25.10.1917.

57 Nicholls, *Cheerful Sacrifice*, p. 62.

58 Bull, *An Officer's Manual*, p. 83.

59 A.W. Green, IWM P101, introduction to his diary.

60 Herbert Hill, *Retreat from Death*, p. 203.

61 Gladden, *The Somme*, p. 148.

62 Gladden, *Ypres*, p. 53.

63 Hiscock, *The Bells of Hell*, p. 84.

64 Hiscock, *The Bells of Hell*, p. 24.

65 Robert F. Feeney, 'Food for the Race to the Pole' in Pieter van der Merwe (ed.), *South: The Race to the* Pole (London, 2000), p. 88.

66 Bell and Valentine, *Consuming Geographies*, p. 51.

67 Transcript of interview with O.I. Dickson dated 10.12.1974, Essex Regimental Archive.

68 Cited in Miller, *The Anatomy of Disgust*, p. 69.

69 Official figures state that by 1918 thirty-two men in every thousand were admitted to hospital for treatment the figure of undiagnosed men, those treated in the line and those treated under another name (e.g. 'urinary infection') must have been far higher. Keith Simpson, 'Dr James Dunn and Shell Shock' in Cecil and Liddle (eds), *Facing Armageddon*, p. 508.

70 *Field Service Pocket Book 1914*, p. 52.

71 *Notes for Infantry Officers on Trench Warfare* (London, 1916), p. 31. See also 'Notes from the Front, Part 3, 1915', in Bull, *An Officer's Manual*, pp. 62–63, which includes a detailed diagram of the optimum position of latrines in the trenches.

72 Brian Keenan, *An Evil Cradling* (London, 1992), pp. 249–251.

73 Nick Bosanquet, 'Health Systems in Khaki: The British and American Medical Experience' in Cecil and Liddle (eds), *Facing Armageddon*, p. 459.

74 Mintz, *Tasting Food*, p. 25.

75 F.B. Smith, *The People's Health*, p. 180.

76 Eleanor. F. Eckstein, *Food, People and Nutrition* (Westport, 1980), p. 53.

77 *Field Service Pocket Book 1914*, p. 52.

78 *Field Service Pocket Book 1914*, p. 53.

79 Jack Halstead, *Jack's War. The Diary and Drawings of Jack Halstead, a Great War Survivor* (Baldock, 2005), diary entry dated 11.1.1917.

80 *Field Service Pocket Book 1914*, p. 53.

81 Murray, *Gallipoli 1915*, p. 71.

82 Tilsley, *Other Ranks*, p. 11.

83 Mark Kurlansky, *Salt: A World History* (New York, 2002), p. 125.

84 J. Williams, IWM 83/14/1, diary entry dated April 1917.

85 Deborah Lupton, 'Food and Emotion' in Carolyn Korsmeyer (ed.), *The Taste Culture Reader. Experiencing Food and Drink* (Oxford, 2007), p. 322.

86 Quinton, IWM 79/35/1, memoir, p. 26.
87 Das, *Touch and Intimacy*, pp. 44–52.
88 Bennett, *Eating Matters*, p. 127.
89 Mark Harrison, 'The Fight Against Disease in the Mesopotamia Campaign', in Cecil and Liddle (eds), *Facing Armageddon*, p. 481.
90 A.P. Herbert, *The Secret Battle* (Oxford, 1982), p. 42
91 Cathryn Corns and John Hughes-Wilson, *Blindfold and Alone: British Military Executions in the Great War* (London, 2005), p. 140.
92 Corns and Hughes-Wilson, *Blindfold and Alone*, p. 137.
93 Miller, *The Anatomy of Disgust*, p. 27.
94 Roper, 'Re-remembering the Soldier Hero' p. 194. See also Bourke, *Fear*, pp. 199–201.
95 Noakes, *The Distant Drum*, p.76.
96 Tilsley, *Other Ranks*, p. 148.
97 Pilcher, *Food in World History*, p. 31.
98 Leslie J. Godden (ed.), *History of the Royal Army Dental Corps* (Aldershot, 1971), p. 1.
99 Godden, *Royal Army Dental Corps*, p. 3.
100 Godden, *Royal Army Dental Corps*, p. 5.
101 Messenger, *Call-to-Arms*, p. 422.
102 *Mr Punch's History of the Great War*, p. 24.
103 Beckett, *Home Front*, p. 12.
104 Silbey, *British Working Class*, p. 44, and Godden, *Royal Army Dental Corps*, p. 6.
105 *Echoes of the Great War*, diary entry dated 15.1.1917.
106 Watts, IWM 01/38/1 memoir, p. 3.
107 C.R. Keller, IWM 02/55/1, memoir, pp. 36–40.
108 F.W. Sutcliffe, IWM 97/26/1, diary entries 7.11.196 to 8.12.1916.
109 Brian Bond and Simon Robbins (eds), *Staff Officer. The Diaries of Lord Moyne 1914–1918* (London, 1987), entry dated 11.10.1915.
110 Coop, IWM 87/56/1, letter dated 6.10.1915; also P.H. Jones, IWM P246, memoir, refers to a man being sent home having 'lost' his dentures, p. 109.
111 Tilsley, *Other Ranks*, p. 74.
112 *Field Service Pocket Book 1914*, p. 51.
113 Eckstein, *Food, People and Nutrition*, p. 193.
114 Harrison, *The Fight Against Disease*, p. 477.
115 Brian A. Fox and Allan G. Cameron, *Food Science, Nutrition and Health* (London, 1989), pp. 352 and 265.
116 See, for example, Reeve, IWM 90/20/1, diary entry dated 31.5.1915.
117 A. Smith, *Four Years on the Western Front*, p. 226.
118 Eckstein, *Food, People and Nutrition*, p. 193.
119 Feeney, 'Food for the Race to the Pole', p. 81.
120 *Field Service Pocket Book 1914*, p. 51.

121 Gray, *Confessions*, p. 60.
122 'Manual of Field Engineering, 1914', in Bull (ed.), *An Officer's Manual*, p. 29.
123 F.J. Prew, IWM 96/42/1, memoir, p. 8.
124 Banks and Chell, *With the 10th Essex*, p. 203.
125 Christopher Haworth, *March to Armistice 1918* (London, 1968), p. 127.
126 Eckstein, *Food, People and Nutrition*, p. 54.
127 *A War of Words*, letter dated 12.9.1916, p. 200.
128 G.L. Raphael, Suffolk Regimental Archive, GB554/Y1/217.
129 Gladden, *Somme*, p. 87.
130 Bet-El, *Conscripts*, p. 110.
131 Groom, *Poor Bloody Infantry*, p. 21.
132 Groom, *Poor Bloody Infantry*, p. 51.
133 Gladden, *Somme*, p. 145.
134 Rogerson, *Twelve Days on the Somme*, p. 25.
135 H.R. Butt, IWM 97/26/1, diary entry dated 12.11.1916.
136 Banks and Chell, *With the 10th Essex*, p. 275.
137 Perriman, IWM 80/43/1, memoir, p. 12.
138 John Keegan, *The Face of Battle* (London, 2004), p. 241.
139 Brigadier-General F.P. Crozier, *A Brass Hat in No Man's Land* (Norwich, 1989), p. 109, and John Blacker (ed.) *Have You Forgotten Yet? The First World War Memoirs of C.P. Blacker M.C. G.M.* (Barnsley, 2000), p. 169.
140 Rosser, *A Sergeant-Major's War*, p. 27. 'Ramsammy' comes from the Hindu 'ramsam', meaning a 'rag or shindig'.
141 Jackson, *Private 12768*, p. 109.
142 McClaren, *Somewhere in Flanders*, letter dated 1.1.1917.
143 W.M. Floyd, IWM 87/33/1, undated diary entry, p. 37.
144 Noakes, *The Distant Drum*, p. 76.
145 James C. Scott, *Domination and the Arts of Resistance: Hidden Transcripts* (New Haven, 1990), p. 172.
146 Roper, *The Secret Battle*, p. 92.
147 See Keith Grieves, 'The Propinquity of Place', in Jessica Meyer (ed.), *British Popular Culture and the First World War* (Leiden, 2008), for a discussion of the role of landscape in sustaining the soldiers.
148 Burke, IWM Con Shelf, letter dated 30.12.1916.
149 Pte Frances Brockett-Coward, London Scottish Regimental Archive, letter dated 30.12.1917.
150 L/Cpl W.H. Petty, London Scottish Regimental Archive, diary entry dated 25.12.1914.
151 Jon E. Lewis (ed.), *The Mammoth Book of War Diaries and Letters. 1775–1991* (London, 1998), letter dated 4.12.1914, p. 256.
152 Stewart, *From Mons to Loos*, p. 212.
153 Sergeant A.G. Beer, NAM Diary 7904-71, entry dated 16.2.1915.
154 Henry Williamson, *The Wet Flanders Plain* (Norwich, 1987), p. 28.

155 Peter Downham (ed.), *Diary of an Old Contemptible. Private Edward Roe, From Mons to Baghdad 1914–1919* (Barnsley, 2004), diary entry dated 20.11.194.

156 Todman, *The Great War*, pp. 22 and 200, for example. See also Rosa Maria Bracco, *Merchants of Hope. British Middlebrow Writers and the First World War, 1919–1939* (Oxford, 1993), p. 154.

157 Wilkinson, *Letters of Captain Jack Oughtred*, letter dated 7.4.1916.

158 Lieutenant C.J. Hapfield, Suffolk Regimental Archive, Bury St Edmunds, GB554/Y1/147a, undated diary entry, p. 35.

159 Clarke, IWM 87/18/1, memoir, p. 6.

6

Beyond the ration: scrounging, supplementing and sharing

Frank Gray, conscripted in 1917, was not a typical ranker: at thirty-seven he was older than the average and his arrival at the barracks in a car driven by 'his man' marked him out as a person of wealth and privilege in civilian life.[1] Although his origins were exceptional, Gray's experience as a ranker on the Western Front reflects that of many of his peers, in particular the impression made upon his memory by the generosity of the soldiers with whom he fought. When he came to recollect his army service in 1920, he recalled:

> A pal and I sat down near a man in another regiment, and he looked at our rations, compared them with his, and then gave each of us a large portion of his supply. I mention this as an example of the generosity that one soldier habitually shows another. It was not a case of giving away superfluity, for we were all hungry.[2]

Difficulties with both the shortfall and the quality of the ration have been considered in earlier chapters; now the strategies men employed to mitigate both the hunger and the monotony engendered by army food will be explored. In addition to their army rations, the rankers often had access to alternative sources of food: parcels from home; provisions purchased locally; meals in estaminets; and items that had been scrounged from farms, fields, orchards and army stores. Regardless of the food's origin, whether it was the official ration as in Gray's description or privately sourced, what was fundamental to the men's eating success was the sharing of the edibles available. In the long term, a ranker's chances of satisfying his hunger increased if he worked on the principle of regularly pooling resources with a group of pals; there was satiety, as well as companionship, in numbers. In addition to the nutritional advantages of sharing, there were emotional benefits: the simulation of another, military 'family', centred on food and an echo of peacetime domesticity. This chapter will explore aspects of the men's eating that were neither determined by nor dependent upon the official ration; the opportunities rankers had to eat in a manner that was dictated by *their* preferences rather than those of the army.

Soldiers were usually quick to find a 'mucking in pal', someone with whom they could share rations and any extras that might come their way. Generally, small groups were formed rather than just a pair, and these sets of pals became dining partners during their service in the line. Comradeship, for many men the only enriching aspect of their war service, was played out in a framework provided by eating. The significance of food, whether in the unselfish sharing of rations by an anonymous ranker as experienced by Gray or in the extra-curricular feasts of egg and chips with 'van blank', is evident. It was the object around which acts of kindness, generosity and pleasure were constructed. Conversely, it could also act as the focal point for less positive emotional states – for example, as discussed at the conclusion of the preceding chapter, the way in which bitterness about lack of food could be used to express a deeper resentment; one that had its roots in the wider injustices the rankers suffered. The position of food at the centre of the men's relationships is reminiscent of its role in their civilian lives, as the medium through which maternal love was conveyed. Food prepared by mothers had a particular savour, as the discussion of the importance of parcels to the men will demonstrate later in this chapter, but even ordinary food had the power to convey feelings that for the soldiers resonated with earlier experiences of maternal care and affection.

The motherless, masculine world of the trenches eroded the civilian fixity of gender roles. Joanna Bourke shows how men assumed tasks that would normally have been performed by their wives, mothers and sisters: laundering, nursing and, of course, cooking.[3] The traditional barriers between male and female tasks were not impermeable as Michael Roper suggests. He notes that for many working-class boys domestic tasks may have been relatively commonplace, for example helping their mothers with the physically taxing extra laundry that many women undertook.[4] John Tosh also demonstrates the way in which men's roles extended beyond the rigid, gendered spheres traditionally regarded as constituting Victorian family life. The men that Tosh describes as 'nursing fathers', as they regularly fed and cared for their children, were from the middle class and inhabited a social stratum distant from that of the great majority of rankers.[5]

While in civilian life some men may have had a wider engagement with certain nurturing tasks than had been previously supposed, the day-to-day preparation of food had remained primarily in the woman's domain. The role of the mother as provider of sustenance gave cooking a specifically feminine quality for the men in the ranks. Part of the scorn heaped upon army cooks came from what was regarded as the feminising effect the role had on them or, more damningly, the supposition that only less than masculine men were attracted to such jobs in the first place. Jack Halstead, a seasoned ranker, describes the arrival in the trenches of a new recruit, Clark, a forty-six-year-old insurance clerk who was bemused by the war conditions. He caused great hilarity when, after a night of heavy shelling, he wanted to know when they would be given a chance to sleep. Halstead reckoned that a week 'roughing it' would have killed Clark, and, as he and his group of pals felt sorry for him, they contrived to arrange matters in such a way that he was never expected to undertake guard or night duty. In return for their consideration, Clark was required to fulfil domestic duties: 'he had to act as our servant. Collect wood, fetch water, sew on buttons, prepare our suppers – the arrangement pleased him and he looked after us very well.' Tellingly, given the nature of his work, the group called him 'Mrs Clark'.[6]

Halstead's group's division of labour was unusual; it was more common for the 'domestic' tasks to be rotated, as with R.S. Ashley and his friends, referenced in the previous chapter, who cut cards to see who would have the privilege of remaining in their homely billet during the day. Experiences such as these appear as echoes of traditional family life within the alien environment of the Western Front. The degree of emotional separation between home and battle fronts has been a subject much explored by historians. Paul Fussell describes the 'adversary atmosphere' of the war, where the men in the line felt themselves estranged from everyone and everything that was not part of their suffering in the trenches. Enmity was directed at the brass hats, the strategists, whom one trench journal defined as 'people who don't care how many lives they risk as long as it isn't their own'.[7] It was also directed towards those at home who were perceived to have no comprehension of the suffering endured.[8] Eric Leed also explores this 'disillusionment with home'; the rejection, or rather, forced abandonment, of the familial context of their earlier existence and the sense of emotional alienation that the men developed.[9] For Fussell and Leeds, the men's lives in the trenches were viewed as a world apart from the families they had left behind, yet, as both Joanna Bourke and Michael Roper have indicated, the trenches were in fact a space where the men were compelled to replicate the very behaviours of the world they were supposed to have rejected. Given that some of the behaviours they replicated were in fact not their own but those of the women in their families, it is debatable whether the acts functioned as comforting memories of domesticity or distressing reminders of lives lost. Eating in the army oscillated between both these extremes. At its worst, the shock of the first camp mess hall or emergency rations in a front line trench, it was the antithesis of home, but at its best, a shared parcel or a Christmas dinner, it had the same power to console that it had possessed in the world before the war.

Sharing with pals

Family meals were predicated upon sharing, an aspect of eating the rankers were keen to reproduce in their military lives. Army rationing was, of course, a complex and institutionalised form of sharing but one that appears to have brought as much resentment as it did satisfaction. In their private eating enterprises, the men aimed to reconstitute the voluntary and equitable sharing of domestic dining. The elective nature of their practices weighted it with a moral superiority, and hence emotional comfort, that army distribution procedures could never emulate. The sharing of food by, not merely amongst, individual rankers was embedded in the British Army's rationing processes. Unlike, for example, the American troops, who received individual ration packs, British soldiers frequently had food distributed in large units. As earlier examples have indicated, it was often a whole loaf, a full jar of jam or a chunk of bacon that then had to be subdivided by the men themselves into single portions. British soldiers took pride in their ability to share food fairly. One NCO recalled the astonishment of American soldiers at the way in which food was issued: "'How on earth can you have rations dished out like that? Our fellows would eat the lot." I said, "Well, our fellows don't."'[10] The number of rankers designated to each item varied depending upon the availability of the ration; when supplies were stretched, a loaf might have to be cut into as many as twenty equal pieces.[11] The soldiers' accounts indicate that men who were skilled and equitable in the apportionment of food were admired and respected by their peers. It is perhaps more likely that it was those men who had already earned the respect of others who were charged with the responsibility of food division. In his analysis of table manners, Norbert Elias notes that traditionally the carving and distribution of meat were honours that fell to the master of the house.[12] Unlike the act of cooking, carving in the army, as it had at home, carried masculine connotations for the rankers. Whatever the honour of the task, shortages of rations could make the extent of the challenge one that even the most able found impossible. P.H. Jones recalled a sergeant who had the unenviable task of cutting a joint of boiled bacon into forty portions with a clasp knife. Bacon complicated the situation as mass alone was an inadequate basis for division; the relative attractiveness of lean meat as opposed to fat fuelled debate amongst the men. Finally, under intense pressure from the complaining men, the sergeant resorted to an autocratic 'take it or leave it.'[13]

Sometimes the rations supplied were in such small quantities that it was regarded as a physical impossibility to divide them equally between the men. In such circumstances it was common practice to raffle the little available. R. Gwinnell remembered that the pieces of cheese his section received were too small to divide into eight portions, so they cut cards with the two highest scorers splitting the ration between them.[14] It was also common for sections to reach an agreement whereby each would take the bacon and cheese ration on alternate days because, as Edward Roe explained, 'it is an impossibility to divide one section's bacon and cheese into eight or ten equal parts, it was that small'.[15] One wonders if it were actually impossible to split the food, as even 1 oz of cheese can be cut into eight, admittedly tiny, pieces. Perhaps the rankers felt the food was so limited that a daily ration would have been insufficient to fill the mouth and give any pleasure to the palate. It would have become more of a torment than a satisfying mouthful. Men in some units preferred to have all or nothing, with the added excitement of a game of chance determining the outcome, gambling being almost as pleasurable as eating for many soldiers. Whilst for Roe a dearth on one day was partly compensated for by the pleasurable anticipation of plenty the next; an eating pattern reminiscent of the prewar traditions of a weekday famine leading up to a Sunday feast.

Parcels from home

The scarcity of rations was compensated for by a number of alternative sources of food, the most significant of which for the soldier in the line was the food sent from home via the parcel post. The volume of packages sent was astounding: between August 1914 and March 1920, 320,409 tonnes of mail and parcels were shipped to the BEF.[16] By 1915, four thousand mail bags crossed the channel daily, a number that rose to over fifty thousand a day in the period before Christmas 1917.[17] Such vast quantities presented problems for the divisional supply trains, who struggled to carry the parcels up the line, alongside the weight of rations, forage and water. On occasion it was an impossible task and one Supply Officer, Major H.A. Stewart recalled that the influx before Christmas 1914 had taxed 'the transport to its fullest carrying capacity'. Ultimately, they had been forced to give up their attempt to carry the mail sacks as far forward as possible. Instead a portion of the church at Westoutre was used as a temporary store until the troops were brought back into reserve and could then collect their post.[18] Stewart's tone implies that this was not an ideal solution. He does not expand upon the unpopular implications of his decision, but the disappointment of soldiers who failed to receive their much anticipated Christmas parcels can be imagined.

Most of the parcels reached their destination within four days of posting, even though at the Post Office Home Depot seven hundred parcels each day had to be repacked as they were so poorly wrapped.[19] The tide of packages was not solely in one direction, and many soldiers sent tokens to their loved ones, particularly their womenfolk; a piece of lace, a handkerchief or costume jewellery were all popular gifts. In addition, some men were keen to post home more explicit evidence of their military experience, and the transport of shells, grenades, detonators and other explosive items had to be prohibited by the authorities. It was not just the obviously hazardous that was vetoed: butter was also added to the soldiers' list of forbidden items. The problem arose from the shortages in Britain, which men hoped to alleviate by sending home the butter they had purchased at market days in France. Unfortunately, the hundreds of pounds of butter in the postal system caused an intolerable amount of mess, particularly on hot days.[20]

Packages bound for Britain were relatively few compared to those arriving on the Western Front. At the beginning of the war, when the army struggled with the provision of rations to the rapidly expanding forces, food parcels were especially significant. Captain J.C. Dunn notes in August 1914 that 'the Staffs of higher formations were . . . living exclusively on hampers supplied by Fortnum and Mason'.[21] Hampers might be ordered from shops by the officers themselves, but most were sent by friends and family as tokens of love and support. The officer class had access to a stream of food of a quality and variety reminiscent of their civilian diet. The Hon. William Fraser requested that, in season, a brace of partridges be sent out each week from the family estate. He also complained about the quality of Fortnum's parcels and requested a change of supplier for his weekly quota of kippers and sausages.[22] Fraser's requests to his family are sharply businesslike in tone, and there is little of the coaxing and gratitude evident in many of the rankers' letters. Peremptoriness was not found exclusively in the correspondence of upper-class officers, but there was a pragmatism that came from a familiarity with the absence of young men from their homes. Such families had a well-established tradition of provision via parcels. The years that upper-class boys spent at prep and public schools had provided ample opportunity for both parties to develop an understanding of the rules of parcel supply and demand. Most importantly, the great majority of the officers would have written their requests home secure in the knowledge that their families would be able to supply them without any financial difficulty. In contrast, many of the rankers were aware that parcels represented a significant portion of the household's income, and their longing was tempered by a concern that they were consuming precious and limited resources.

The conditions on the Western Front, however, tended to militate against unselfish behaviour. The boys of the Stopher family, George, Albert and Percy, who had found the food in his training camp less then comely, came from the agricultural poor and their letters reflect their limited education. They made no attempt at literary polish, nor did they parrot the clichés that both the censoring officers at the time and historians have highlighted as the favoured solution to the challenge of translating emotional bonds into text. In fact, some of their letters have a brevity similar to that of the Hon. William Fraser, but the Stophers' sprang from an almost total lack of literary skill rather than a sense of entitlement. Geoff Dyer suggests that 'a lack of linguistic self-consciousness exacerbated the tendency to express the experience of war through the words of others'.[23] Whilst this may have been true for many, at least those who had a familiarity with 'the words of others', the Stophers' lives in the depths of rural Suffolk left them relatively unexposed to the manifestations of popular culture that fed the consciousness of urban men. Bessie, Albert's sweetheart, had to undertake a lengthy bicycle ride to the nearest small town in order to have her photograph taken and then wait three months for it to be ready. Such a slow process suggests a rural isolation that was uncommon in the urbanised ranks. In addition to the directness and insistence of their language, the Stopher letters display a profound lack of certainty in the ability of those at home to keep them properly supplied.

Money, or its absence, was clearly a determining factor for the Stophers, and their correspondence is testimony to the struggle of an impoverished labouring family to sustain the appetites of its soldiering sons. The letters from the men were full of demands for more parcels, most fiercely articulated by their longing for home baking: 'Please send me some cake or make a nice batter pudding so I can cut a bit and have some butter on it.'[24] They were less demanding of other correspondents, including cousin Ethel, who was in domestic service. In a letter to her, George acknowledges the expense involved for those at home: 'you don't want to worry about sending parcels as they cost to [*sic*] much to send.'[25] The food-related requests and complaints were mainly directed to their parents, who were deemed to be in dereliction of their fundamental duty to feed their children, even though they were now grown men. There is a plaintive, childlike tone to their grievances, a feeling of thwarted entitlement resulting from parental failure. The Stopher boys frequently complain not only about the lack of parcels but about an associated absence of letters. There is a sense that the parents, who clearly did not have the money to send the flow of food the boys demanded, were embarrassed by their failure. The boys' comments make it clear that a letter was not regarded as an acceptable substitute for the more expensive parcel, perhaps causing their parents to prefer not to communicate at all. In one letter, George begs his mother and father to do everything in their power to support the men at the front. He assures them that there is no shame in asking neighbours and acquaintances for the necessary funds and urges them: 'do not be afraid to ask anybody for a little gift'.[26] It seems unlikely that such an approach would have been free of shame for the elder Stophers. While it was common practice for officers to canvass friends and family for sweets and cigarettes for 'their boys', it was far more unusual for it to be sought actively by a parent for their sons alone.

The Stophers were not unusual in struggling to keep up a steady stream of packages to the soldiers at the front. Men were aware of financial pressures and, as the war progressed, worsening food shortages. S.J. Hounsom wrote to his wife, 'I get twice as good food as you do, and as much as I want. Please don't send foodstuffs again, you naughty girl.'[27] Hounsom's solicitude was founded upon his favoured position at the company's HQ, where food was considerably more plentiful than it was in the line.[28] Concerns for those at home were usually overwhelmed by the men's own need. A number of soldiers viewed the privations on the home front with a certain amount of derision: lack of butter was a negligible price for civilians to pay compared with the sacrifice that was being extracted from the men in the trenches. Lawrence Attwell dismissed the trials of queues at the grocer's when he wrote to his family: 'the food shortage at home will soon seem a small item when the clash of the great offensive begins to fill the granaries of death.'[29] Nevertheless, it appears that, as time wore on, initial irritation at complaints from home regarding lack of food was replaced by a growing concern amongst the soldiers. Men who had been called upon to risk their lives for their country strongly resented its inability to provide for their families during their enforced absence. Edie Bennett made no attempt to protect her husband, who was serving in Mesopotamia, from the shortages at home: 'I have no good news to tell you as things here are getting in a terrible state . . . Oh darling to think we should ever get to this terrible state of starvation.'[30] One can only imagine the distress this must have caused her husband when he opened the letter – although the florid tone of Edie's correspondence indicates a tendency to the dramatic, his knowledge of which would hopefully have attenuated his response. The letters from families at home struggling with food shortages ultimately had a discernible impact on the soldiers' outlook. Bernard Waites notes a decline in morale in 1918, when those letters home read by the censors appeared to reflect the complaints that the men had received from their womenfolk regarding the queues and shortages. Additionally, fewer and less generous food packages may have been a contributory factor in formulating the men's understanding that all was not well in the eating aspects of the home front.[31]

Parcels from other sources

Family or friends were the issue point for the majority of parcels, but this was not the only source. A 5s donation to the Queen Alexandra's Field Force Fund Despatches would send a gift of food and toiletries to a soldier at the front.[32] Comforts Funds were created to provide the men with treats, such as the one organised by Mrs E.D. Stephens, the wife of the Colonel of the Second Rifle Brigade. This particular fund was a large-scale operation, organising the purchase and transport of significant quantities of food. The Battalion Orders of 16 November 1915 state that in the previous four months the fund had provided: 1,008 tins of milk, 51 lb of sweets, 32 lb of curry powder and 72 large tins of bloater paste.[33] Curry powder was very popular with the soldiers and was no doubt a familiar flavouring for those regulars who had served in India. It is not much referenced in accounts of prewar working-class diet, and although

Eliza Acton's 1845 *Modern Cookery for Private Families* contains a recipe for curry powder, hers is a book aimed at the middle classes.[34] The strong flavouring appears to have been swiftly adopted by the rankers, despite its novelty. The heat of the spices would have helped make palatable any poor-quality fresh meat, as well as enlivening a tin of bully. It was clear from the correspondence that the fund was not merely for the provision of 'extras' to the men; it compensated for shortcomings in the basic ration. The Quartermaster's letters indicate that the ASC had failed to supply sufficient sugar and milk, both fundamental to the men's diet and the ration, and these gaps had been filled through the efforts of the Comforts Fund.[35]

Employers were another possible source of supply for the soldiers, and a number were linked by geography to particular regiments. On Christmas Day 1916, J. Player of Nottingham gave each Sherwood Forester the gift of twenty cigarettes and a bar of chocolate, together with a greetings card.[36] British shops were quick to maximise the possibilities of combining patriotism with profit and many devised ranges of hampers specifically for men on active service. Harrods set up a 'War Comforts Department' where all those items that might be necessary for a soldier, from food to socks, were grouped together in one area of the store. In this way, the men's relatives were saved from having to navigate the whole shop in order to select the contents of their parcels, and no doubt encouraged to purchase items they might not have previously considered.[37] At the other end of the gift-giving spectrum, many schools encouraged pupils to use their pocket money to send letters and gifts to soldiers as small tokens of appreciation of their sacrifice. Rankers could be mercenary in their desire for parcels. George Hewins, who was married with numerous children, formed a relationship with a woman unaware of his marital status at his home training camp. His sole intention appears to have been to ensure an extra source of food supply, something of which he was in particular need as money was very short in the family home.[38] Hewins was quite clear, although obviously not to her, that the only reason for his interest in the woman was the chocolate she sent him: he called her his 'Cadbury's Girl'. Hewins's behaviour was unusually blatant, but the unreal conditions of wartime facilitated these strangely unformed emotional relationships, a number of which seem to have been predicated upon prosaic transactions. Margaret Semple corresponded for two years with Jock McLeod and there are two striking and interlinked factors in the seventy letters that remain, almost all of which are from Jock. When on leave and convalescence, Jock used every excuse possible to avoid meeting Margaret, although he was exceedingly grateful for the parcels she regularly sent him. After their initial contact, all of Margaret's attempts to meet with Jock come to nothing. Whether he is on leave or convalescing, he always has a reason for being unavailable or indeed standing-up the ever keen Margaret. On one occasion, Jock's letter explains that as much as he would love to see her, he is still feeling weak and as 'any excitement of any kind nearly kills me altogether', it would be inadvisable. The correspondence clearly indicates his lack of interest in her, at least to the objective eye, and eventually he writes to inform her of his love for a nurse. Margaret was valued not for herself but for the provisions and requisites she unfailingly sent him.[39]

Food from parcels could be of critical nutritional importance when rations were short or inedible. When Hugh Mann was ill with dysentery he could not stomach army rations and the food from home became exponentially important: 'I got your last fine parcel and the biscuits kept me in life for three days when I could eat nothing else'.[40] Parcels from home, individually gathered and packed by loved ones, were regarded as 'the most powerful emblem of sentiment and affection'.[41] Pre-packaged commercial products were not imbued with the same levels of familial love; they did not resonate with the care and intimacy evidenced in a home-packed gift. In addition to the food they supplied, the parcels had a clear emotional content: they were the point of contact between men and their families and a tangible reminder of the world they had left, but to which they longed to return.[42] A regular supply of parcels embodied the care and affection that families, deprived of the physical presence of their loved ones, communicated through the postal service. Consequently, an interruption of the supply caused dismay and, in the manner of the hungry Stophers, men would chide their relatives if they felt that they were not sending packages as often as they could or should. C.R. Jones wrote home wistfully, 'I am rather in the cold because fellows are continually getting parcels', wondering why he was not in receipt of a similar display of care.[43] His earlier letters are a litany of requests and it is unsurprising that his relatives were unable to meet his demands. The reproachful tone must have wounded them, as it is touching to note that after his death in 1916, before his family gave his letters to the Imperial War Museum, they annotated his complaint with the qualification that they had sent out four to six parcels a month. The poignant afterword ensures that subsequent readers will never doubt their love and concern.

Parcels did not consist entirely of foodstuffs, and soldiers requested a range of items from camp cookers to lice powder. Medicines and toiletries were popular because, as the headline of an advertisement that Boots The Chemist ran in *The Daily Chronicle* ominously stated, 'Remember there are no Chemists' Shops in the Trenches'.[44] Regardless of contents, the receipt of the package was satisfying in itself, as S.J. Hounsom explained to his family: 'You don't know the pleasure there is in merely unpacking it.'[45] It was the edible items that most fuelled the enjoyment in the contents of the parcels received. Food had a far greater power to elicit an excited response and generate pleasure than, for example, a box of candles. The sheer range of food posted to the men was remarkable. Walter Holyfield was grateful for the fresh eggs he had received and made a point of congratulating his mother on her highly superior packing skills.[46] Prepared meat was popular, particularly items that were not included in the ration, such as chicken. However, the families at home could be over-ambitious with the food gifts they sent, and delivery time and temperature often conspired against them. H.M. Adams was not unusual in having to throw away a chicken which had 'been too long on the road' by the time he received it.[47] Adams was fortunate, as the meat was sufficiently far along the road to decay to advertise the inadvisability of its consumption. C.P. Blacker ate a pot of brawn which manifested its unsuitability only once he had eaten it and had become very unwell.[48]

For wives and mothers, the satisfaction of the needs of their men provided a welcome area of shared interest and safe ground, where the traditional roles of feminine nurture could be continued despite the wartime separation. Sometimes there is a trace of an inversion of the civilian balance of power in the correspondence. The soldiers' reliance on their families for support gave their women a more explicitly critical role than they had had in peacetime. Sustaining men at the front was a significant responsibility and one that gave wives and mothers an additional authority in their relationships with their men. Edie Bennett wrote to her husband on 20 October 1916, 'glad you were pleased with the parcel and you don't want to thank me so, as you must remember it's my duty to look after you especially when you are in need'. While over-analysis of the letter would be unwise, the statement of duty and the emphasis that it was now her husband who was in need, may speak to a shift of power within their relationship. The role of gratitude in the prewar relationship between mothers and sons has been noted by Ellen Ross, who comments upon the thread of indebtedness that runs through so many memoirs of Edwardian childhood.[49] For many working-class men, the gratitude had a fundamental basis, as evidenced by the sacrifices (explored earlier) that mothers made just to ensure that their children ate. Gratitude, whether between mothers and sons or husbands and wives, was an emotion in which undercurrents of resentment or domination might sometimes be detected.

Unspoken emotions were integral to the gifts sent to the rankers; parcels and their contents helped to occupy the space in correspondence which could not be filled by the less palatable aspects of the men's war experience. In general, men did not want, or were unable whether in terms of literary skills or emotional anguish, to write home with details of the extremes of their service: the filth, injury, death and terror. The horrors punctuated long periods of waiting and preparation behind the front line, a tedium that presented a different challenge to the correspondent. W.V. Tilsley neatly summed up the shortage of suitable subject matter for a man's letters: 'What could one say beyond asking for parcels, exchanging healths, and exhorting the recipient to keep smiling?'[50] Consequently, many letters were a litany of items required or no longer needed, dependent upon the vagaries of the army's rationing system. Bert Bailey's letter to his wife is indicative of the detailed requirements: 'Don't send me any more Oxo or Bovril until I ask you to, Darling, will you. The little pat of butter is always welcome . . . Good substitutes for things I have asked you not to send would be sardines, pickles, or a bit of cheese.'[51] The mundanity of the dialogue was perhaps the essence of its comfort. The epistolary conversation was little different from a discussion the couple might have had over their breakfast table, regarding that evening's meal. A husband's, and a son's, preferences had shaped the eating experience of the working- and lower-middle-class families in prewar Britain, as explored in Chapter 2. The position of main wage earner had given their appetites first call on the food budget. The man of the house's likes and dislikes had traditionally dictated the purchases of their womenfolk, and despite geographical distance that privilege remained. Parcels permitted families some continuance, even pretence, of an ordinary existence. They gave access to a world where inadequate supplies of pickles or a surfeit of chocolate were matters of concern; an imaginative space that was comfortingly distant from the frightening possibilities of the Western Front.

A taste of home

For the men, unwrapping their packages in trenches, billets and camps, each represented a fragment of home, lovingly captured in brown paper and string. The touch and taste of the items reconnected soldiers with their loved ones nutritionally and also emotionally, stimulating their memory and imagination to recreate a picture of family and friends. It is difficult to assess how much time the soldier was able to devote to dreams of home, given both the demands placed upon his time and the psychic risks inherent in allowing his thoughts to dwell on a world denied him. Henry Williamson noted the dangers of taking one's mother to war, and contact with home was viewed by others as problematic. Herbert Read, commenting upon another man's cowardice, ascribed it to his repeated letters home: 'he never got free from his home thoughts . . . his mind . . . was not free . . . to create the conditions of its own existence'.[52] For most, emotional survival was achieved by total immersion in the military world; wistful but hopeless yearnings, even home leave, were ultimately painful and even unhelpful.[53] To some degree, the tension between the two fronts was balanced through the medium of parcels. Unlike letters, where the baldness of love and loss was all too painfully obvious, packages conveyed love in an implicit and comforting form. The gifts formed a connection between the parties, completing an emotional circuit through which affection could flow without the dangerous explicitness of words. The offerings of Knightsbridge grocers paled in the presence of a homemade cake; as Kenneth Addy wrote home, nothing is 'as good as mother makes'.[54] The desire for food cooked by mothers is a dominant theme in the rankers' references to parcels. B. Britland was delighted with the homemade cake his mother had sent him; he and his friends consumed it swiftly: '[the cake] melted like snow . . . we didn't half enjoy it, I can tell you'.[55] While C.R Jones was grateful for the packages his family had posted to him, his letter of thanks did include the comment that he preferred homemade cake to the shop-bought one that had been sent.[56] The picture at Figure 6.1 of men celebrating the arrival of a homemade Christmas pudding neatly illustrates the connection between food and memory.

The special comfort of food cooked by mother was less prevalent amongst the middle and upper classes, where domestic servants mediated this nurturing role. On a more prosaic level, many of the flattering references to home cooking found in letters home are no doubt indicative of the men's consideration of future supplies. They were keen to do all they could to encourage further packages, and criticism of a burnt cake or a leaden sponge might have dampened the enthusiasm of mothers and wives to send their baking to the front.

Sometimes it was not the cake alone that triggered comforting memories. Lance-Corporal W.H. Petty wrote in his diary how delighted he was with the cake his wife had baked and sent to him, but it was the container

Home Stirred and Stirring Thoughts of Home

" Home made, my lads ! " Apart from its symbolism as a British institution, Christmas plum-pudding is mighty good stuff which will be hailed with delight in the trenches. It is good to know that arrangements have been made whereby every man on active service will receive his share of pudding this Christmas Day.

6.1 Image from *The War Illustrated*, 1916

in which it was sent that appears to have given him the greatest pleasure. He ends his entry with the comment, 'it [the cake tin] reminded me very much of home as I recognised the tins that are usually on the kitchen shelf'.[57] The synchrony described at the end of the last chapter, where soldiers were able to imagine an escape from their military world and envision themselves inhabiting their past lives is poignantly captured in Petty's response to the cake tin. The apparent insignificance of an inconsequential, homely object, perhaps even to the wife who packed the parcel, is disproportionate to its impact on the recipient for whom it unlocks a world laden with the weight of emotion and memory.

Ironically, whilst so many of the parcels were the quintessence of a deeply personal and intimate relationship, they were simultaneously public property. Their receipt was a matter of celebration, not just for the addressee but also for his particular pals. Sharing was both a manifestation of friendship and a practical survival tool. Anthropological study has identified the importance of co-operation in hunting and eating in primitive societies, where without combining their effort men would have been unable to obtain sufficient supplies for their families.[58] Erratic food supplies ensure that people are sustained by a 'web of mutual obligation', where edible gifts are given as an insurance against future hunger.[59] A.P. Burke reassured his family in a letter home that, even though their parcel had not arrived and rations were stretched, '[I] never go short of anything, there are some good lads here'.[60] Burke was fortunate to receive regular gifts from home; not all men were so privileged. Ben Clouting remembered that in his unit the men pooled their gifts with two orphans who received nothing, saying that 'it was only fair that those who received parcels from home shared out the contents, particularly food'.[61] His emphasis on food is interesting, as a packet of cigarettes or candles could have been equally easily divided. There was something elemental in the sharing of food; to witness a neighbour's hunger in the presence of one's own plenty would have contravened every sensibility, whether anthropological, social or religious.

The pooling of parcels could extend beyond a soldier's life when parcels sent to men killed in action were shared amongst the survivors. It was regarded as only sensible to open them and eat the contents which, after all, were likely to spoil if returned to the sender. Jack Ashley echoed the experience of the majority of the rankers when he wrote in his diary: 'There were a week's parcels and, as two thirds of the men were killed or wounded, there was plenty for everybody.'[62] The division of the parcels of casualties amongst the living did not always take place; sometimes they were returned to the senders. Mrs Rosamund Wordsworth wrote to Mrs E.D. Stephens, the organiser of a Rifle Brigade Comforts Fund, to say that, following her son's death, all her parcels had been returned, 'Xmas pudding and all . . . Our system of postal arrangements is truly wonderful.'[63] It is hard to believe that the loss of a beloved son could in some way be compensated for by the success of post office procedures.

The criteria for keeping or returning parcels are not clear and it seems likely that the decision rested with the officers in the field. It was determined by a combination of their sensitivities and the practical implications of having to transport the surplus packages. For the surviving rankers, hunger took precedence over delicacy, just as it did when it came to dividing up the extra army rations that arrived when there had been no recalculation to reflect casualty figures. A few were diffident, F.E. Noakes recalled: 'it was not pleasant to think that we might be enjoying dainties which had been prepared with loving care for someone we had known and who might now be dead – but we did not refuse them on that account.'[64] The only circumstances in which such food might become wholly unpalatable was when it was too closely identified with the dead man and his family. P.H. Jones was unable to stomach a plum cake sent by a loving mother to her recently dead son because of the note that accompanied it: '"To dear Reggie with best wishes for a Happy Christmas and a safe return home, from Mother."'[65] The tangible and unequivocal evidence of love made public by loss was too much for Jones, and to eat the cake would have been to intrude upon an intimacy. Here, the tension between the private and public aspects of the parcel was insoluble. A man was generally required to give permission for the admission of his family's gift to the common pool; it was possible to presume his tacit acceptance if he were killed or wounded, but not if the presence of his family, and hence the personal nature of the gift, was made so explicit. However, the timing of Jones's scruples may have been pertinent: it was Christmas and parcels were in abundance. Perhaps on a cold, hungry day in January the personalisation of the cake might not have had quite the same impact.

In the majority of circumstances, the sharing of parcels was a universally accepted behaviour, or perhaps a disinclination to share was something soldiers were unwilling to articulate, whether at the time or in their memoirs. George Herbert Hill, unusually, did acknowledge reluctance, and wrote of the disappointment felt when he could not keep all of the contents of a parcel to himself: 'I shared it unwillingly with them, only keeping the lion's share of the [much prized apple] tart by right of ownership.'[66] Hill wrote his memoir as a novel, and it may have been easier to present ignoble thoughts in a depersonalised, fictional format. Similarly, in A.P. Herbert's *The Secret Battle*, the bad feeling between Penrose and his fellow officers is increased by the resentments arising from the inequitable sharing of parcels.[67]

Stories of the need for generosity in times of hunger can be found in the histories of other traumatic events. Memories of the Irish Famine contain a number of moralistic tales of charity rewarded, where those who helped their starving neighbours were later blessed with good luck.[68] In a similar fashion, the accounts of the rankers emphasise the generosity of sharing amongst the soldiers; a selfish, greedy man did not convey the image of self-sacrifice central to both their own belief and others, expectations. Amongst the virtually unanimous accounts of unchallenged sharing, the plain-speaking George Stopher stands out. He wrote to his cousin, 'don't send me more sweets as they all want some and I cannot say no to them but you can send me all the money you like'.[69] Stopher resented both the assumption that gifts would be shared and also the pressure exerted to ensure that he complied. The letter was written from a training camp in Wiltshire, at the beginning of his military service and there are no similar complaints in later correspondence. It may be that his attitude to the pooling of provisions changed as time went on, enhancing both his relationships with other rankers and his understanding of the benefits of sharing in the face of army privations.

Judicious sharing of parcels could not fully compensate for the shortfalls in, and boredom with, army rations. The soldiers' response was to undertake a more unilateral type of sharing of the other food available, that is scrounging from the local population and the army. Shortages meant that officers tended to ignore the illegality of the men's efforts to supplement their diet, and in certain circumstances encouraged, even ordered, the soldiers to take extra food wherever they could. Often the only interventions were orders to avoid confrontation with the locals, such as ensuring that orchards were raided under cover of darkness, something upon which Captain J.C. Dunn insisted.[70] Stealing fruit was common and virtually impossible to prevent, even becoming a suitable subject for official artists such as John Singer Sargent, whose picture ironically titled *Thou Shalt Not Steal* is reproduced on the cover of this book. The evidence suggests that the only surprising aspect of the drawing of two soldiers taking apples in an orchard is the fact that the man eating the spoils is looking around in a rather furtive fashion.[71] The frequent references to taking fruit found in the men's accounts indicate that it was an unremarkable event. It had a greater significance for its victims, and local farmers were generally less accepting. Jack Halstead was uncomprehending, but rather impressed by the furious language of the farmer that resulted from his raid on a tempting cherry tree.[72] Stealing fruit could be a highly dangerous occupation, and on occasion it was hard to balance the longing for something delicious with the risks that had to be taken to acquire it. The fruit-loving Halstead bagged some plums from a tree that stood in an exposed position between the front and the second line trenches, but reflected that he was unsure whether it was worth the 'uncalled risk'.[73]

Chickens, pigs, horses and other game

At times of real crisis, when the supply lines had broken down, 'scrumping' was insufficient, and a concerted raid on available provisions was required. In 1918, J. Sanderson noted in his diary that 'some of the men had actually been detailed by the Major to go out looking for food, wines etc in the deserted houses'.[74] When rations and men failed to connect, COs were compelled to do what they could for their men. Sanderson's use of 'actually' implies that it was unusual for such a direct order to be issued, although his diary has numerous matter-of-fact references to his and his pals' habitual scrounging. These were actions which directly contravened the letter from Lord Kitchener, held in each soldiers' pay book, which advised them to 'always look upon looting as a disgraceful act'.[75] Unsurprisingly, direct orders to undertake such acts were uncommon, and rankers tended to be circumspect in their activities. Ben Clouting noted that stolen chickens were always skinned, never plucked, to ensure that evidence of the crime could be more easily concealed.[76] On occasion complaints were made by the locals and acted upon. Captain C.P. Blacker had to actively dissuade his men from poaching, after the 'garde forestière' of the woods in which they were based protested that their activities were excessive.[77] Deer and chickens were larger and more expensive and attracted a degree of attention not accorded an apple pulled from a tree, or a swede from a field.

Retribution for the stealing of provisions from the local populace was generally unforthcoming, owing in part to the officers' own proclivities. It was difficult for an officer to punish his rankers when he was also happy to take what he could from the locale. Gentlemen continued their enjoyment of country pursuits, and, whilst the Western Front may not have been as well stocked with game as the grouse moors of Scotland, it did provide opportunities for both sport and an enhanced dinner table.[78] It paid to be cautious, however, as an officer discovered when resting with the unit he had just joined. He was about to shoot one of the large hares he saw nibbling at the hedge only to be bellowed at by an irate Sergeant Major: 'For ***** sake, don't touch them hares! Them's our mascots.'[79] It was not only fur and feathered game that was under threat from the officers: canals, rivers and lakes were fished for their edible contents. For some rankers, untutored in the sportsmanlike behaviour of their officers, rods and lines could prove too slow a method and successful catches were ensured through unsporting means. Ben Clouting recalled a particularly enterprising scrounger who closed the sluice gates of a river in order to lower the water level and strand the fish. He was successful and quantities of fish were picked from the puddles; unfortunately his methods caused localised flooding in the villages upstream.[80] On occasion the tools of the soldier's trade assisted successful scrounging strategies; F.A.J. 'Tanky' Taylor wrote that he had used purloined grenades to stun fish.[81] Officers, sustained by better food and therefore motivated more by sport than hunger, were unlikely to have been tempted by the snatched vegetables the men sometimes ate raw.[82] Fresh game was a different matter, and incidents such as that of an officer fleeing angry villagers with a live stolen salmon struggling in his breeches made the imposition of discipline difficult.[83] This entertaining anecdote may border on the apocryphal, but it conveys the message that officers were frequently as culpable as their men when it came to scrounging.

Opportunities to supplement the diet did not always arise from sport; sometimes they were a direct consequence of shelling. Horses were frequent victims of the barrage, but the response to their meat was mixed. Horsemeat was alien to the British diet and, while popular amongst the French working classes, it was taboo in many parts of the world for both religious and sentimental reasons. Lance-Corporal W.H. Petty was enthusiastic about French bread and butter when he arrived in France in September 1914, but deeply suspicious of the meat. He found it very amusing when his pals ordered 'beefsteak' at a café, but then discovered half-way through its consumption that it was in fact horsemeat.[84] In addition to the unfamiliarity of the meat, many units, given the widespread use of horses in supporting the war effort, would be eating their own charges. Close relationships with the horses may have influenced the ability of some of the men to ingest what the day before had been a carefully nurtured dependant. It has been suggested that the carnage of the war was a turning point in attitudes towards animals. After 1918, the similarities between man and beast were more widely acknowledged, reflected in the upsurge of interest in vegetarianism in the interwar period.[85] Fortunino

Matania's popular painting *Good-Bye Old Man* at Figure 6.2 vividly illustrates the powerful bond that could develop between soldiers and their
charges. The sight of the grieving man cradling the dying horse's head
in his hands is an image at odds with the notion of horses as food. Even
the generally inarticulate William Hate, whose stilted letters home were
discussed in Chapter 1, was moved to comment in his diary on the pain
he endured at the sight of the horses' suffering.[86]

For some, the eating of horse would have introduced a suggestion of
cannibalism to the meal. Reactions did vary: Ben Clouting, a cavalryman,
thoroughly enjoyed his meal of horse liver, but some of his neighbours
were sick once they discovered what they had eaten.[87] William Carr
served in an artillery company which used horses to transport the guns,
but this proximity to the animals did not prevent his unit enjoying
'tasty steaks' from a horse they had butchered. Their feasting had to be
curtailed when the CO appeared and told them that the consumption
of horsemeat was against army regulations and ordered the remainder destroyed.[88] Army Orders seem to be silent on the consumption
of horsemeat; there are instructions on the disposal of dead horses by
burial, but nothing that explicitly states that their meat was forbidden.[89]
Indeed, other officers were happy to make the most of extra food, including the captain recalled by F.W. Sutcliffe, who shot a horse with a broken
leg and invited the men to have 'a steak off it'.[90] The army's dietary
manuals did contain information on the correct method of butchering
cows, but they make no mention of similar for horses.[91] The potential
inclusion of horsemeat in the ration would have been a discomfiting
possibility for many, at least when they were full of normal rations. For
some officers, perhaps the sight of men ingesting such an alien foodstuff
was too distressing; it suggested a breakdown of civilised order through
the assumption of eating habits that, while long acceptable in France and
Germany, were not British. It appears that the decision on whether or not
to eat the horses rested with the officers present, just as it did with many
other aspects of day-to-day army life.

Despite the butchery instructions in the dietary manual, soldiers'
accounts make no mention of the availability of extra beef, although the
occasional pint of fresh milk was appreciated. In quieter sections, some
units like the 5th Gloucesters kept a 'trench cow' for this purpose.[92] Pigs
were a far more accessible livestock, in terms of both size and availability.
Many rural households kept a single animal for their own meat, so their
ubiquity ensured that they frequently crossed the paths of the hungry
soldiers. On occasion, a pig might be a shelling casualty; Billy Congreve

6.2 *Good-Bye Old Man* by Fortunino Matania, 1916

wrote delightedly in his diary: 'we have had splendid pork chops . . . shrapnel-killed pork! Quite a new diet!'[93] More frequently the pig's death was non-accidental, and Sergeant Major Shephard shot one that was 'foolish enough to come down the road'.[94] It took time and immobility to butcher and cook a pig, conditions that were rare when an army was on the move. In the rapid and hungry retreat of March 1918, William Carr's unit killed an abandoned sow and carried the carcass away with them but had no opportunity to cook it before it rotted, a misfortune he described as a 'tragedy' for the hungry men.[95] Perhaps the men's disappointment would have been tempered by the knowledge that the consequences of eating too much pork could be equally unfortunate. In *All Quiet on the Western Front*, after preparing a sumptuous dinner of the pigs they had found abandoned, the men were very ill, their digestive systems being unused to such rich and plentiful food.[96]

The rankers' relationship with the local population's food supplies was not purely predatory, and there were acts of generosity. E. Brunsdon remembered distributing tins of bully beef to hungry villagers and the joyful welcome they received.[97] Brunsdon does not date the occasion but the assumption must be that it was later in the war, when food was an increasingly pressing problem for the local population. At the start of the conflict, the civilians on whose land the battles were fought could be very generous to the soldiers, and provisions were given freely. Sergeant E.C.H. Rowland noted that, during the retreat from Mons, the French 'have been more than kind to us giving us of their best food, fruit, wine'.[98] Private George Wilson landed in France in September 1914 and describes in his diary how his repeated shouts of 'Vive La France!' were 'answered with a shower of grub'.[99] Local enthusiasm had worn thin after four years of the locust-like presence of the armies of the Western Front, as had food supplies, given that the growing of crops in the proximity of the battlefields was fraught with difficulty. The soldiers' unpopularity was not related solely to the stealing of food; a potentially more dangerous issue was the fires they unwittingly started in the barns and farm buildings in which they were billeted. Between January and March 1915, there were eighty-one, and damages in just fifty of them amounted to 250,000 francs (£10,000).[100] The relationship with local farmers was not an easy one, despite the efforts of the army to provide manpower for the agricultural jobs left vacant by the absent French men. Despite the general reluctance to work the fields, E. Brunsdon remembered that informal arrangements were sometimes made in his sector. These men appeared to have had a particularly good relationship with the local population and 'many of the troops help villagers with their crops etc in the few spare hours'.[101]

Scrounging or stealing?

The efforts described by Brunsdon were unusual. Generally the rankers were far less helpful to the local population, though few went quite as far as T. Dalziel, who admitted to the stealing of bread from the French workers who passed through his sentry post.[102] Scrounging, like grousing, was a traditional part of a soldier's life; the position of armed men in the countryside gave them a power that was hard to resist. Dalziel's description of outright robbery from an identifiable individual was extremely unusual. Taking extra food was usually perceived as a victimless crime, an acceptable pastime, where men who were inventive and successful scroungers were lauded by their peers. Occasionally, however, the praise was tinged with a degree of revulsion. Frederic Manning neatly sums up the ambivalence when, in *Her Privates We*, Corporal Tozer admonishes two of the men: '"You two are the champion bloody scroungers in the battalion," he said; and it was impossible to know whether he was more moved by admiration or by disgust.'[103] The majority of men took food when the chance arose because they either were hungry or knew they were likely to be so in the future. Army life made soldiers opportunistic; finding extra food was not an everyday occurrence and it was wise to capitalise upon the availability of additional supplies.

The principled certainties of respectable civilian life, where theft was both morally and legally defined, were somewhat blurred by military service, and the taking of food was mitigated by both physical hunger and the general frustrations and resented exploitations of military life. Perhaps life in the army partly redefined the men's civilian views of ownership, as the soldiers found themselves in a world where normal determinations of property were less applicable. The British Army ranked its strategic needs above the concerns of local farmers, and their occupation and use of agricultural land was a visible demonstration of the fragility of civilian ownership in wartime to the soldiers.[104] For many men, wartime made theft a less heinous crime. Frank Gray wrote the ranker 'does not steal, for that is a word unknown to the British soldier . . . we may go out early or late to "win" what is wanted, but steal never'.[105] The verb 'win' was commonly used by the agricultural poor researched by Barry Reay, who employed it as an acceptable alternative to 'poaching'. For example, a man described how 'you sometimes won a pheasant accidentally and you won a fish'.[106] The notion that food somehow fell into a man's hands without the need for him to accept any agency for its presence was a comforting explanation for poachers, whether of game or army supplies.

The conflict caused an adjustment to peacetime morality; it was necessary for the state to endorse violence and murder in the furtherance of its war aims, and this appears to have had a concomitant impact on the army's perception of other crimes, theft in particular. Many of the rankers would have had the childhood experience of snatching any extra food that presented itself. The poorest of the working class had learnt young to take whatever food was available from market stalls or open fields, regardless of the niceties of ownership. Hungry times on the Western Front encouraged the reassertion of an opportunism which had lain dormant in their earlier adult lives. Certainly the attitude of many of the officers serving at the front, as we have already seen, displayed a lack of interest in prosecuting their men to the letter of the law and a willingness to accommodate stealing in a way that the Army Regulations did not. In his exploration of the sexual behaviour of British soldiers on the Western Front, K. Craig Gibson notes both the unwillingness of regiments to report sexual crimes committed by the men and the tendency to punish at company level those offences which ought to have led to a court martial.[107] It could reasonably be assumed that a similar attitude would have applied to property crimes. Therefore, while the *Field Service Pocket Book* issued to every soldier pronounced that they faced a maximum of fourteen years' imprisonment if court-martialled and convicted of theft, the reality seemed some way distant from the letter of the law.[108] The statistics of the courts martial held during the war state that a total of 9,322 soldiers were tried for theft, while in the same period 87,131 were prosecuted for being absent without leave and 39,906 for drunkenness.[109] The official position, as evidenced in both the *Pocket Book* and *The Manual of Military Law*, was one of fierce approbation but the full strictures of the law were probably less frequently employed than the regulations imply and only the very worst cases were pursued in the military courts. Surviving details of wartime courts martial relate to capital offences such as desertion rather than the less serious crimes, but it is likely that prosecuting minor incidences of theft was low on the army's list of priorities. As a *maire*, exasperated by the pillaging of the village's potato fields, complained to a British officer, 'giving orders is well and good, ensuring their enforcement would be better still'.[110]

Shifts in wartime morality did not make all theft acceptable, and the soldiers' accounts indicate a complicated ethical code. Christopher

Haworth defined a difference between 'scrounging' for personal consumption, which was 'not morally bad', and 'flogging' or thieving to sell for gain, which was regarded as unacceptable.[111] His definition was underpinned by the assumption that none of these acts was committed against individual soldiers. Acceptable theft had to be 'victimless' and that meant goods taken from either the civilian population or the army, both of whom were regarded as occupying a far more fortunate position than the beleaguered ranker. Haworth's explanation is a reflection of the view expressed in *The Manual of Military Law* which stresses that 'stealing from a comrade is regarded as peculiarly disgraceful' because the open nature of barrack life meant that a man's possessions were usually accessible to his fellow soldiers.[112] Haworth describes life in the trenches, half-jokingly, as a truly Socialist world, where limited resources were equitably shared, in sharp contrast to the exploitative capitalists he perceived to be profiteering on the home front. Accounts from other soldiers indicate that Howarth may have had a rather romantic view of the rankers' honesty, as there are a number of references to pilfering amongst the men. A.P. Burke wrote home about 'a big rat (a two-legged one) nibbling at my choc'; he was not too distressed as it turned out to be 'one of the lads' with whom he generally shared food.[113] In his diary, Edward Roe bitterly denounced the 'rascal [who] pinched my emergency rations of tea and sugar'. Roe was especially angry as the absence contravened the rules and resulted in him being sentenced to the indignity of Field Punishment Number One.[114] It transpired that the supplies were stolen by a man from another regiment, when Roe had been separated from his own in the confusion of September 1914. No doubt it was easier for a ranker to steal from a stranger, even if he did wear a similar uniform. It appears that, for less scrupulous men, the concept of the theft of food as a victimless crime extended to any soldier to whom they had no personal attachment. W.M. Floyd, who served as an orderly in various hospitals in France, cheerfully recorded the 'good feeds' he obtained by rifling through the bedside cupboards of the patients.[115]

Pilfering from a fellow soldier was, at least publicly, regarded as offensive unless of course they had been killed. Eating the rations of a casualty was permitted because George Coopard noted, not unreasonably, 'a tin of bully in a dead man's pack can't help him'.[116] Not all soldiers had such a pragmatic approach and squeamishness could inhibit men. Captain J.C. Dunn recorded in his diary that a new soldier's nerves had 'given way' at the sight of rankers eating a tin of sardines they had just taken from a corpse.[117] Similarly, the belongings of an officer might be regarded as fair game if the opportunity arose; their superior supplies and elevated status militated against the protection that was usually afforded to the rankers. Indeed, the opportunity to eat an officer's food seemed to give it a particularly enjoyable savour. Jack Halstead's diary registers the resentment a fellow ranker felt when ordered to take care of an officer's kit; his angry reaction was 'I'm a fighting soldier not a ****** officer's servant, anyway, he'll be sorry he left it to me.'[118] Revenge took the form of 'losing' one of the officer's parcels; the chocolates and biscuits obtained were enjoyed by the men as much for the redress they signified as for their actual calorific value. Such taking of food from those who had plenty is reminiscent of the function similar acts had for the slaves in the antebellum South. Stealing from a plantation owner or an officer represented a range of possibilities and meanings: it assuaged hunger pangs, provided the pleasure of adventure and indirectly chastened a despised master.[119]

Whilst theft from live rankers was, at the very least, frowned upon, taking food from army supplies for personal consumption was acceptable, even commendable: a form of legitimate appropriation. Purloining food from officers was defensible in the 'Robin Hood spirit' of taking from the rich to feed the poor, and the stealing of army supplies was justifiable as the seizure by the rankers of that which was rightly theirs. However, moral acceptability disappeared if soldiers stole large quantities to sell for profit, the 'flogging' that Howarth so despised. A number of the rankers' stories have a hint of entertainment rather than authenticity about them, for example Roe's anecdote of the estaminet that paid three francs a tin for the anti-frostbite grease the men were supposed to rub on their feet and used it to fry chips.[120] Practical problems of access to stores meant that the most persistent offenders, as has been discussed in earlier chapters, were likely to be the ASC, HQ staff or the cooks. Ordinary soldiers might have had the occasional opportunity to grab an extra loaf or tin of bully whilst on a ration or work detail, but that was usually the extent of their gains. The example of Joseph Murray is typical; he was detailed to help unload a supply ship at Gallipoli and was delighted when he managed to drop a tin of condensed milk into the sea in order to retrieve it later.[121]

Scrounging was not the only option by which soldiers could supplement their diet; the estaminets that abounded in the reserve areas offered another possibility. The local population was quick to take advantage of its captive clientele and set up small eateries. Many of the establishments frequented were little more than a family's kitchen or front room, converted into a commercial café for the duration. In the manner of on-duty eating, the venues for off-duty meals tended to be segregated on the basis of rank. The sharing of dining space by officers and men 'was apt to cause to all parties confusion and embarrassment'.[122] Frank Richards recalled that he saw officers and men sharing a café on only one occasion during his four years on the Western Front.[123] Men of all ranks were drawn to the two key centres of recreation, Poperinghe for the troops around Ypres, and Amiens for those serving on the Somme. A day's entertainment in these places was not easily embarked upon; a key obstacle for the rankers was that of transport from the reserve areas. Officers had access to motor vehicles in their off-duty hours or could use their rank to hitch a ride with a convoy, options unavailable to the men. Even if rankers were able to reach the towns, popular and stylish restaurants such as Godbert's in Amiens and Cyril's in Poperinghe were expensive for a man on a rankers' pay. The average infantryman received 1s 9d a day, a sum that included additions for length of service and specific skills.[124] Many men had part of their pay deducted at source and forwarded to their families, leaving them with an even more restricted income. For many soldiers the money that remained was dedicated to the purchase of additional food: as S.T. Eachus recorded in his diary, 'am spending a good deal of money upon the important function of eating'.[125]

A lack of funds, combined with the unavailability of transport, ensured that rankers gravitated to the more convenient, smaller, local estaminets where prices were lower than those in the centres populated by the officers. Perhaps many of them were attracted to the homely environment of these establishments, which was less daunting than the formal venues. Opportunities for the working classes to eat out had been relatively limited before the war, as discussed in Chapter 2. Restaurants such as Godbert's were more reminiscent of the Café Royal than a Lyons Corner House or Chop House, representing unfamiliar territory for the majority of the men. The restricted menus of the smaller venues did not present a problem, as the British ranker was not renowned for his sense of culinary adventure. Forays into unfamiliar food types were infrequent and doomed to failure. There were numerous jokes comparing the smell of French cheese, which was especially unpopular, to unwashed socks, and it was widely rejected as 'white and soapy, looking and tasting like curdled milk'.[126] Concerns about the alien aroma of Camembert lingered on into the Second World War. Claude Lévi-Strauss describes how American soldiers, advancing through Normandy in 1944, occasionally blew up dairies without entering them, believing that their strong smell was indicative of decomposing corpses not cheese.[127] The intimate

6.3 'More German Atrocities', postcard by Donald McGill

relationship between food and identity means that unappealing foreign foodstuffs could be construed as representative of national barbarity, as the Donald McGill postcard (Figure 6.3) indicates. S.T. Eachus, at the beginning of the preceding chapter, declared that the lack of vegetables provided by the British Army was cruelty on a par with anything the Germans had been accused of, and here McGill also uses food as a potential source of anguish, admittedly in a more humorous vein.

Eggs and women

The First World War rankers were more adventurous when it came to alcohol. Many enjoyed their first taste of 'van' (wine), whether red or white; Oliver Coleman was delighted with his and described it as 'hot!' in his diary.[128] The quality varied, as Lance-Corporal W.H. Petty recorded. He was initially very pleased with the red wine served at 'only 4d' a pint, but less than two weeks later he complains about a café where the glass tasted 'more like red ink and water'.[129] The men drank what they could when they could, but alcohol was frequently expensive and in short supply, so it was food to which they turned most regularly for comfort. The staple, often the only dish on the estaminets' menus was egg and chips, for which the men had 'an unconquerable passion'.[130] Captain C.L.

Overton wrote to his fiancée of the dish's popularity amongst the men. He describes an enterprising old couple who had set up a venture selling only eggs and chips, and managed to sell as many as four hundred eggs a day.[131] The number of eggs men were able to consume was impressive. A.P. Burke wrote home that he was delighted to have found a place where he could indulge: 'have had 3 everyday for my dinner ... & 4 today – one extra as a souvenir – what a treat from stew'.[132] Pleasure in eggs was not confined to the men; they were favoured by officers as well, and W.J. Bunbury managed to eat nine over a consecutive supper and breakfast.[133]

There were many reasons for the popularity of the egg, an item that had much to recommend it nutritionally. Clearly, a change from the main source of protein, the relentless bully beef, was a major factor in its favour: the crispness of egg and chips contrasted pleasingly with the oleaginous tinned meat. The dish was usually cooked to order, arriving on the hungry soldier's plate with a speed that ensured a degree of freshness difficult for army cooks to replicate. Accounts indicate that eggs were something of a 'comfort food' for the men. For the very poorest, eggs represented a treat, offered only on high days and holidays, but for many of the men they were perhaps reminders of childhood breakfasts and teatimes of boiled eggs and toast soldiers. It is difficult to ascertain levels of egg consumption before 1914, as they were not recorded separately in the food statistics collected by nineteenth- and early twentieth-century investigators. In their study of the British diet, Drummond and Wilbraham state that the numbers eaten 'approximately doubled between 1909–13', but do not provide detailed figures.[134] The lunches that working- and lower-middle-class men ate at cafés and eating houses were usually of the 'meat and two veg' variety, although eggs were included on the prewar menu at the Bournville canteens, alongside the roast beef, sausages and pies.[135] There is a wealth of evidence indicating the growing role of chips in the prewar working-class diet, but they were more usually accompanied by fish rather than eggs.

The popularity of eggs amongst the men was likely to have had its basis in the conditions of active service. The fears and tensions of war stimulated a retreat to the familiar, and eggs were a plain, easily digestible and tasty foodstuff. Eggs offered a stable, unthreatening point of nutritional reference in the unfamiliar terrain of the Western Front. The egg-loving Bunbury noted, 'It is curious how childlike we have all become, as it seems to me that we are all rather like schoolboys and simply love receiving such delicacies as cake, chocolate, sweets &c'.[136] The childlike solace found in sugar could equally be located in eggs. The army regarded eggs as a luxury item and they were rarely issued as part of the ration. The exception to this was in military hospitals, where they were fed to the sick and wounded men as part of an invalid diet. After George Stopher's death on 19 May 1917, Sister Lenard, who had nursed him at Casualty Clearing Station 32, sent a letter of comfort to his bereaved mother. She wrote that it had been 'very difficult to get him comfortable', a phrase that can only hint at the unspeakable nature of his wounds and the pain he endured. On a more reassuring note, Sister Lenard added, 'He had everything he liked and was very fond of a little champagne and an egg with his tea.'[137] Impoverished rural Suffolk would have provided few opportunities for champagne, but Mrs Stopher like her poor dead son would have recognised eggs as a nurturing and comforting food, a taste of maternal care provided in her absence by the caring Sister.

Eggs had much to recommend them to the soldiers, not least the security of their goodness and fitness for consumption. The natural packaging their shell provides uniquely protects them from contamination to which all types of meat and fish products were prone. Susanne Friedberg describes how nineteenth-century farmers devised a method of keeping eggs fresh for years by storing them in a mixture of brine and quicklime. Eggs were a safe food, and if they had gone bad it was unmistakable, unlike meat products which could conceal their toxic state from the consumer until it was too late. Friedberg points out that tending the flocks of chickens on the farms was traditionally regarded as women's work. She also quotes an early twentieth-century manual that explains that this division of labour was due 'to the fact that they seem to understand the temperament of the sitting hen better than men', a comment that further cements the reassuring femininity of the egg.[138] Warren Belasco, in a discussion of the power of Proust's madeleine to conjure memories, describes eggs as being 'particularly evocative' in this way, something that he attributes to their 'reproductive significance'.[139] The soldiers' consumption of eggs had implications beyond their nutritional value; the ingestion of an item so complete in itself, and both female and maternal by definition, afforded a high level of comfort.

The female comfort men sought was also present in the running of the estaminets, where memories of home and an approximation of maternal care resurfaced, even if the men did have to pay for it. The women, the wives and mothers who ran the bulk of these establishments, reminded men of their prewar existence: to have a meal prepared and served by a female in domestic surroundings was a welcome relief from the masculinity of the military. Occasionally the references were derogatory, the woman was unattractive, grubby or she overcharged, although in the latter circumstance soldiers might make their own amends: 'Had a rather dear dish of chips & steak so pinched a fork to put things a bit square.'[140] In the main the soldiers viewed the women, if not reverentially, certainly with at least a degree of respect and often one of warmth. Such feelings could be reciprocated, as in the case of Madame who ran an establishment in Beuvry and whom Captain J.C. Dunn noted 'was a motherly soul who delighted to bake a cake for someone's birthday, or do a kindly service for a customer'.[141] Of course, estaminets could provide feminine attractions of a different kind, and men like F. Rawnsley were able to record a visit that provided a 'fine feed also nice kiss'.[142] For many men, romance may have been something that owed more to imagination than reality, given the great numbers of soldiers compared to the limited availability of young women. Descriptions of such contacts are infrequently recorded. An assignation with a girl from the local café was hardly the stuff of letters home or of the subsequent memoirs written as testimonies to noble sacrifice. In addition, diaries were not wholly private as they, too, were often intended for family consumption. Sergeant Arthur Bridges made several references to the kind attentions in his diary of a 'Mamzelle', who prepared especially tasty meals for him. He also included the comment, 'Hope Em won't be jealous when she reads this but we must make the best of things here.' Bridges seemed to be prepared for the fact that the contents of his diary would at some point have a wider audience, including his fiancée or girlfriend.[143]

The Reverend Andrew Clark, whose own diary paints a riveting picture of the home front, wrote that the soldiers using a canteen at Woolwich hated being served by 'young ladies, whom they are shy of, but would like a motherly working woman'.[144] Clark's comment may have been as much a reflection of his personal morality and class inhibitions; the 'ladies' suggests females of a different class from both the men and the 'working woman' of Clark's ideal. Certainly, soldiers on the Western Front were generally pleased to have contact with young women, especially if they were English. John Jackson remembered the pleasure of meeting the girls from home who served in the canteen 'Angelina's', set up by Lady Angela Forbes at Etaples.[145] The contrast between the brutality of the camp and the gentility of Lady Forbes's enterprise was striking.

Around the Western Front, women who did not run an actual estaminet were often happy to provide ad hoc private dining arrangements for soldiers. They had both the cooking skills and the domestic space for those men who had purchased foodstuffs and wanted them prepared and served in a more convivial environment than the camp. The provisions for such meals tended to be purchased locally, as parcels often contained ready-prepared foodstuffs. Buying food was not easy; the problem in centres such as Poperinghe was the expense: as Aubrey Smith recalled, 'we could buy any extra food we required – at a price'.[146] In smaller places supplies were limited and concerns regarding civilians' requirements often resulted in local orders limiting soldiers' access to food. S.T. Eachus noted that, in one village, bakers were forbidden to sell bread to the troops and, in another, soldiers were banned from entering food shops until after 4 pm, presumably to allow the locals first choice of what was available.[147] If the makings of a good meal could be obtained, a sympathetic local woman might transform it into a feast. C.R. Jones wrote home admiringly, 'These French women know how to cook!', although he was referring to a 'ripping fine egg & chips' he had just consumed, rather than any gourmet offering.[148] At least that most popular dish had a currency that crossed national boundaries unlike the suet pudding with treacle that the soldiers in *Her Privates We* had hoped the farmer's wife would prepare for them. Sadly, she was unable to translate the dish into her own culinary repertoire and a compromise had to be reached, a sweet omelette and jam that suited both parties.[149]

Canteens

Local shops were not the sole source of ingredients for such feasts; canteens and rest huts were established in or near most army camps at home and abroad. They were run by a variety of organisations as well as the army itself, mainly churches and charitable institutions such as the YMCA, which had ten rest huts in the Ypres Salient alone.[150] In addition to the supplies and refreshments offered, they provided what was regarded as a morally healthy alternative to the temptations on offer elsewhere. Refreshments available were limited, the staple being a cup of tea and a bun, both of which could usually be obtained for twopence.[151] The rankers were not necessarily drawn to them for the food they offered, but they did enjoy their relatively convivial environment. The YMCA Handbook instructed that the huts should be 'homelike and comfortable . . . more like a club and . . . less like a barrack-room'.[152] The unmilitary setting was appreciated by the men, and the billiards, concerts and books provided were much enjoyed, but the food they offered was limited. Canteens, as well as providing refreshments, aimed to sell a wider range of food. Availability was best in the permanent establishments sited in the camps; the mobile outfits, which travelled to be near the men, were more basic. The Salvation Army and the YMCA set up temporary establishments close to the front; soldiers were very grateful for their willingness to dispense snacks and hot drinks in forward positions. In his journal, Captain Henry Ogle notes the shocking contrast between the Battle of the Somme and the excellent food provided by the YMCA canteen within earshot of the guns.[153]

Running such canteens could be a dangerous responsibility: those within shell range were sometimes hit and then had to be evacuated. This was not wholly disastrous, certainly not for the soldiers in the vicinity for whom, like A.J. Jamieson, it might be a beneficial event. Jamieson recalled that 'as food had been very scanty for two days we were told to lift what we could from the [abandoned] canteen'.[154] The risk of operating a forward canteen was an integral aspect of its attraction for some. C.P. Blacker noted the efforts of E.W. Hornung, whose son, Oscar, had been killed and who had subsequently felt 'a strong desire to have personal experience of the sort of life Oscar had led'. The result of this was his decision to run a YMCA canteen in a sunken road close to the front line near Arras. It was thought odd that an asthmatic old man should choose such a dangerous position but 'the worse the hardship, the more he was pleased; the nearer he felt to Oscar'.[155] The image of a grieving father, striving to bridge the chasm between the civilian and military fronts through his own sacrifice, is touching. It is significant that Hornung chose to do this through the medium of food; despite having lost his own child he was able to assume a nurturing *loco parentis* role to the stranger soldiers who ate and drank from his supplies.

Walking to and from the front, weary men were grateful for a cup of tea and a biscuit but in their rest and reserve areas their demands were greater. The men's desire for edible treats was often thwarted by the deficiencies of the canteens' stocks. Ivor Gurney wrote to a friend of the inadequacy of his unit's canteen, where 'the only thing one is certain of getting is boot polish'.[156] Stores were sporadically received, and F.E. Noakes queued for two-and-a-half hours for 'one franc's worth of biscuits and a tin of herrings – all the variety there was to buy'.[157] Availability was often determined by rank; the goods offered to officers were far more desirable. Bourne in *Her Privates We* was thrilled at the sight of sweets, bottled fruit and olives in a canteen, but was told they were for officers only and he could get 'cocoa and biscuits round the back'.[158] Even when items were available, men were concerned about the variation in prices charged at the different facilities. For example, the same packet of cigarettes could cost thirty centimes at a regimental canteen, fifty centimes at an Expeditionary Force canteen, or one franc at a Church Army Hut.[159]

The efforts of charitable organisations, welfare sections of the army, local estaminets and shops, families at home and the men's own initiative provided the possibility of extra food for the men. In their accounts, the rankers generally portrayed themselves as equitable and generous, with few examples of less than exemplary behaviour. Norman Gladden did recall serving in one unhappy platoon where 'it was every man for himself and if anyone went without he got no sympathy', but went on to say that this was not his normal army experience.[160] An unwillingness to share food was widely condemned. W.V. Tilsley describes a much disliked man as a '"Bleedin' scrounger!"', because, although not an actual thief, he kept extra bread rations for himself rather than share them with the other men. Tilsey also writes that 'Men would have choked each other for half a loaf', yet this view is not supported in the rest of his book, which highlights the generosity men showed to their fellows.[161] Parcels, in particular, were regarded as objects for distribution within a set of friends. Initially, families shared food with their men, who then did the same with their own group of pals. The behaviour of the majority of the rankers reinforces John Bourne's assertion that 'sharing was at the heart of working-class culture. Its importance was learned at home.'[162]

Of course, officers shared food too, whether their parcels or in their messes but theirs was the sharing of plenty. To offer food to another when the donor had access to plentiful supplies, whether through rank, wealth or both, did not carry the same weight as it did amongst the less privileged rankers. Many officers were industrious in writing home for gifts of food or cigarettes for their men, and some became famous for their generosity, such as Major General Sir Robert Fanshawe, nicknamed the 'Chocolate Soldier' because of his regular distribution of chocolate bars in the trenches.[163] The rankers' accounts, except at Christmas, make relatively few references to gifts from their officers, whereas it is a matter that features prominently in the writing of those that gave the presents. It appears that what was perceived as generosity by the officers was received as their due by the rankers; an acknowledgement of their greater sacrifice and need. Indeed, the debt that existed between the two parties may have, subconsciously, motivated the officers' actions. Paul Fieldhouse discusses the role of food as a gift which can assuage guilt, and the officers' largesse may have had its foundations in their knowledge that the conditions, including the food, the men endured were far worse than their own.[164]

The same small set of pals who shared food, both rations and extras, was for many the only stable and comforting feature of the rankers' military existence, and, while even these groups could be transitory, they were less risky than forming one close friendship with another man. The precarious nature of their world, where soldiers that they had lived alongside for months could suddenly disappear, whether through death, injury or army organisational changes, made traditional friendship both difficult to maintain and prone to an enforced, external failure. Bourne, in *Her Privates We*, differentiates between 'good comradeship' and friendship; the latter, he believed, 'implies rather more stable conditions, don't you think?'[165] He suggests that friendship involves a degree of choice that was not present in the war environment. In the early months; men may have joined up with their friends in 'Pals Regiments', but the introduction of conscription at the start of 1916, and the frequent regimental reorganisations following heavy battle casualties, militated against close friends either starting or staying together in the ranks. Soldiers made the best of the companionship on offer and their memoirs reflect their closeness to a small group rather than one man in particular. The communal life of the army facilitated this with its emphasis on the formation of sets of men, whether in terms of ration distribution or, quite often, in shared billets or tents. When Manning describes the difference between comradeship and friendship, he writes that the former could 'rise on occasion to an intensity of feeling which friendship never touches'.[166] Perhaps it was the difficulty of the external conditions that enhanced the warmth of the camaraderie, rather than any intrinsic quality. It may have been that the collective nature of the experience created a synergy that allowed this group affection to exceed the levels of emotion present in one-to-one friendships. Manning, an educated, middle-class professional writer, may have had a different sensibility from the majority of rankers; a distance from and a perception of his peers that may not have been shared by them. The small sets of pals, initially formed around the need to share food and subsequently bonded by that process, provided the individual soldiers with an emotional refuge from the miseries of army life; a place of affective, if not physical, safety and support. The cliché of 'safety in numbers' was certainly true in these circumstances, where to concentrate all one's affection into an intimate friendship with only one other soldier was high-risk, and had a far less certain future than comradeship with a number. These groups were structured in an environment similar to that which they had known at home, where positive emotion and food were inextricably intertwined.

Demonstrations of affection, and even acts of bravery, were frequently associated with food in the memories of the rankers. W. Clarke recalled crouching cold, wet and hungry in a shell hole: 'when I heard a voice say "Want a drop of hot soup Clarke?" And there was a friend of mine . . . with a soup container and he was dodging about from shell hole to shell hole with the soup.'[167] The soldier remembered the pleasure this soup gave him with an enthusiasm that does not appear to have been related purely to the physical hunger it satisfied. Food was endowed with particular savour when a soldier was prepared to risk his own safety in order to share it with his friend. Acts of sharing could engender subsequent acts of sacrifice in its beneficiaries, and soldiers who were generous with their extra food, especially beyond the confines of their own chosen group, were regarded with admiration and respect. In *Her Privates We*, a soldier, Smart, who was something of an outsider and not at all well-liked, volunteers for a dangerous raid because of the past kindnesses of its leader, Bourne; he remembered the food and drink he had received and says, 'tha'lt share all th'as got wi' us'ns'.[168] Smart was prepared to risk his life with Bourne because of the loyalty created by his earlier acts of generosity.

The even-handed division of food was a subject that the rankers referenced repeatedly; it was crucial to their war experience and reflected upon with even greater fervour in their memoirs. The sharing of food in a just and proper fashion recreated, to some small degree, a microcosm of an ordered, civilised world in the ranks. The element of justice, so often denied the ranker in their position at the bottom of the military hierarchy, could be reinstated in one part of their lives: the equitable apportionment of food.

Notes

1 Gray, *Confessions*, p. 2.
2 Gray, *Confessions*, p. 50.
3 Joanna Bourke, *Dismembering the Male: Men's Bodies, Britain and the Great War* (London, 1999), pp. 133–136.
4 Roper, *The Secret Battle*, p. 183.
5 John Tosh, *A Man's Place. Masculinity and the Middle-Class Home in Victorian England* (Bath, 1999), p. 87.
6 Halstead, *Jack's War*, diary entry dated 8.12.1917.
7 Robb, *British Culture*, p. 183.
8 Fussell, *The Great War*, p. 86.
9 Leed, *No Man's Land*, p. 189.
10 Sergeant Perry Webb, cited in Arthur, *Forgotten Voices*, p. 288.

11 See Corporal Goffee in Gladden, *Ypres*, p. 53.

12 Elias, *Civilizing Process*, p. 119.

13 P.H. Jones, IWM P246, memoir, p. 208.

14 Gwinnell, IWM 01/38/1, memoir, p. 110.

15 Downham, *Diary of an Old Contemptible*, p. 70.

16 *Statistics of Military Effort*, p. 521.

17 Howard Robinson, *Britain's Post Office* (London, 1953), p. 237.

18 Stewart, *From Mons to Loos*, p. 211.

19 Denis Winter, *Death's Men*, p. 164.

20 Robinson, *Britain's Post Office*, p. 237.

21 Dunn, *The War the Infantry Knew*, p. 14.

22 David Fraser (ed.), *In Good Company. The First World War Letters and Diaries of the Hon. William Fraser, Gordon Highlanders* (Salisbury, 1990), letters dated 5.10.1917 and 15.10.1917.

23 Geoff Dyer, *The Missing of the Somme* (London, 2001), p. 81.

24 Albert Stopher, Ipswich Records Office, letter to his mother dated 27.10.1915.

25 George Stopher, Ipswich Records Office, letter dated 17.8.1915.

26 George Stopher, Ipswich Records Office, letter dated 29.4.1916.

27 S.J. Hounsom, IWM 99/56/1, letter dated 10.5.1918.

28 See, for example, Gray, who compared rations he found at HQ with those he experienced in the line: 'the food conditions . . . were fully fifty per cent better than what I had been used to' *Confessions*, p. 181.

29 Atwell, *Letters of Lawrence Attwell*, letter dated 4.3.1917.

30 E.S. Bennett, IWM 96/3/1, letter dated 24.1.1918.

31 Waites, *A Class Society at War*, p. 231.

32 Denis Winter, *Death's Men*, p. 165.

33 Letters of Mrs E.D. Stephens, NAM 8902-201-1088.

34 Recipe cited in Lizzie Collingham, *Curry: A Tale of Cooks and Conquerors* (London, 2005), p. 142.

35 Stephens, NAM 8902-201-1066, letter dated 21.7.1915, and NAM 8902-201-1074, letter dated 23.8.1915.

36 M. Bacon and D. Langley, *The Blast of War: A History of Nottingham's Bantams, 15th (S) Battalion Sherwood Foresters 1915–1919* (Nottingham, 1986), p. 51.

37 Alan Wakefield, *Christmas in the Trenches* (Stroud, 2006), p. 38.

38 Hewins, *The Dillen*, p. 143.

39 Miss M. Semple, IWM 96/50/1 and Con Shelf.

40 Brid Hetherington (ed.), *Under the Shadow. Letters of Love and War 1911–1917* (Dunfermline, 1999), letter dated 7.8.1915.

41 Herbert, *Secret Battle*, p. 83.

42 See also Roper, *The Secret Battle*, chapter two 'Separation and support' for a discussion of the significance of parcels.

43 C.R. Jones, IWM 05/9/1, letter dated 3.1.1916.

44 Bull, *An Officer's Manual*, inside front cover.

45 Hounsom, IWM 99/56/1, letter dated 16.5.1916.

46 Holyfield, Essex Regimental Archive, letter dated 6.8.1916.

47 H.M. Adams, *A War Diary: 1916–1918* (Worcester, 1922), entry dated 11.9.1916.

48 Blacker, *Have You Forgotten Yet?*, p. 61.

49 Ross, *Love and Toil*, p. 24.

50 Tilsley, *Other Ranks*, p. 149.

51 MacDonald, *Voices and Images of the Great War*, p. 110.

52 Herbert Read, *In Retreat* (London, 1991), p. 46.

53 W. Clarke, IWM 87/18/1, recalled his home leave thus: 'I remember how wonderful it was at first and then within a week I was itching to get back to the front. I wanted to be with my mates', memoir, p. 6.

54 G.H. Addy, *A Memoir of his Son Kenneth James Balguy Addy, Second Lieutenant* (London, 1916), letter dated 20.4.1915.

55 Britland, IWM 88/57/1, letter dated 30.12.1914.

56 C.R. Jones, IWM 05/9/1, letter dated 8.4.1916.

57 Petty, London Scottish Regimental Archive, diary entry dated 17.11.1914.

58 See Sherwood L. Washburn and C.S. Lancaster, 'The Evolution of Hunting,' in Richard B. Lee and Irven DeVore (eds), *Man the Hunter* (Chicago, 1968), pp. 293–303.

59 Harris, *Good to Eat*, p. 27; see also Marcel Mauss, *The Gift: Forms and Functions of Exchange in Archaic Societies* (London, 1980).

60 Burke, IWM Con Shelf, letter dated 17.12.1915.

61 Van Emden, *Tickled to Death to Go*, p. 92.

62 Stone, *War Diary of Pte. R.S. Ashley*, entry dated 19.9.1916.

63 Stephens, NAM 8902-201-1044, letter dated 21.1.1915.

64 Noakes, *The Distant Drum*, p. 177.

65 P.H. Jones, IWM P246, p. 81.

66 Herbert Hill, *Reteat from Death*, p. 275.

67 Herbert, *Secret Battle*, p. 50.

68 Cormac Ó Gráda, *Black '47 and Beyond. The Great Irish Famine in History, Economy and Memory* (Princeton, 1999), p. 213.

69 George Stopher, Ipswich Records Office, letter dated 14 &15.5.1915.

70 Dunn, *The War the Infantry Knew*, p. 138.

71 John Singer Sargent, *Thou Shalt Not Steal*, IWM ART 1609.

72 Halstead, *Jack's War*, diary entry dated 15.6.1917.

73 Halstead, *Jack's War*, diary entry dated 22.8.1917.

74 J. Sanderson, IWM 87/33/1, diary, entry dated 11.4.1918.

75 Jack Alexander, McCrae's *Battalion. The Story of the 16th Royal Scots* (Edinburgh, 2003), p. 117.

76 Van Emden, *Tickled to Death to Go*, p. 79.

77 Blacker, *Have you Forgotten Yet?*, p. 93.
78 See Dunn, *The War the Infantry Knew*, p. 64.
79 Stewart, *On the Road from Mons*, p. 74.
80 Van Emden, *Tickled to Death to Go*, p. 89.
81 Taylor, *The Bottom of the Barrel*, p. 158.
82 For example, Lieutenant C.J. Hapfield, Suffolk Regimental Archive, GB554/Y1/147a, diary and memoir, p. 10, and O. Coleman, Ipswich Records Office, diary, entry dated 17.10.1917.
83 Van Emden, *Tickled to Death to Go*, p. 90.
84 L/Cpl W.H. Petty, London Scottish Regimental Archive, diary entries 17.9.1914 and 28.9.1914.
85 Carol J. Adams, *The Sexual Politics of Meat. A Feminist-Vegetarian Critical Theory* (New York, 2000), p. 137.
86 W.T. Hate, IWM 86/51/1, diary.
87 Van Emden, *Tickled to Death to Go*, p.142.
88 Carr, *Time to Leave the Ploughshares*, p. 29.
89 *Army Orders 1916*, No. 135.
90 F.W. Sutcliffe, IWM 97/26/1 diary entry for 14.6.1917.
91 See *Manual of Military Cooking and Dietary Mobilization* (London, 1917).
92 P.L. Wright, *The First Buckinghamshire Battalion 1914–1919* (London, 1920), p. 17.
93 Terry Norman (ed.), *Armageddon Road. A VC's Diary, 1914–1916* (London, 1982), entry dated 15.11.1914.
94 Rosser, *Sergeant Major's War*, p. 20.
95 Carr, *Time to Leave the Ploughshares*, p. 111.
96 Remarque, *All Quiet*, pp. 153–6. Banks and Chell recalled a similar incident when the unit 'gorged on fowl and pig. So lavishly did we feed on these, that for long afterwards the sight of feathered fowl and bristled beast awakened the feelings of a sea voyage!', *With the 10th Essex*, p. 275.
97 E. Brunsdon, IWM 85/15/1, memoir, p. 72.
98 Sergeant E.C.H. Rowland, NAM 1986-01-31, diary, entry dated 27.8.1914.
99 Pte George Wilson, London Scottish Regimental Archive, diary entry 16.9.1914.
100 Gibson, 'The British Army, French Farmers and the War', p. 185.
101 Brunsdon, IWM 85/15/1, memoir, p. 22.
102 T. Dalziel, IWM 85/51/1, diary entry dated 26.12.1914.
103 Manning, *Her Privates We*, p. 14.
104 See Gibson, 'The British Army, French Farmers and the War'.
105 Gray, *Confessions*, p. 83.
106 Reay, *Rural Englands*, p. 76.
107 K. Craig Gibson, 'Sex and Soldiering in France and Flanders: The British Expeditionary Force along the Western Front, 1914–1919', *The International History Review*, 13:3 (2001), p. 563.

108 *Field Service Pocket Book*, p. 225.
109 *Statistics of Military Effort*, p. 669. It should be noted that the figures available are for the period 4 August 1914 to 31 March 1920.
110 Gibson, 'The British Army, French Farmers and the War', p. 196.
111 Haworth, *March to Armistice*, pp. 94–5.
112 *Manual of Military Law*, p. 20.
113 Burke, IWM Con Shelf, letter dated 20.7.1915.
114 Downham, *Diary of an Old Contemptible*, p. 47- 9.
115 W.M. Floyd, IWM 87/33/1, diary entry dated 24.9.1914.
116 Coppard, *With a Machine Gun*, p. 85.
117 Dunn, *The War the Infantry Knew*, p. 385.
118 Halstead, *Jack's War*, entry dated 19.10.1917.
119 Scott, *Domination*, p. 188.
120 Downham, *Diary of an Old Contemptible*, p. 78.
121 Murray, *Gallipoli 1915*, p. 92.
122 Bryan Latham, *A Territorial Soldier's War* (Aldershot, 1967), p. 7.
123 Richards, *Old Soldiers*, p. 16.
124 Denis Winter, *Death's Men*, p. 148.
125 Eachus, IWM 01/51/1, diary entry dated 25.1.1917.
126 Herbert Hill, *Retreat from Death*, p. 163.
127 Lévi-Strauss, *The Origin of Table Manners*, p. 478.
128 Coleman, Ipswich Records Office PR654/1, diary entry for 31.3.1917.
129 Petty, London Scottish Regimental Archive, diary entries 17.9.1914 and 28.9.1914.
130 P.H. Jones, IWM P246, memoir and letters, p. 187.
131 Captain C.L. Overton, IWM 67/300/1, letter dated 19.2.1918.
132 Burke, IWM Con Shelf, letter dated 5.5.1916.
133 W.J. Bunbury, *A Diary of an Officer: With the 4th Northumberland Fusiliers in France and Flanders from April 20th to May 24th 1915* (Hexham, undated), entry dated 4.5.1915.
134 Drummond and Wilbraham, *An Englishman's Food*, p. 458.
135 Burnett, *Eating Out*, p. 112.
136 Bunbury, *Diary of an Officer*, diary entry dated 6.5.1915.
137 Stopher Family Correspondence, Ipswich Records Office HD825, letter to Mrs Stopher dated 19.5.1917.
138 Susanne Friedberg, *Fresh: A Perishable History* (Cambridge, MA, 2009), pp. 90–91.
139 Warren Belasco, *The Key Concepts of Food* (New York, 2008), p. 28.
140 Coleman, Ipswich Records Office PR654/1, diary entry dated 23.12.1917.
141 Dunn, *The War the Infantry Knew*, p. 175.
142 F. Rawnsley, IWM 80/40/1, diary, entry dated 7.10.1916.
143 Sgt Arthur Bridges, Suffolk Regimental Archive, GB554/Y1/398a, diary entries for 23.11.1914 and 27.11.1914.

144 Munson, *Echoes of the Great War*, entry dated 16.9.1915.
145 Jackson, *Private 12768*, p. 89.
146 Smith, *Four Years on the Western Front*, p. 105.
147 Eachus, IWM 01/51/1, diary, entry dated 4.3.1917. Gladden remembered a similar restriction on the purchase of bread in *Ypres*, p. 111. Eachus, diary entry dated 14.4.1917.
148 C.R. Jones, IWM 05/9/1, letter dated 6.11.1915.
149 Manning, *Her Privates We*, p, 100.
150 Jeffrey Reznick, *Healing the Nation. Soldiers and the Culture of Caregiving in Britain during the Great War* (Manchester, 2004), p. 21.
151 Bet-El, *Conscripts*, p. 51.
152 Reznick, *Healing the Nation*, p. 23.
153 Glover, *The Fateful Battle Line*, p. 129.
154 A.J. Jamieson, IWM, memoir, 85/52/1.
155 Blacker, *Have You Forgotten Yet?*, p. 205.
156 Thornton, *Ivor Gurney Letters*, letter dated 7.8.1916.
157 Noakes, *The Distant Drum*, p. 201.
158 Manning, *Her Privates We*, p. 189.
159 Dunn, *The War the Infantry Knew*, p. 249.
160 Gladden, *Somme*, pp. 126–7.
161 Tilsley, *Other Ranks*, pp. 102 and 160.
162 Bourne, 'The British Working Man in Arms', p. 346.
163 Ian Beckett, 'The Territorial Force in the Great War', in P.H. Liddle (ed.), *Home Fires and Foreign Fields. British Social and Military Experience in the First World War* (London, 1985), p. 31.
164 Fieldhouse, *Food and Nutrition*, p. 201.
165 Manning, *Her Privates We*, p. 80.
166 Manning, *Her Privates We*, p. 79.
167 Clarke, IWM 87/18/1, memoir, p. 1.
168 Manning, *Her Privates We*, p. 242.

Conclusion

The ranker's relationship with food was a constant thread, woven throughout his army experience: men came and went, strategies changed, battles passed, even the trench mud disappeared each summer, but every day, wherever he was, a man needed to eat. The fundamental simplicity of food's physiological role was combined with the overwhelming complexity of its social and emotional associations and attempts to separate the interlocking strands are fraught with difficulty.

When I first embarked upon this research, my ambition was to isolate what I perceived to be the different factors that together created the rankers' eating experience of the war. Firstly, I confidently expected to be able to recreate an accurate and detailed picture of what the men were given by the army. Secondly, this data could then be cross-referenced with the soldiers' own accounts, in order to determine whether their complaints arose from calorific shortfalls or a dislike of the adequate but unpalatable food provided. Thirdly, I anticipated the ability to discern distinct emotional responses to particular foods, meals or situations. I also strongly believed that, for the mass of relatively inarticulate men who formed the ranks, food had a weightier significance in their communications with the families at home than it did for their officers. None of these aims has emerged unscathed.

The bulk of records related to military food have not had the longevity granted to the official War Diaries or service records. Information pertaining to provisioning seems to have been regarded as transitory and unimportant compared to the real business of war. The army's rations scales and supply procedures remain as theoretical examples, but the calculation of the gap between the theory and practice is not possible.

Failures in feeding were glossed over in the official army statistics; an acknowledgement of the military's inability to provide for the most basic of human needs would have been embarrassing in the postwar world. Yet the problems did seep into official records, although specific difficulties with the rations have remained relatively unpublicised. The 1922 report of the War Office Committee of Enquiry into Shell Shock heard evidence that determined 'unsavoury cooking and feeding' as a significant factor in its cause.[1]

In the absence of detailed official accounts, I tried to find a veteran who had left both a collection of letters or a diary and a memoir, providing the opportunity to compare contemporaneous opinions with subsequent reflections. An analysis of the possible change of views over time would have confirmed or rebutted the notion that army food was not as bad as the men were to claim later. Comparisons between sources had indicated that, in memory, food appeared to become a signifier for wider injustices than those committed at the mess table. The search was unsuccessful but, as my research progressed, I realised that the mechanistic calculation of a specifiable gap between the army's provisioning ambitions and the men's dinners was less critical than originally thought.

The rankers' own accounts make it clear, even without the definitive corroboration of the exact supply details, that many of their demands were not predicated upon the calories available. There were occasions when there was no food at all, but these were relatively rare, although not as unusual as the official records would suggest. More commonly, there was food but it was not what the men wanted to eat or there was acceptable food served in an environment they found distressing. It seems that shortages of bully beef and hardtack biscuit were uncommon, but at times of troop movement even these essentials could be absent. The army's records suggest that there were always enough provisions for the men, but the presence of sufficient stores does not guarantee freedom from hunger. The experience of modern famine indicates that the issue is not the total quantity of food available but the difficulties in its distribution.[2] In the main, the British Army's supply procedures operated satisfactorily, but there were occasions when they failed to deliver. In static times, and this was to be the more usual experience of the soldiers, there was sometimes a surfeit of the unpopular tins of beef, which were put to use as flooring in dug-outs by men who preferred not to consume their contents.

Further research into the medical problems of the rankers would no doubt indicate that they were far less well nourished than has been suggested. The army operated within the restrictions of early twentieth-century nutritional science where calorie count was paramount, and there was only a partial awareness of the true complexity of a healthy diet. Low-level, sub-medical vitamin deficiencies were likely to have been widespread, an assumption supported by the minor health complaints of boils, bad teeth and sore gums frequently mentioned in the men's accounts. The lack of fruit and vegetables and the long stewing of much of their meat, both tinned and fresh, were likely to have resulted in low levels of ascorbic acid in the soldiers' diet. The ration's emphasis on large quantities of meat presented another problem. The World Health Organisation currently recommends that 8 to 15 per cent of total energy consumption should come from protein, and, of this, 10 to 25 per cent should be of animal origin.[3] These figures illustrate how far the rankers' high-protein diet, predicated as it was on tins of processed meat, was from the physiological optimum. It was a diet to which most rankers were unused, and the numerous complaints regarding both constipation and diarrhoea are indicative of the widespread digestive problems that persisted independent of outbreaks of dysentery or food poisoning. Private John F. Knowles wrote to a friend from France in 1915:

> I do not think you would stand the life out here. It requires a much better digestion than Providence has blessed you with to stand the kind of food we get here. Of course it is quite good and nourishing but somehow or other nearly everybody is suffering from some bowel complaint.[4]

Knowles's letter encapsulates the paradox of army provisioning. He is positive about the food, pronouncing it to be wholesome, yet at the same time he declares it to be indigestible; the men are well nourished, but they all suffer from bowel complaints.

A further apparent contradiction is the soldiers' preparedness to ignore the rations, to choose not to eat even when food is available. The problems of feeding an army are considered in a 2005 document produced for the Ministry of Defence, *The Commander's Guide to Nutrition*. The paper states that, while soldiers may not consciously starve themselves, it is common that they will eat 20 to 40 per cent less than their actual energy needs when on active service. The possible reasons for insufficient nutrition, in addition to that of unavailability of supplies, are given as: 'inadequate time to eat, lack of education and menu fatigue'.[5] Contemporary research confirms that the presence of food does not guarantee its consumption. The issue of 'menu fatigue' is particularly pertinent to the experience of the First World War rankers, whose accounts make it clear that boredom with the food provided was a major problem. It was a problem exacerbated by the narrowness of the prewar working-class diet, which had created a rank and file for whom a desire to escape dietary monotony was counterbalanced by a fear of the new. This aversion to untried foods may have been particularly strong amongst the British. It is a conservatism that can be identified in Scott's 1911 expedition to the South Pole, where the party's unwillingness to eat their dogs had a detrimental impact on their nutrition and the outcome of the project. This contrasted strongly with the successful Norwegian team who overcame their initial unwillingness, and the killing and eating of their dogs became acceptable. Their vitamin C levels were boosted accordingly, and Amundsen came to relish the food, writing in his diary that his mouth watered at the prospect of fresh dog cutlets.[6]

Poor nutrition can present significant difficulties in terms of performance and this can be a particular problem for adolescents in the army. The *Commander's Guide* explains that the growth spurts common during this period require extra food, if soldiers are to develop properly and retain fitness and normal energy levels.[7] It seems likely that the young men in the First World War would have had similar physiological needs, but this additional requirement was not catered for in the field. The army had some awareness of the extra nutritional requirements of young men; its rations for the troops at home indicate that those under nineteen years of age had their scale fixed at the November 1916 level while the older men's food continued to be reduced over the last two years of the war.[8] There is nothing to indicate that additional rations were made available on active service.

The winter conditions on the Western Front may also have been instrumental in increasing the men's hunger. The *Commander's Guide* points out that cold conditions can radically increase energy expenditure. It notes that 'severe cold stress' is not confined to areas with sub-zero air temperatures, but often occurs in North-West Europe where above-freezing temperatures combine with wind and rain to create an equally detrimental environment. Aside from inadequate clothing, a key problem is that of the soldiers remaining stationary; twice the amount of energy can be used up in static shivering than would expended if the troops were walking or marching.[9] The fixed nature of the cold, wet trenches, and the lack of appropriate weatherproof clothing, would appear to have been a recipe for hunger.

The exploration of the First World War soldiers' diet in the context of contemporary knowledge highlights its inadequacies. The widely held opinion amongst historians of the war that the men were far better fed than in their civilian lives, and therefore pleased with army provisioning, is a belief that has only a limited basis in reality. Extra military calories, even if they were all available in the variety described in the menu plans, did not automatically equate to satisfied soldiers. An analysis based solely upon the notion that there is an unequivocal correlation between calories and consumer satisfaction is fundamentally unsound, ignoring as it does the complexities of eating. The fact that the stated military ration – and this was often not delivered in its entirety – had higher energy values than the prewar diet of many of the rankers is only one aspect of the nuanced relationship between the men and their meals.

However hard the army tried, it is unlikely that it could ever have satisfied the rankers. Eating could not be separated from the world of the war: physically, for those who ate their rations in trenches amongst the corpses of earlier casualties, and psychically, for all civilian soldiers everywhere, whose daily army food intake was an inescapable reminder of all that the military had taken from them. As modern studies of food disorders indicate, eating is about control and this was equally true for the soldiers of the First World War. Rankers had no say in the rations they were given, but they could sometimes exert control over how they ate and with whom. The cloth and flowers on the billet table described in Chapter 5 are vivid evidence of the dining choices men might make when the opportunity arose. In the restricted monotony of the rankers' diet, the ability to vary their meal restored some element of choice to them. Frederic Manning described the pleasure a group of pals derived from a special dinner they were planning: 'they would have some wine, some variation of food, and some quiet talk, before turning over to sleep. They were the masters of the moment at least.'[10]

The power that soldiers exercised in choosing to share their food with others was particularly important. Ilana Bet-El describes how it permitted an element of self-determination that was generally denied them.[11] It was a fundamental evocation of natural justice in an unjust world; the division of limited supplies between the groups of pals was a moral choice as well as a source of comfort. Alexander Watson has written a fascinating article on the 'mental coping strategies' men developed on the Western Front.[12] Watson, within the context of life in the trenches, considers the assertions of psychologists regarding the innate human need to predict the future and control events. In his analysis of life in the front line, he stresses the importance of a strong sense of personal control in discouraging the soldiers from sinking into a dangerously apathetic state.

Watson does not make the connection in his writing, but eating was, of course, of major importance in sustaining feelings of self-determination in a world of oppression. The details of the planning, preparation and consumption of meals which filled the men's accounts were an indication of food's role in the reassertion of their existence: I eat therefore I am and, even more importantly, I believe I will eat tomorrow.

In addition to food providing a transitory element of control in a world where the rankers had little freedom, it also provided them with opportunities of intimacy with other men that helped to make the unbearable bearable. Responses to food transcended national boundaries and Erich Maria Remarque was lyrical in this description of his characters sharing extra food: 'two soldiers in shabby coats, cooking a goose in the middle of the night. We don't talk much, but I believe we have a more complete communion with one another than even lovers have.'[13] Most rankers' accounts do not have the literary polish of Remarque's but they still contrive to convey the companionship that sustained them, much of which was structured around food and eating. Their writing reveals the affective complexity of this 'language of food', its use as a vocabulary for emotion and familial love amongst a community that did not possess the ability to capture their feelings in the abstract parlance of the better educated. For so many families, mothers and sons, husbands and wives, food was about love: in fact food often *was* love. Of course, it was not all positive; food could elicit bad behaviour as well, and not just on the part of selfish officers or an uncaring army; sometimes even rankers behaved badly. The picture constructed from the men's accounts is no doubt biased as few were willing to acknowledge greed in the ranks, even in the relative privacy of their diaries. Negative emotions associated with food tended to be directed away from the ranks, whether upwards to the officers and faceless senior commanders, or to the cooks and the ASC whose privileges fuelled the other soldiers' resentment.

Wilfred Owen famously wrote of the men who died like cattle in the human shambles of the Western Front.[14] The analogy stands in other aspects of their military lives: men who died like animals also lived like them. The conditions of the rankers' existence were frequently poor and food was a key privation. Even if the food were good, it was difficult for it to overcome the feelings of anger, fear and resentment that sprang from the ranker's captivity in an army he hated. The officers were rarely consciously demeaning or cruel, often quite the opposite, but the paternalistic concern they demonstrated could speak more to the squire in his stable than of one man to another. The rankers were treated as an aggregated mass by the army, they were fed in order that they might work, or, in a bitter inversion of nurture, die.

The rankers' resentment concerning food was fundamental to their war experience but their deprivation was as much emotional as calorific, a response to a variety of distressing stimuli. The practical challenges and tasks associated with food, its procurement, preparation and consumption, were of great importance: food was central to nurturing expressions of the men's concern for each other. In a world where soldiers were distanced from their homes and the normal demonstrations of familial affection, they came to recreate the emotional comfort of these relationships around the rituals of eating. Food gained an emotional significance that had perhaps always existed, although implicitly, in civilian life but which was made explicit by the rigours and deprivations, both physical and affective, of the war.

Notes

1 Corns and Hughes-Wilson, *Blindfold and Alone*, p. 419.
2 Amartya Sen cited in Ó Gráda, *Black '47 and Beyond*, p. 122.
3 Christopher Wanjek, *Food at Work: Workplace Solutions for Malnutrition, Obesity and Chronic Diseases* (Geneva, 2005), p. 28. These figures are endorsed by the modern British Army, which recommends a level of 15 per cent protein in the diet of its soldiers.
4 John McConachie, *The Student Soldiers: The Aberdeen University Company 4th Gordons* (Elgin, 1995), p. 75.
5 Paula Messer, Gail Owen and Anna Casey, *Commander's Guide: Nutrition for Health and Performance* (QINETIQ/KI/CHS/CR021120, 2005) (Farnborough, 2005), pp. 36 and 42.
6 Feeney, 'Food for the Race to the Pole', pp. 83 and 89.
7 QinetiQ ltd, *Commander's Guide*, p. 36.
8 *Statistics of Military Effort*, p. 585. For example, the younger soldiers' meat ration remained at 12 oz per day, while that of other soldiers had been reduced to 8 oz by the end of the war.
9 QinetiQ ltd, *Commander's Guide*, pp. 26–27.
10 Manning, *Her Privates We*, p. 195.
11 Bet-El, *Conscripts*, p. 129.
12 Alexander Watson, 'Self-deception and Survival: Mental Coping Strategies on the Western Front', *Journal of Contemporary History*, 41 (2006), pp. 247–268.
13 Remarque, *All Quiet*, p. 66.
14 Wilfred Owen, 'What passing-bells for these who die as cattle?', 'Anthem for Doomed Youth', in Jon Silkin (ed.), *The Penguin Book of First World War Poetry* (London, 1979), p. 178.

Bibliography

Imperial War Museum

Diaries

Bolton, H.T., P262.
Butt, H.R., 97/26/1.
Cubbon, T.H., 78/4/1.
Dalziel, T., 85/51/1.
Eachus, S.T., 01/51/1.
Floyd, W.M., 87/33/1.
Fraser, P., 85/32/1.
Gameson, Captain L., P395–396 & Con Shelf.
Green, A.W., P101.
Hardwick, Major A.G.P., 98/14/1.
Poulton, S.W., 88/57/1.
Pritchard, Captain N.P., 03/17/1.
Rawnsley, F., 80/40/1.
Rees, I.T., 87/55/1.
Reeve, A., 90/20/1.
Sanderson, J., 87/33/1.
Sellors, Reverend J., 87/10/1.
Speed, S.E., 86/36/1.
Sutcliffe, F.W., 97/26/1.
Williams, J., 83/14/1.

Letters

Bennett, E.S., 96/3/1.
Britland, B., 88/57/1.

Burke, A.P., Con Shelf.
Coop, Canon J.O., 87/56/1.
Harpin, Miss H.M., Con Shelf.
Harris, Miss D., Con Shelf.
Hate, W.T., 86/51/1.
Hollister, J., 98/10/1.
Hounsom, S.J., 99/56/1.
Jones, C., Con Shelf.
Jones, C.R., 05/9/1.
Overton, Captain C.L., 67/300/1.
Scammell, S.J., Con Shelf.
Semple, Miss M., 96/50/1 & Con Shelf.
Spencer, Lieutenant W.B.P., 87/56/1.
Sweeney, D.J., 76/226/1 & 1A & Con Shelf.
Trafford, E.H., 98/32/1.
Whitby, Miss B., 95/38/1.

Memoirs

Aston, S.J., 98/24/1.
Brunsdon, E., 85/15/1.
Clarke, W., 87/18/1.
Gwinnell, R., 01/38/1.
Hall, P.R., 87/55/1.
Jamieson, A.J., 88/52/1.
Johnston, J.A., 02/29/1.
Jones, P.H., P246.
Keller, C.R., 02/55/1.
Lewis, A.W., 98/2/1.
McCauley, J., 97/10/1.
Perriman, A E., 80/43/1.
Prew, F.J., 96/42/1.
Quinton, W.A., 79/35/1.
Sambrook, A., 95/16/1.
Simmons, A.J., Misc 163 (2503).
Watts, G., 01/38/1.

IWM Miscellaneous

Food Ephemera, EPH.C.FOOD.
Jesse Short Collection, 220 (3152).
Miss Gladys Storey's Scrapbook, 96/1813.

Bibliography

National Army Museum

Diaries

Beer, A. G., 7904–71.
Clark, R., 7606–45.
Littler, J., 2001-10-4.
Rowland, E.C.H., 1986-01-31.
Willison, D., 7001/2.

Letters

Down, A. 1969-10-19.
Ely, Captain D., 2000-03-167.
Fraser, Lieutenant C., 2004-03-4-11.
'MGF'. 91-01-72.
Rose, J. 2000-02-94.
Stephens, Mrs E.D., 8902-201-1043-1396.

Miscellaneous
Wilkins, C. (Notes on Cooking), 2004-10-78.

Essex Regimental Archive

Diaries

Dean, J.D.
Gale, F.
Maitland, A.E.
Ricketts, W.R.
Williams, H.J.

Letters

Folkard, F.T.
Holyfield, W.
Liddell, A.
Liddell, S.
Sneezum, G.W.

Miscellaneous

Essex Regiment Gazette.
The Rifle Brigade Chronicle for 1906.

Bibliography

London Scottish Regimental Archive

Diaries

Black, L/Cpl Walter Cairns.
Cowper, L/Cpl J.B.F.
Fowler, Pte Henry J.
France, Pte Bert F.
Hose, Pte C.
Innes, A.G.S.
Kinross, Pte Ernest A.
Maben, Herbert.
Park, Pte William G.
Petty, L/Cpl W.H.
Wilson, Pte George.

Letters

Brockett-Coward, Pte Francis.

Suffolk Regimental Archive

Diaries

Allman, GB554/Y1/2b.
Barton, Lieutenant, GB554/Y1/18d.
Bridges, A., GB554/Y1/398a.
Brown, Lieutenant, GB554/Y1/42b.
Fenn, GB554/Y1/109.
Hapfield, Lieutenant C.J., GB554/Y1/147a.
Raphael, G.L., GB554/Y1/217.
Unidentified Soldier, GB554/Y3/7.

Letters

Allman, GB 554/Y1/2a.

Miscellaneous

The Queue (POW magazine), GB554/Y1/20.
Suffolk Regimental Gazette 1916.

Ipswich Records Office

Diary

Coleman, O., PR654/1.

Bibliography

Letters
Lady Stradbroke's Correspondence, HA11/A16/11.
Stopher Family Correspondence, HD825.

Private collections

Mark Ashmore
Bunting, Will.
Ward, Fred.

Bill Fulton
Fulton Family Papers.
Kendrick, George.

Printed primary sources

Imperial War Museum
Army Orders 1914, 1915, 1916, 1917 and 1918
The Cookhouse and Simple Recipes. SS 606 (London, 1916)
Cooking in the Field. SS 615 (London, 1917)
The Duties of an Officer. Knowledge and Character, SS 415 (London, undated)
Hints on Cooking in the Field. SS 469 (London, 1916)
Manual of Military Cooking and Dietary Mobilization (London, 1915)
Manual of Military Cooking and Dietary Mobilization (London, 1917)
Manual of Military Cooking and Dietary Mobilization (London, 1918)
Manual of Military Law (London, 1918)
Messing and Economy. SS 613 (London, 1917)
Ration Pamphlet. Scales of Rations, Forage, Fuel & Light as Authorised for the British Armies in France. SS 571 (London, 1917)
Reductions in the Scale of Rations in the German Army. SS 474 (London,1916)
Some of the Many Questions a Platoon Commander Should Ask Himself on Taking over a Trench and at Intervals Afterwards. SS 408 (London, undated)
Supplies and Supply Transport in the 38th (Welsh Division) by a Senior Supply Officer (London, undated)

National Army Museum
Report of Inspections at Certain of the Meat Canning Factories in the United States of America as Affecting the Supply of Preserved Meat to the British Army (London, 1906)
Report of the Royal Commission on Supply of Food and Raw Material in Time of War: Volume 1: The Report (London, 1905)
Supply Manual (War) (London, 1909)

Bibliography

Published diaries

Adams, H.M., *A War Diary: 1916–1918* (Worcester, 1922)

Bickersteth, John (ed.), *The Bickersteth Diaries 1914–1918* (London, 1995)

Bird, Antony (ed.), *Unversed in Arms: A Subaltern on the Western Front. The First World War Diary of P.D. Ravenscroft M.C.* (Swindon, 1990)

Bishop, Alan (ed.), *Vera Brittain: Chronicle of Youth Great War Diary, 1913–1917* (London, 1981)

Bond, Brian and Robbins, Simon (eds), *Staff Officer. The Diaries of Lord Moyne 1914–1918* (London, 1987)

Briscoe, Diana (ed.), *The Diary of a World War I Cavalry Officer. Brigadier General Sir Archibald Home* (Tunbridge Wells, 1985)

Bunbury, W.J., *A Diary of an Officer. With the 4th Northumberland Fusiliers in France and Flanders from April 20th to May 24th, 1915* (Hexham, undated)

Cooper, A.M. (ed.), *We Who Knew. The Journal of an Infantry Subaltern during the Great War: Matthew Cooper* (Lewes, 1994)

Dearden, Harold, *Medicine and Duty. A War Diary* (London, 1928)

Downham, Peter (ed.), *Diary of an Old Contemptible. Private Edward Roe East Lancs. Regiment: From Mons to Baghdad 1914–1919* (Barnsley, 2004)

Glover, Michael (ed.), *The Fateful Battle Line. The Great War Journals and Sketches of Captain Henry Ogle, MC* (London, 1993)

Halstead, Jack, *Jack's War. The Diary and Drawings of Jack Halstead, a Great War Survivor* (Baldock, 2005)

Hitchcock, Captain F.C., *'Stand To': A Diary of the Trenches 1915–18* (Norwich, 1988)

Lewis, Jon E. (ed.), *The Mammoth Book of War Diaries and Letters. 1775–1991* (London, 1998)

MacDonagh, Michael, *In London During the Great War. The Diary of a Journalist* (London, 1935)

Middlebrook, Martin (ed.), *The Diaries of Pte Horace Bruckshaw Royal Marine Light Infantry 1915–1916* (London, 1979)

Munson, James (ed.), *Echoes of the Great War. The Diary of Reverend Andrew Clark, 1914–1919* (Oxford 1985)

Murray, Joseph, *Gallipoli 1915* (Bristol, 2004)

Norman, Terry (ed.), *Armageddon Road. A VC's Diary, 1914–1916. Billy Congreve* (London, 1982)

Palmer, S. and Wallis S., (eds), *A War in Words. The First World War in Diaries and Letters* (London, 2003)

Stewart, Major H.A., *From Mons to Loos. Being the Diary of a Supply Officer* (London, 1916)

Stone, Philippa (ed.), *War Diary of Private R.S. Ashley 2472 7th London Regiment 1914–1918* (South Woodford, 1982)

Taylor, A. (ed.), *From Ypres to Cambrai: The 1914–1919 Diary of Infantryman Frank Hawkings* (Morley, 1974)

Bibliography

Vaughan, E. C., *Some Desperate Glory. The Diary of a Young Officer, 1917* (London, 1981)

Published Letters

Addy, G.H. (ed.), *A Memoir of His Son Kenneth James Balguy Addy* (London, 1916)

Attwell, W.A. (ed.), *Lawrence Attwell's Letters from the Front* (Barnsley, 2005)

Barnett, Denis Oliver, *In Happy Memory. His letters from France and Flanders October 1914 – August 1915* (Stratford, 1915)

Bell, John (ed.), *Wilfred Owen. Selected Letters* (Oxford, 1998)

Bickerstaffe-Drew, P. (ed.), *John Ayscough's Letters to His Mother 1914–1916* (London, 1919)

Bishop, Alan and Bostridge, Mark (eds), *Letters from a Lost Generation: The First World War Letters of Vera Brittain and Four Friends* (London, 1998)

Butterworth, Hugh M., *Letters from Flanders* (Wellington, 1916)

Cook, Don (ed.), *1914 Letters from a Volunteer* (London, 1984)

Feilding, R., *War Letters to a Wife: France and Flanders, 1915–1919* (Staplehurst, 2001)

Fraser, David (ed.), *In Good Company. The First World War Letters and Diaries of the Hon. William Fraser, Gordon Highlanders (Salisbury, 1990)*

Hetherington, Brid (ed.), *Under The Shadow. Letters of Love and War 1911–1917* (Dunfermline, 1999)

Housman, Laurence (ed.), *War Letters of Fallen Englishmen* (Philadelphia, 2002)

Laffin, John, *Letters from the Front, 1914–1918* (London, 1973)

Liddiard, Jean (ed.), *Isaac Rosenberg. Selected Poems and Letters* (London, 2003)

McClaren, S.J. (ed.), *Somewhere in Flanders. Letters of a Norfolk Padre in the Great War* (Dereham, 2005)

Morten, Sheila (ed.), *I Remain, Your Son Jack. Letters from the First World War* (Manchester, 1993)

Rosser, Bruce (ed.), *A Sergeant-Major's War: From Hill 60 to the Somme, Ernest Shephard* (Marlborough, 1987)

Sanger, Ernest, *Letters from Two World Wars* (Stroud, 1993)

Sheffield, G. and Inglis G., (eds), *From Vimy Ridge to the Rhine. The Great War Letters of Christopher Stone DSO MC* (Marlborough, 1989)

Thornton R.K.R. (ed.), *Ivor Gurney. War Letters* (London, 1984)

Townshend E. (ed.), *Keeling Letters & Recollections* (London, 1918)

Wilkinson, Alan (ed.), *The War Letters of Captain Jack Oughtred M.C. 1915–1918* (Beverley, 1996)

Published memoirs

Adams, Bernard, *Nothing of Importance. A Record of Eight Months at the Front with a Welsh Battalion* (London, 1917)

Bibliography

Aitken, Alexander, *Gallipoli to the Somme. Recollections of a New Zealand Infantryman* (London, 1963)

Anon., *A Cornish Waif's Story: An Autobiography* (London, 1956)

Anon., *Tale of a Territorial* (Wellingborough, 1917)

The Army from Within, by the Author of 'An Absent Minded War' (London, 1901)

Austin, Brigadier-General H.H, *Some Rambles of a Sapper* (London, 1928)

Banks, Lieutenant-Colonel T.M. and Chell, Captain R.A., *With the 10th Essex in France* (London, 1924)

Blacker, John (ed.), *Have You Forgotten Yet? The First World War Memoirs of C.P. Blacker M.C. G.M.* (Barnsley, 2000)

Bloch, Marc, *Memoirs of War 1914–15* (Cambridge, 1988)

Blunden, Edmund, *Undertones of War* (London, 2000)

Bourke, Joanna (ed.), *The Misfit Soldier. Edward Casey's War Story, 1914–1918* (Cork, 1999)

Brittain, Vera, *Testament of Youth* (London, 2004)

Carr, William, *A Time to Leave the Ploughshares. A Gunner Remembers 1917–18* (London, 1985)

Cartmell, H., *For Remembrance. An Account of Some Fateful Years* (Preston, 1919)

Church, Richard, *Over the Bridge* (London, 1974)

Clark, Captain A.O.T., *Transport and Sport in the Great War Period* (London, 1938)

Colman, Sir Jeremiah, *Reminiscences of the Great War 1914–1918* (Norwich, 1940)

Compton H. (ed.), *Edwin Mole: The King's Hussar. The Recollections of a 14th (King's) Hussar During the Victorian Era* (Leonaur, 2008)

Coppard, George, *With a Machine Gun to Cambrai* (London, 2003)

Crozier, F.P., *A Brass Hat in No Man's Land* (Norwich, 1989)

Dayus, Kathleen, *Her People* (London, 1982)

Dolden, A. Stuart., *An Infantryman's Life on the Western Front 1914–18* (Poole, 1980)

Downing, W. H., *To the Last Ridge* (London, 2005)

Dunn, Captain J. C., *The War the Infantry Knew 1914–1919* (London, 1987)

Eberle, V.F., *My Sapper Venture* (Bath, 1973)

Edmonds (Carrington), Charles, *A Subaltern's War* (London, 1930)

Emden, Richard van (ed.), *Tickled to Death to Go. Memoirs of a Cavalryman in the First World War* (Staplehurst, 1996)

Foley, Alice, *A Bolton Childhood* (Manchester, 1973)

French, Anthony, *Gone for a Soldier* (Warwick, 1972)

Fussell, Paul (ed.), *The Ordeal of Alfred M. Hale. The Memoir of a Soldier Servant* (London, 1975)

Gask, G.E., *A Surgeon in France. The Memoirs of George E. Gask 1914–1919* (London, 2002)

Bibliography

Gladden, E.N., *The Somme, 1916: A Personal Account* (London, 1974)

Gladden, E.N., *Ypres, 1917: A Personal Account* (London, 1967)

Graham, Stephen, *A Private in the Guards* (London, 1928)

Graves, Robert, *Goodbye to All That* (London, 1960)

Gray, Frank, *The Confessions of a Private* (Oxford, 1920)

Green, John, *A Soldier's Life 1805–1815* (Wakefield, 1973)

Griffiths, W., *Up to Mametz* (London, 1931)

Groom, W.H.A., *Poor Bloody Infantry. A Memoir of the First World War* (London, 1976)

Harris, Brigadier L.H., *Signal Venture* (Aldershot, 1951)

Haworth, Christopher, *March to Armistice 1918* (London, 1968)

Herbert, A.P., *The Secret Battle* (Oxford, 1982)

Hewins, A. (ed.), *The Dillen. Memories of a Man of Stratford-upon-Avon* (London, 1981)

Hill, George Herbert, *Retreat from Death: A Soldier on the Somme* (London, 2005)

Hiscock, Eric, *The Bells of Hell Go Ting-a-Ling-a-Ling* (London, 1976)

Hodges, Frederick James, *Men of 18 in 1918* (Ilfracombe, 1988)

Jackson, John, *Private 12768: Memoir of a Tommy* (Stroud, 2005)

Junger, Ernst, *Storm of Steel* (New York, 1996)

Latham, Bryan, *A Territorial Soldier's War* (Aldershot, 1967)

Levy, Stanley J., *Memories of the 71st and 83rd Companies RASCMT 1914–1918* (private publication, 1931)

MacBride, H., *A Rifleman Went to War* (Mt Ida, AR, 1987)

MacGill, Patrick, *Children of the Dead End: The Autobiography of a Navvy* (London, 1918)

MacGill, Patrick, *The Great Push* (Edinburgh, 2000)

Manning, Frederic, *Her Privates We* (London, 1999)

Mark VII (Max Plowman), *A Subaltern on the Somme in 1916* (London, 1927)

Mayo, Virginia (ed.), *Harry's War. A British Tommy's Experience in the Trenches in World War One* (London, 2002)

Montague, C.E., *Disenchantment* (London, 1934)

Nettleton, John, *The Anger of the Guns* (London, 1979)

Noakes, F.E., *The Distant Drum* (Tunbridge Wells, 1952)

On the Road from Mons with an Army Service Corps Train. By Its Commander (London, 1916)

Parker, E., *Into Battle 1914–18* (London, 1964)

Perkins, A.M., *Between Battles: At a Base in France* (London, 1918)

Read, Herbert, *In Retreat* (London, 1991)

Remarque, Erich Maria, *All Quiet on the Western Front* (London, 1991)

Richards, Frank, *Old Soldiers Never Die* (Sleaford, 1994)

Rogerson, Sidney, *Twelve Days on the Somme. A Memoir of the Trenches, 1916* (London, 2006)

Sassoon, Siegfried, *The Complete Memoirs of George Sherston* (London, 1949)

Smith, Aubrey, *Four Years on the Western Front* (London, 1922)
Tawney, R.H., *The Attack and Other Papers* (London, 1953)
Taylor, F.A.J., *The Bottom of the Barrel* (Bath, 1978)
Thompson, Flora, *Lark Rise to Candleford* (London, 1984)
Thompson, Thea, *Edwardian Childhoods* (London, 1983)
Tilsley, W.V., *Other Ranks* (London, 1931)
Uttley, Alison, *Country World: Memories of Childhood* (London, 1984)
Voigt, F.A., *Combed Out* (London, 1929)
Watcyn-Williams, M., *From Khaki to Cloth* (Cardiff, 1949)
Wilberforce-Bell, Captain H., *War Vignettes: Being the Experiences of an Officer in France and England during the Great War* (Bombay, 1916)
Williamson, Henry, *The Wet Flanders Plain* (Norwich, 1987)
Wright, P.L., *The First Buckinghamshire Battalion 1914–1919* (London, 1920)
Wyndham, Horace, *The Queen's Service* (London, 1899)

Other published primary sources

Arthur, Max, *Forgotten Voices of the Great War* (St Helens, 2002)
Arthur, Max, *When This Bloody War Is Over. Soldiers' Songs of the First World War* (London, 2001)
Beveridge, Sir William, *British Food Control* (London, 1928)
Booth, William, *In Darkest England and The Way Out* (London, 1890)
Boyd, Colonel J.A., *Supply Handbook for the Army Service Corps* (London, 1899)
Bull, Stephen, *An Officer's Manual of the Western Front 1914–1918* (London, 2008)
Chew, Ada Nield, *The Life and Writings of a Working Woman* (London, 1982)
Field Service Pocket Book 1914 (Reprinted with Amendments, 1916). General Staff, War Office
Grossmith, George and Weedon, *The Diary of a Nobody* (London, 2006)
Harrison, M., Stuart-Clark, C. and Marks, A. (eds), *Peace and War: A Collection of Poems* (Oxford, 1989)
Hartman, Geoffrey F. (ed.), *The Selected Poetry and Prose of Wordsworth* (New York, 1980)
Klein, Melanie, *Envy and Gratitude and Other Works, 1946–1963* (New York, 1984)
Laffin, John, *On the Western Front. Soldiers' Stories from France and Flanders 1914–1918* (Gloucester, 1985)
Laffin, John, *World War I in Postcards* (Gloucester, 1988)
Liddell Hart, B.H., *Thoughts on War* (Staplehurst, 1999)
MacDonald, Lyn, *1914–1918. Voices and Images of the Great War* (London, 1991)
McGuffie, T.H., *Rank and File. The Common Soldier at Peace and War 1642–1914* (London, 1964)
Moran, Lord, *The Anatomy of Courage* (London, 1945)

Bibliography

Mr Punch's History of the Great War (Stroud, 2007)

Nicholson, J. Shield, *War Finance* (London, 1917)

Notes for Infantry Officers on Trench Warfare (1916). General Staff, War Office

Oldmeadow, Ernest, *Home Cookery in War-Time* (London, 1915)

Palmer, Roy, *The Rambling Soldier: Life in the Lower Ranks, 1750–1900, through Soldiers' Songs and Writings* (Harmondsworth, 1977)

Report of the War Office Committee of Enquiry into 'Shell-Shock' (1922) (London, 2004)

Rivers, W.H.R., *Instinct and the Unconscious. A Contribution to a Biological Theory of the Psycho-neuroses* (London, 1920)

Sassoon, Siegfried, *Counter-Attack: and Other Poems* (London, 1919)

Sherriff, R.C., *Journey's End* (London, 2000)

Stallworthy, Jon (ed.), *The Oxford Book of War Poetry* (Oxford, 1990)

Statistics of the Military Effort of the British Empire during the Great War (London, 1999)

Williams, Captain Basil, *Raising and Training the New Armies* (London, 1918)

Unpublished PhD theses

Coss, E.J., *All for the King's Shilling. An Analysis of the Campaign and Combat Experiences of the British Soldier in the Peninsular War 1808–14*. Ohio State University, 2005

Duffett, Rachel. *A War Unimagined: Food and the Rank and File Soldiers of the First World War*. University of Essex, 2009

Rich, Rachel. *Bourgeois Consumption: Food, Space and Identity in London and Paris, 1850–1914*. University of Essex, 2005

Unpublished MA dissertation

Duffett, Rachel. *'I believe 'e'd sell 'imself for a tin o'toffee'. The significance of food in the memoirs of the rank and file soldiers of the First World War*. University of Essex, 2005.

Secondary sources

Adams, Carol J., *The Sexual Politics of Meat: A Feminist-Vegetarian Critical Theory* (New York, 2000)

Akiyama, Yuriko, *Feeding the Nation. Nutrition and Health in Britain before World War One* (London, 2008)

Alexander, Jack, *McCrae's Battalion. The Story of the 16th Royal Scots* (Edinburgh, 2003)

Allen, D.E., *British Tastes: An Enquiry into the Likes and Dislikes of the Regional Consumer* (London, 1968)

Bibliography

Allen, Keith, 'Food and the German Home Front: Evidence from Berlin', in Gail Braybon (ed.), *Evidence, History and the Great War* (New York, 2003), pp. 172–197

Allinson, Sidney, *The Bantams: The Untold Story of World War I* (London, 1981)

Allison, W. and Fairley, J., *The Monocled Mutineer* (London, 1978)

Ashplant, T., Dawson, G. and Roper M., (eds), *The Politics of War Memory and Commemoration* (London, 2000)

Ashworth, Tony, *Trench Warfare 1914–1918. The Live and Let Live System* (London, 2000)

Atkins, Peter J., Lummell, Peter and Oddy, Derek J., (eds), *Food and the City in Europe since 1800* (Aldershot, 2007)

Atkinson, Paul, 'Eating Virtue', in Anne Murcott (ed.), *The Sociology of Food and Eating* (Aldershot, 1986) pp. 9–17

Attar, Dena, *A Bibliography of Household Books Published in Britain 1800–1914* (London, 1987)

Auster, Paul, *The Art of Hunger* (New York, 1993)

Babington, Anthony, *For the Sake of Example. Capital Courts-Martial 1914–1920* (London, 1993)

Bacon, M. and Langley, D., *The Blast of War: A History of Nottingham's Bantams 15th (S) Battalion Sherwood Foresters 1915–1919* (Nottingham, 1986)

Bailey, Peter, 'White Collars, Gray Lives? The Lower Middle Class Revisited', *Journal of British Studies*, 38:3 (1999), pp. 273–290

Barker, T.C., McKenzie, J.C. and Yudkin, J. (eds), *Our Changing Fare: Two Hundred Years of British Food Habits* (London, 1966)

Barnett, L. Margaret, 'Fletcherism: The Chew-Chew Fad of the Edwardian Era', in David F. Smith (ed.), *Nutrition in Britain. Science, Scientists and Politics in the Twentieth Century* (London, 1997), pp. 6–28

Barrie, Alexander, *War Underground. The Tunnellers of the Great War* (Staplehurst, 2000)

Barthes, Roland, 'Toward a Psychosociology of Contemporary Food Consumption', in Robert Forster and Orest Ranum (eds), *Food and Drink in History: Selections from the Annales* (Baltimore, 1979), pp. 139–165

Barton, Peter, Doyle, Peter and Vandewalle, Johan, *Beneath Flanders Field. The Tunnellers' War 1914–18* (Staplehurst, 2004)

Baynes, John, *Morale. A Study of Men and Courage* (London, 1987)

Beadon, Colonel R.H., *The Royal Army Service Corps. A History of Transport and Supply in the British Army* (Cambridge,1931)

Beardsworth, Alan and Keil, Teresa, *Sociology on the Menu. An Invitation to the Study of Food and Society* (London, 1997)

Beckett, Ian F.W. 'The Territorial Force in the Great War', in P.H. Liddle (ed.) *Home Fires and Foreign Fields. British Social and Military Experience in the First World War* (London, 1985), pp. 21–37

Bibliography

Beckett, Ian F.W. 'The Nation Arms 1914–1918,' in Ian F.W. Beckett and Keith Simpson (eds), *A Nation in Arms. A Social Study of the British Army in the First World War* (Manchester, 1985), pp. 1–36

Beckett, Ian F.W., *Home Front 1914–1918. How Britain Survived the Great War* (Richmond, 2006)

Beckett, Ian F.W., *The Victorians at War* (London, 2003)

Beckett, Ian F.W., *Victoria's Wars* (Princes Risborough, 1998)

Beckett Ian F.W. and Simpson Keith, (eds), *A Nation in Arms. A Social Study of the British Army in the First World War* (Manchester, 1985)

Belasco, Warren, *The Key Concepts of Food* (New York, 2008)

Bell, David and Valentine, Gill, *Consuming Geographies: We Are Where We Eat* (London, 2003)

Bennett, Gerald, *Eating Matters: Why We Eat What We Eat* (London, 1988)

Bergonzi, Bernard, *Heroes' Twilight. A Study of the Literature of the Great War* (London, 1965)

Berking, Helmuth, *Sociology of Giving* (London, 1999)

Bet-El, Ilana, *Conscripts: Forgotten Men of the Great War* (Stroud, 2003)

Bond, Brian, *The Unquiet Western Front* (Cambridge, 2002)

Booth, D.A., *Psychology of Nutrition* (London, 1994)

Bosanquet, Nick, 'Health Systems in Khaki: The British and American Medical Experience', in Hugh Cecil and Peter Liddle (eds), *Facing Armageddon: The First World War Experienced* (London, 1996), pp. 451–465

Bourke, Joanna, *Dismembering the Male: Men's Bodies, Britain and the Great War* (London, 1999)

Bourke, Joanna, *Fear: A Cultural History* (London, 2005)

Bourke, Joanna, *An Intimate History of Killing: Face to Face Killing in Twentieth-Century Warfare* (London, 1999)

Bourke, Joanna, 'New Military History', in Matthew Hughes and William J. Philpott (eds), *Palgrave Advances in Modern Military History* (Basingstoke, 2006) pp. 258–280

Bourke, Joanna, '"Remembering" War', *Journal of Contemporary History*, Special Issue: Collective Memory, 39:4 (2004), pp. 473–485

Bourke, Joanna, *Working-Class Cultures in Britain 1890–1960. Gender, Class and Ethnicity* (London, 1994)

Bourne, John, *Britain and the Great War 1914–1918* (London, 1994)

Bourne, John, 'The British Working Man in Arms', in Hugh Cecil and Peter Liddle (eds), *Facing Armageddon: The First World War Experienced* (London, 1996), pp. 336–352

Bowley, A.L. and Burnett-Hurst, A.R., *Livelihood and Poverty. A Study in the Economic Conditions of Working-Class Households in Northampton, Warrington, Stanley and Reading* (London, 1915)

Bracco, Rosa Maria, *Merchants of Hope. British Middlebrow Writers and the First World War, 1919–1939* (Oxford, 1993)

Bibliography

Brears P., Black, M., Corbishley, G., Renfrew, J. and Stead, J., *A Taste of History: 10,000 Years of Food in Britain* (London, 1997)

Broomfield, Andrea, *Food and Cooking in Victorian England. A History* (Westport, CT, 2007)

Brophy, John and Partridge, Eric, *The Daily Telegraph Dictionary of Tommies' Songs and Slang, 1914–18* (London, 2008)

Brown, Ian Malcolm, *British Logistics on the Western Front 1914–1919* (Westport, CT, 1998)

Brown, Malcolm, *Tommy Goes to War* (Stroud, 1999)

Bryder, Linda, 'The First World War: Healthy or Hungry?', *History Workshop Journal*, 24 (1987), pp. 141–157

Burnett, John, 'Trends in Bread Consumption', T.C Barker, J.C. McKenzie and J. Yudkin (eds), *Our Changing Fare: Two Hundred Years of British Food Habits* (London, 1966), pp. 61–75

Burnett, John, *Destiny Obscure: Autobiographies of Childhood, Education and Family from the 1820s to the 1920s* (London, 1984)

Burnett, John, *England Eats Out. 1830 – Present* (Harlow, 2004)

Burnett, John, *Plenty and Want. A Social History of Diet in England from 1815 to the Present Day* (London, 1979)

Campbell, R.H., 'Diet in Scotland. An Example of Reagional Variation', in T.C. Baarker, J.C. McKenzie and J.Yudkin (eds), *Our Changing Fare: Two Hundred Years of British Food Habits* (London, 1966), pp. 47–60

Caplan, Pat, Keane Anne, Willets Anna and Williams Janice, 'Studying Food Choice in its Social and Cultural Contexts: Approaches from a Social Anthropological Perspective', in Anne Murcott (ed.), *The Nation's Diet: The Social Science of Food Choice* (Harlow, 1998), pp. 168–82

Caruth, Cathy, *Unclaimed Experience. Trauma, Narrative and History* (Baltimore, 1996)

Carver, Field Marshal Lord, *Britain's Army in the Twentieth Century* (London, 1998)

Clayton, Anthony, *The British Officer. Leading the Army from 1660 to the Present* (London, 2006)

Cobley, Evelyn, *Representing War: Form and Ideology in First World War Narratives* (Toronto, 1996)

Cole, Howard N., *The Story of the Army Catering Corps* (London, 1984)

Collingham, Lizzie, *Curry: A Tale of Cooks and Conquerors* (London, 2006).

Connelly, Mark, *Steady the Buffs! A Regiment, a Region and the Great War* (Oxford, 2006)

Corley, T.A.B., *Huntley & Palmers of Reading 1822–1972: Quaker Enterprise in Biscuits* (London, 1972)

Corns, Cathryn and Hughes-Wilson, John, *Blindfold and Alone. British Military Executions in the Great War* (London, 2005)

Corrigan, Gordon, *Mud, Blood and Poppycock* (London, 2004)

Coveney, John, *Food, Morals and Meaning: The Pleasure and Anxiety of Eating* (London, 2000)

Crew, Graeme, *The Royal Army Service Corps* (London, 1970)

Crossick, Geoffrey (ed.), *The Lower Middle Class in Britain 1870–1914* (London, 1977)

Curtis-Bennett, Sir Noel, *The Food of the People: The History of Industrial Feeding* (London, 1949)

Darby, Robert, 'Oscillations on the Hotspur-Falstaff Spectrum: Paul Fussell and the Ironies of War', *War in History*, 9 (2002), pp. 307–331

Das, Santanu, '"Kiss me", Hardy: The Dying Kiss in the First World War trenches', in Karen Harvey (ed.), *The Kiss in History* (Manchester, 2005), pp. 166–186

Das, Santanu, *Touch and Intimacy in First World War Literature* (Cambridge, 2005)

Davidoff, Leonore and Westover Belinda, (eds), *Our Work, Our Lives, Our Words. Women's History and Women's work* (Basingstoke, 1986)

Davies, Margaret Llewelyn (ed.), *Life As We Have Known It: By Co-Operative Working Women* (London, 1982)

Davin, Anna, *Growing up Poor: Home, School and Street in London, 1870–1914* (London, 1996)

Davin, Anna, 'Loaves and Fishes: Food in Poor Households in Late Nineteenth-Century London', *History Workshop Journal*, 4 (1996), pp. 167–192

Davis, Belinda J., *Home Fires Burning. Food, Politics, and Everyday Life in World War I Berlin* (Chapel Hill, NC, 2000)

Dawson, Graham, *Soldier Heroes: British Adventure, Empire and the Imaginings of Masculinities* (London, 1994)

Douglas, Mary, *Implicit Meanings. Essays in Anthropology* (London, 1975)

Douglas, Mary, *Purity and Danger. An Analysis of the Concepts of Pollution and Taboo* (London, 1985)

Drummond, J.C. and Wilbraham Anne, *The Englishman's Food. A History of Five Centuries of English Diet* (London, 1964)

Duffett, Rachel, 'A Taste of Army Life: Food, Identity and the Rankers of the First World War', *Cultural and Social History*, 9 (2012)

Duffett, Rachel, 'A War Unimagined: Food and the Rank and File Soldier of the First World War', in Jessica Meyer (ed.), *British Popular Culture and the First World War* (Leiden, 2008), pp. 47–70

Duffett, Rachel, 'What Do We Want with Eggs and Ham: Food on the Western Front, 1914–1918', *BBC History*, December 2009

Dwork, Deborah, *War Is Good for Babies and Other Young Children* (London, 1987)

Dyer, Geoff, *The Missing of the Somme* (London, 2001)

Eckstein, Eleanor, *Food, People and Nutrition* (Westport, 1980)

Elias, Norbert, *The Civilizing Process. The History of Manners* (Oxford, 1978)

Bibliography

Ellis, John, *Eye Deep in Hell* (Abingdon, 1976)

Emden, Richard van, and Humphries Steve (eds), *All Quiet on the Home Front. An Oral History of Life in Britain during the First World War* (London, 2004)

Engels, Friedrich, *The Condition of the Working Class in England* (London, 2005)

Englander, David and Osborne, James, 'Jack, Tommy and Henry Dubb: The Armed Forces and the Working Class', *The Historical Journal*, 21:3 (1978), pp. 593–621

Feeney, Robert F., 'Food for the Race to the Pole', in Pieter van der Merwe (ed.), *South: The Race to the Pole* (London, 2000)

Ferguson, Niall, *The Pity of War* (London, 1999)

Fernandez-Armesto, Felipe, *Food: A History* (London, 2001)

Fiddes, Nick, *Meat: A Natural Symbol* (London, 1992)

Fieldhouse, Paul, *Food and Nutrition: Customs and Culture* (Beckenham, 1988)

Floud, Roderick, Wachter, Kenneth and Gregory, Annabel *Height, Health and History: Nutritional Status in the United Kingdom, 1750–1980* (Cambridge, 2006)

Fox, Brian A. and Cameron, Allan G. *Food Science, Nutrition and Health* (London, 1989)

Franklyn, Julian, *The Cockney: A Survey of London Life and Language* (London, 1953)

Friedberg, Susanne, *Fresh: A Perishable History* (Cambridge, MA, 2009)

Fuller. J.G., *Troop Morale and Popular Culture in the British and Dominion Armies 1914–1918* (Oxford, 2001)

Furse, Colonel G.A., *Provisioning Armies in the Field* (London, 1899)

Fussell G.E. and Fussell K.R, *The English Countrywoman: A Farmhouse Social History 1500–1900* (London, 1953)

Fussell, Paul, *The Great War and Modern Memory* (Oxford, 2000)

Gagnier, Regina, *Subjectivities. A History of Self-Representation in Britain 1832–1920* (New York, 1991)

Geertz, Clifford, *The Interpretation of Cultures: Selected Essays* (London,1993)

Gennep, Arnold van, *The Rites of Passage* (London, 1965)

Germov, John and Williams, Lauren (eds), *A Sociology of Food and Nutrition: The Social Appetite* (Melbourne, 2008).

Gibson, Craig, 'The British Army, French Farmers and the War on the Western Front 1914–1918', *Past and Present*, 180 (2003), pp. 175–239

Gibson, K. Craig, 'Sex and Soldiering in France and Flanders: The British Expeditionary Force along the Western Front, 1914–1919', *The International History Review*, 13:3 (2001), pp. 535–579

Gill, Douglas and Dallas Gloden, 'Mutiny at Etaples Base in 1917', *Past and Present*, 69 (1975), pp. 86–103

Godden, Leslie J. (ed.), *History of the Royal Army Dental Corps* (Aldershot, 1971)

Goffman, Erving, *The Presentation of Self in Everyday Life* (New York, 1959)

Goody, Jack, *Cooking, Cuisine and Class: A Study in Comparative Sociology* (Cambridge, 1984)

Goody, Jack, *Food and Love. A Cultural History of East and West* (London, 1998)

Gratzer, Walter, *Terrors of the Table. The Curious History of Nutrition* (Oxford, 2005)

Gregory, Adrian, *The Last Great War. British Society and the First World War* (Cambridge, 2008)

Grieves, Keith, 'The Propinquity of Place', in Jessica Meyer (ed.), *British Popular Culture and the First World War* (Leiden, 2008), pp. 21–46

Hammerton, J., 'The English Weakness? Gender, Satire and "Moral Manliness" in the Lower Middle Class 1870–1920', in Alan Kidd and David Nicholls (eds), *Gender, Civic Culture and Consumerism: Middle Class Identity in Britain, 1800–1914* (Manchester, 1999), pp. 164–197

Harding, Marion (ed.), *The Victorian Soldier. Studies in the History of the British Army 1816–1914* (London, 1993)

Hardyment, Christina, *From Mangle to Microwave. The Mechanization of Household Work* (Cambridge, 1988)

Harries-Jenkins, Gwyn, *The Army in Victorian Society* (London, 1977)

Harris, Marvin, *Good to Eat: Riddles of Food and Culture* (London, 1986)

Harrison, Mark, 'The Fight Against Disease in the Mesopotamia Campaign', in Hugh Cecil and Peter Liddle (eds), *Facing Armageddon: The First World War Experienced* (London, 1996), pp. 475–489

Hibberd, D., *Wilfred Owen. A New Biography* (London, 2002)

Hickman, Tom, *The Call-Up. A History of National Service* (London, 2004)

Higonnet, M.R., Jenson, J., Michel, S., and Weitz, M.C. (eds), *Behind the Lines. Gender and the Two World Wars* (New Haven, 1987)

Holmes, Richard, 'Battle. The Experience of Modern Combat', in Charles Townshend (ed.), *The Oxford Illustrated History of Modern War* (Oxford, 1997), pp. 194–212.

Holmes, Richard, *Tommy: The British Soldier on the Western Front 1914–1918* (London, 2005)

Hope, Annette, *Londoners' Larder: English Cuisine from Chaucer to the Present* (Edinburgh, 1990)

Hynes, Samuel, *The Soldiers' Tale* (New York, 1997)

Hynes, Samuel, *A War Imagined: The First World War and English Culture* (London, 1992)

James, Lawrence, *The Middle Class: A History*, (London, 2006)

Jerrold, Douglas, *The Lie about the War* (London, 1930)

Jones, Martin, *Feast: Why Humans Share Food* (Oxford, 2007)

Jones, Max, *The Last Great Quest. Captain Scott's Antarctic Sacrifice* (Oxford, 2003)

Kamm, Anthony and Jeffares, Norman, (eds), *A Jewish Childhood* (London, 1988)

Keegan, John, *The Face of Battle* (London, 2004)

Bibliography

Keegan, John, Holmes, Richard, and Gau, John, *Soldiers. A History of Men in Battle* (London, 1985)

Keenan, Brian, *An Evil Cradling* (London, 1993)

Kidd, Alan and Nicholls, David (eds), *Gender, Civic Culture and Consumerism: Middle Class Identity in Britain, 1800–1914* (Manchester, 1999)

Kittler, P.G. and Sucher K.P., *Food and Culture* (Belmont, 2004)

Klein, Holger (ed.), *The First World War in Fiction* (London, 1976)

Knight, Jill, *'All Bloody Gentlemen': The Civil Services Rifles in the Great War* (Barnsley, 2005)

Korsmayer, Carolyn (ed.), *The Taste Culture Reader. Experiencing Food and Drink* (Oxford, 2007)

Kurlansky, Mark. *Salt: A World History* (New York, 2002)

Leed, Eric J., 'Class and Disillusionment in World War I', *The Journal of Modern History*, 50:4 (1978), pp. 680–699

Leed, Eric, *No Man's Land. Combat and Identity in World War I* (Cambridge, 1979)

Leese, Peter, *Traumatic Neurosis and the British Soldier of the First World War* (Basingstoke, 2002)

Lévi-Strauss, Claude, *The Origin of Table Manners* (London, 1978)

Lévi-Strauss, Claude, *The Raw and the Cooked* (London, 1970)

Lewis, Jane (ed.), *Labour and Love: Women's Experience of Home and Family, 1880–1914* (Manchester, 1993)

Liddle, P.H. (ed.), *Home Fires and Foreign Fields. British Social and Military Experience in the First World War* (London, 1985)

Liddle, P.H., *The Soldier's War 1914–18* (London, 1988)

Liddle, P.H. and Richardson, M.J., 'Voices from the Past: An Evaluation of Oral History as a Source for Research into the Western Front Experience of the British Soldier 1914–18', *Journal of Contemporary History*, 31:4 (1996), pp. 651–674.

Loane, M., *The Queen's Poor: Life as They Find It in Town and Country* (London, 1998)

Lockwood, David, *The Black Coated Worker* (Oxford, 1989)

Logue, A.W., *The Psychology of Eating and Drinking* (New York, 2004)

Lupton, Deborah, *Food, the Body and the Self* (London, 1998)

Lupton, Deborah, 'Food and Emotion', in Carolyn Korsmeyer (ed.), *The Taste Culture Reader. Experiencing Food and Drink* (Oxford, 2007), pp. 315–328

McCartney, Helen B., *Citizen Soldiers. The Liverpool Territorials in the First World War* (Cambridge, 2005)

McConachie, John, *The Student Soldiers: The Aberdeen University Company 4th Gordons* (Elgin, 1995)

McIntosh, Wm. Alex, *Sociologies of Food and Nutrition* (New York, 1996)

McNamee, Betty, 'Trends in Meat Consumption', in T.C. Barker, J.C. McKenzie and J. Yudkin (eds), *Our Changing Fare: Two Hundred Years of British Food Habits* (London, 1966), pp. 76–93

Bibliography

McPhail, Helen, *The Long Silence. Civilian Life under the German Occupation of Northern France 1914–1918* (London, 1999)

Makepeace, Clare, 'Male Heterosexuality and Prostitution during the Great War. British Soldiers' Encounters with *Maison Tolérées*' in *Cultural and Social History*, 9, 2012

Marsay, Mark (ed.), *The Bairnsfather Omnibus: 'Bullets & Billets' and 'From Mud to Mufti'* (Scarborough, 2000)

Moson, Betty, 'Everything Stops for Tea', in C.Anne Wilson (ed.) *Luncheon, Nuncheon and Other Meals: Eating with the Victorians* (Stroud, 1994), pp. 71–90

Mathias, P., 'The British Tea Trade in the Nineteenth century', in D.J. Oddy and D. Miller (eds), *The Making of the Modern British Diet*, pp. 91–100

Mauss, Marcel, *The Gift: Forms and Functions of Exchange in Archaic Societies* (London, 1980)

Mennell, Stephen, *All Manners of Food. Eating and Taste in England and France from the Middle Ages to the Present* (Oxford, 1985)

Mennell, S., Murcott, A., and Otterloo, A. van, (eds), *The Sociology of Food: Eating, Diet and Culture* (London, 1992)

Messenger, Charles, *Call-to-Arms: The British Army 1914–18* (London, 2005)

Messinger, Gary S., *British Propaganda and the State in the First World War* (Manchester, 1992)

Middleton, T.H., *Food Production in War* (London, 1923)

Miller, William Ian, *The Anatomy of Disgust* (Cambridge, MA, 1997)

Milner, N.P. (trans.), *Vegetius: Epitome of Military Science* (Liverpool, 1993)

Mintz, Sidney, *Sweetness and Power. The Place of Sugar in Modern History* (New York, 1985)

Mintz, Sidney, *Tasting Food, Tasting Freedom. Excursions into Eating, Culture and the Past* (Boston, 1996)

Moir, Guthrie, *The Suffolk Regiment* (London, 1969)

Morgan, D.H.J. and Scott, Sue, 'Bodies in the Social Landscape', in Sue Scott and David Morgan (eds), *Body Matters: Essays on the Sociology of the Body* (London, 1996), pp. 1–21

Murcott, Anne, 'Cooking and the Cooked: A Note on the Domestic Preparation of Meals', in Anne Murcott (ed.), *The Sociology of Food and Eating* (Aldershot, 1986), pp. 178–185

Murcott, Anne, 'Purity and Pollution: Body Management and the Social Place of Infancy', in Sue Scott and David Morgan (eds), *Body Matters: Essays on the Sociology of the Body* (London, 1996), pp. 122–134

Nemeroff, Carole and Rozin, Paul, '"You Are What You Eat": Applying the Demand-Free "Impressions" Technique to an Unacknowledged Belief', *Ethos*, 17:1 (1989), pp. 50–69

Nicholls, Jonathan, *Cheerful Sacrifice. The Battle of Arras 1917* (London, 1995)

Noakes, Vivien (ed.), *Voices of Silence. The Alternative Book of First World War Poetry* (Stroud, 2006)

Bibliography

Ó Gráda, Cormac, *Black '47 and Beyond. The Great Irish Famine in History, Economy and Memory* (Princeton, 1999)

Oddy, Derek, 'A Nutritional Analysis of Historical Evidence: The Working-Class Diet, 1880–1914', in D.J. Oddy and D. Miller (eds), *The Making of the Modern British Diet* (London, 1976), pp. 214–231

Oddy, Derek, 'Food, Drink and Nutrition', in F.M.L. Thompson (ed.), *The Cambridge Social History of Britain 1750–1950* (Cambridge, 1990), Vol.2, pp. 251–278

Oddy, Derek, 'The Paradox of Diet and Health: England and Scotland in the Nineteenth and Twentieth Centuries', in Alexander Fenton (ed.), *Order and Disorder. The Health Implications of Eating and Drinking in the Nineteenth and Twentieth Centuries* (Edinburgh, 2000)

Oddy, Derek, 'Working-Class Diets in Late Nineteenth-Century Britain', *The Economic History Review*, 23:2 (1970), pp. 314–323

Oddy, Derek and Miller Derek, (eds), *The Making of the Modern British Diet* (London, 1976)

Offer, Avner, *The First World War. An Agrarian Interpretation* (Oxford, 1989)

Olson, M., *The Economics of Wartime Shortage* (Durham, 1963)

Orwell, George, *The Road to Wigan Pier* (London, 2001)

Othick, J.,' The Cocoa and Chocolate Industry in the Nineteenth Century', in D.J. Oddy and Derek Miller (eds), *The Making of the Modern British Diet* (London, 1976), pp. 77–90

Palmer, Arnold, *Movable Feasts: A Reconnaissance of the Origins and Consequences of Fluctuations in Meal-Times with Special Attention to the Introduction of Luncheon and Afternoon Tea* (Oxford, 1953)

Paris, Michael, *Warrior Nation. Images of War in British Popular Culture 1850–2000* (London, 2000)

Patterson, Lieut-Colonel J.H., *With the Judæans in the Palestine Campaign* (London, 1922)

Pegler, Martin, *British Tommy 1914–18* (Oxford, 1996)

Petter, Martin, '"Temporary Gentlemen" in the Aftermath of the Great War: Rank, Status and the Ex-Officer Problem', *The Historical Journal*, 37:1 (1994), pp. 127–152

Pilcher, Jeffrey M., *Food in World History* (Abingdon, 2006)

Pilgrim, Francis J., 'The Components of Food Acceptance and Their Measurement', *The American Journal of Clinical Nutrition*, 5 (1957), pp. 171–175

Pill, Roisin, 'An Apple a Day . . . Some Reflections on Working Class Mothers' Views on Food and Health', in Anne Murcott (ed.), *The Sociology of Food and Eating* (Aldershot, 1986), pp. 117–127

Plummer, Alfred, *New British Industries in the Twentieth Century* (London, 1937)

Portelli, Alessandro, *The Battle of Valle Giulia: Oral History and the Art of Dialogue* (Madison, 1997)

Bibliography

Pound, Reginald, *A.P. Herbert: A Biography* (London, 1976)

Priestland, Gerald, *Frying Tonight: The Saga of Fish & Chips* (London, 1972)

Putkowski, Julian, *British Army Mutineers 1914–1922* (London, 1998)

Putkowski, Julian and Sykes, Julian, *Shot at Dawn* (London, 1992)

Pyke, Magnus, *Townsman's Food* (London, 1952)

Rawson, Andrew, *The British Army Handbook* (Stroud, 2006)

Reader, William, *Metal Box: A History* (London, 1976)

Reay, Barry, *Rural Englands: Labouring Lives in the Nineteenth Century* (Basingstoke, 2004)

Reeves, Maud Pember, *Round About a Pound a Week* (London, 1913)

Reznick, Jeffrey, *Healing the Nation: Soldiers and the Culture of Caregiving in Britain during the Great War* (Manchester, 2004)

Richardson, D.J., 'J. Lyons &Co. Ltd.: Caterers and Food Manufacturers, 1894 to 1939', in D.J Oddy and Derek Miller (eds), *The Making of the Modern British Diet* (London, 1976), pp. 161–172

Robb, George, *British Culture and the First World War* (Basingstoke, 2002)

Roberts, Elizabeth, *A Woman's Place. An Oral History of Working Class Women 1890–1940* (Oxford, 1984)

Roberts, Robert, *The Classic Slum: Salford Life in the First Quarter of the Century* (Harmondsworth, 1971)

Robinson, Howard, *Britain's Post Office (London, 1953)*

Roper, Michael, 'Between Manliness and Masculinity: The "War Generation" and the Psychology of Fear in Britain, 1914–1950', *Journal of British Studies*, 44 (2005), pp. 343–362

Roper, Michael, 'Maternal Relations: Moral Manliness and Emotional Survival in Letters Home during the First World War', in S. Dudink, K. Hagermann and J. Tosh (eds), *Masculinity in Politics and War: Rewritings of Modern History* (Manchester, 2004), pp. 295–316.

Roper, Michael, 'Re-remembering the Soldier Hero: The Psychic and Social Construction of Memory in Personal Narratives of the Great War', *History Workshop Journal*, 50 (2000), pp. 181–204

Roper, Michael, *The Secret Battle: Emotional Survival in the Great War* (Manchester, 2009)

Roper, Michael, 'Slipping Out of View: Subjectivity and Emotion in Gender History', *History Workshop Journal*, 59 (2005), pp. 58–72

Rose, Jonathan, *The Intellectual Life of the British Working Classes* (London, 2001)

Ross, Ellen, *Love and Toil. Motherhood in Outcast London 1870–1918* (New York, 1993)

Ross, Ellen, 'Survival Networks: Women's Neighbourhood Sharing in London Before World War I', *History Workshop Journal*, 15 (1983), pp. 4–28

Rozin, Paul, 'Why We Eat What We Eat, and Why We Worry about It', *Bulletin of the American Academy of Arts and Science*, 50:5 (1997), pp. 26–48

Rozin, Paul, Markwith, Maureen and Stoess, Carolyn, 'Moralization and Becoming a Vegetarian: The Transformation of Preferences into Values and the Recruitment of Disgust', *Psychological Sciences*, 8:2, pp. 67–73

Ryan, M.P., *Mutiny at the Curragh* (London, 1956)

Samuel, Raphael and Thompson, Paul (eds), *The Myths We Live By* (London, 1990)

Saunders, Nicholas J. *Trench Art* (Princes Risborough, 2002)

Scholliers, Peter (ed.), *Food, Drink and Identity. Cooking, Eating and Drinking in Europe since the Middle Ages* (Oxford, 2001)

Schouten, Steven, 'Fighting a Kosher War: German Jews and Kashrut in World War 3, 1914–1918', in Ina Zweiniger-Bargielowska and Rachel Duffett (eds), *Food and War in Twentieth Century Europe* (Farnham, 2012)

Scott, James C., *Domination and the Arts of Resistance: Hidden Transcripts* (New Haven, 1990)

Shaw, Lieutenant-Colonel, G.C., *Supply in Modern War* (London, 1938)

Sheffield, G.D., *Forgotten Victory. The First World War: Myths and Realities* (London, 2001)

Sheffield, G.D., *Leadership in the Trenches. Officer–Man Relations, Morale and Discipline in the British Army in the Era of the First World War* (London, 2000)

Sheffield, G.D., 'Officer–Man Relations, Discipline and Morale in the British Army of the Great War', in Hugh Cecil and Peter Liddle (eds), *Facing Armageddon: The First World War Experienced* (London, 1996), pp. 413–424

Shephard, Ben, *A War of Nerves. Soldiers and Psychiatrists 1914–1994* (London, 2000)

Showalter, Elaine, *The Female Malady: Women, Madness and English Culture 1830–1980* (London, 1987)

Silbey, David, *The British Working Class and Enthusiasm for War 1914–1916* (Abingdon, 2005)

Simkins, Peter, 'Soldiers and Civilians: Billeting in Britain and France', in Ian F.W. Beckett and Keith Simpson (eds), *A Nation in Arms. A Social Study of the British Army in the First World War* (Manchester, 1985), pp.165–192

Simkins, Peter, *Kitchener's Army: The Raising of the New Armies 1914–16* (London, 1988)

Simkins, Peter, 'The War Experience of a Typical Kitchener Division: The 18th Division', in Hugh Cecil and Peter Liddle (eds), *Facing Armageddon: The First World War Experienced* (London, 1996), pp. 297–313

Simpson, Andy, *Hot Blood & Cold Steel. Life and Death in the Trenches of the First World War* (Staplehurst, 1993)

Simpson, Keith, 'Dr James Dunn and Shell Shock', in Hugh Cecil and Peter Liddle (eds), *Facing Armageddon: The First World War Experienced* (London, 1996), pp. 508–520

Sims, George R., *How the Poor Live and Horrible London* (London, 1889)

Skelley, Alan Ramsay, *The Victorian Army at Home. The Recruitment and Terms and Conditions of the British Regular, 1859–1899* (London, 1977)

Smith, David, 'The Discourse of Scientific Knowledge of Nutrition and Dietary Change in the Twentieth Century', in Anne Murcott (ed.), *The Nation's Diet: The Social Science of Food Choice* (Harlow, 1998), pp. 311–331

Smith, David F., 'Nutrition Science and the Two World Wars', in David F. Smith (ed.), *Nutrition in Britain. Science, Scientists and Politics in the Twentieth Century* (London, 1997), pp. 142–165

Smith, F.B., *The People's Health 1830–1910* (London, 1979)

Smurthwaite, David, 'A Recipe for Discontent', in Marion Harding (ed.), *The Victorian Soldier. Studies in the History of the British Army 1816–1914* (London, 1993), pp. 69–78.

Snowden, Philip, *The Living Wage* (London, 1912)

Solomon, Susan, *The Coldest March. Scott's Fatal Antarctic Expedition* (London, 2001)

Spagnoly, Tony and Smith, Ted, *Cameos of the Western Front. Salient Points Two. Ypres Sector 1914–18* (Barnsley, 1998)

Spencer, Colin, *The Heretic's Feast: A History of Vegetarianism* (London, 1993)

Spencer, William, *Army Service Records of the First World War* (Kew, 2001)

Spiers, Edward, 'The Late Victorian Army 1868–1914', in David G. Chandler (ed.), *The Oxford History of the British Army* (Oxford, 2003), pp. 187–210

Stargardt, Nicholas, *Witnesses of War. Children's Lives under the Nazis* (London, 2005)

Steedman, Carolyn, *Landscape for a Good Woman. A Story of Two Lives* (London, 1993)

Steedman, Carolyn, *The Radical Soldier's Tale* (London, 1988)

Strange, Julie-Marie, *Death, Grief and Poverty in Britain, 1870–1914* (Cambridge, 2005)

Sutton, David E., *Remembrance of Repasts. An Anthropology of Food and Memory* (Oxford, 2001)

Tames, Richard, *Feeding London: A Taste of History* (London, 2003)

Tannahill, Reay, *Food in History* (London, 2002)

Teuteberg, Hans J., 'The Discovery of Vitamins: Laboratory Research, Reception, Industrial Production', in Alexander Fenton (ed.), *Order and Disorder: The Health Implications of Eating and Drinking in the Nineteenth and Twentieth Centuries* (Edinburgh, 2000), pp. 253–280

Thompson, E.P., 'The Moral Economy of the English Crowd in the Eighteenth Century', *Past and Present*, 50 (1971), pp. 76–136

Thompson, Major General, Julian, *The Lifeblood of War. Logistics in Armed Conflict* (London, 1991)

Thompson, Paul, *The Edwardians: The Remaking of British Society* (London, 1992)

Thomson, Alistair, *Anzac Memories: Living with the Legend* (Melbourne, 1994)

Thomson, Mathew, 'Psychology and the "Consciousness of Modernity" in Early Twentieth-Century Britain', in Martin Daunton and Bernhard Reiger (eds),

Meanings of Modernity. Britain from the Late-Victorian Era to World War II (Oxford, 2001), pp. 97–115

Todman, Dan, *The Great War: Myth and Memory* (London, 2005)

Torode, Angeliki, 'Trends in Fruit Consumption', in T.C. Barker, J.C. McKenzie and J. Yudkin (eds), *Our Changing Fare: Two Hundred Years of British Food Habits* (London, 1966), pp. 115–134

Tosh, John, *A Man's Place. Masculinity and the Middle-Class Home in Victorian England* (Bath, 1999)

Townshend, Charles (ed.), *The Oxford Illustrated History of Modern War* (Oxford, 1997)

Travers, Tim, *The Killing Ground. The British Army, the Western Front and the Emergence of Modern War 1900–1918* (Barnsley, 2003)

Trentmann, Frank and Just, Flemming, (eds), *Food and Conflict in Europe in the Age of the Two World Wars* (Basingstoke, 2006)

Trustram, Myna, *Women of the Regiment: Marriage and the Victorian Army* (Cambridge, 1984)

Tucker, Albert V., 'Army and Society in England 1870–1900: A Reassessment of the Cardwell Reforms', *The Journal of British Studies*, 2:2 (1963), pp. 110–141

Turner, E.S., *Dear Old Blighty* (London, 1980)

Turner, Victor, 'Betwixt and Between: The Liminal Period in *Rites de Passage*', in *The Forest of Symbols. Aspects of Ndembu Ritual* (Ithaca, 1989), pp. 93–111

Turner, Victor, *The Ritual Process* (London, 1969)

Twigg, Julia, 'Vegetarianism and the Meanings of Meat', in Anne Murcott (ed.), *The Sociology of Food and Eating* (Aldershot, 1986), pp. 18–30.

Ulio, James A., 'Military Morale', *The American Journal of Sociology*, 47:3 (1941), pp. 321–330

Venning, Annabel, *Following the Drum. The Lives of Army Wives and Daughters Past and Present* (London, 2005)

Vernon, James, *Hunger – A Modern History* (Cambridge, MA, 2007)

Vincent, David, *Bread, Knowledge and Freedom: A Study of Nineteenth-Century Working Class Autobiography* (London, 1981)

Visser, Margaret, *The Rituals of Dinner. The Origins, Evolution, Eccentricities and Meaning of Table Manners* (London, 1992)

Waites, Bernard, *A Class Society at War. England 1914–1918* (Leamington Spa, 1987)

Waites, Bernard, 'The Effect of the First World War on Class and Status in England, 1910–20', *Journal of Contemporary History*, 11:1 (1976), pp. 27–48

Wakefield, Alan, *Christmas in the Trenches* (Stroud, 2006)

Walton, John K., *Fish & Chips & the British Working Class 1870–1940* (Leicester, 1992)

Wanjek, Christopher, *Food at Work: Workplace Solutions for Malnutrition, Obesity and Chronic Diseases* (Geneva, 2005)

Ward, Major V.H., *Dentists at War* (London, 1996)

Bibliography

Warde, Alan and Martens, Lydia, *Eating Out. Social Differentiation, Consumption and Pleasure* (Cambridge, 2000)

Washburn, S.L. and Lancaster C.S., 'The Evolution of Hunting', in Richard B. Lee and Irven DeVore (eds), *Man the Hunter* (Chicago, 1968), pp. 293–303

Watson, Alexander, *Enduring the Great War: Combat, Morale and Collapse in the German and British Armies, 1914–1918* (Cambridge, 2008)

Watson, Alexander, 'Self-deception and Survival: Mental Coping Strategies on the Western Front', *Journal of Contemporary History*, 41 (2006), pp, 247–268

Watson, Janet, *Fighting Different Wars. Experience, Memory and the First World War in Britain* (Cambridge, 2004)

Waugh, Alec, *The Lipton Story* (London, 1952)

Weeks, Alan, *Tea, Rum and Fags. Sustaining Tommy 1914–18* (Stroud, 2009)

Westlake, Ray, *Kitchener's Army* (Staplehurst, 1998)

Whetham, Edith, 'The London Milk Trade, 1900–1930', in D.J. Oddy and Derek Miller (eds), *The Making of the Modern British Diet* (London, 1976), pp.65–76

White, Cynthia L., *Women's Magazines 1693–1968* (London, 1970)

Wild, Jonathan, '"A Merciful, Heaven-Sent Release?" The Clerk and the First World War in British Literary Culture', *Cultural and Social History*, 4:1 (2007), pp. 73–94

Wilson, Bee, *Swindled: From Poison Sweets to Counterfeit Coffee – the Dark History of the Food Cheats* (London, 2008)

Wilson, C. Anne (ed.), *Luncheon, Nuncheon and Other Meals* (Stroud, 1994)

Wilt, Alan, *Food for War: Agriculture and Rearmament in Britain before the Second World War* (Oxford, 2001)

Winter, Denis, *Death's Men. Soldiers of the Great War* (London, 1978)

Winter, J.M. *The Great War and the British People* (Basingstoke, 1987)

Winter, J.M., 'Military Fitness and Civilian Health in Britain during the First World War', *Journal of Contemporary History*, 15:2 (1980), pp. 211–244

Winter, J M., *Sites of Memory, Sites of Mourning* (Cambridge, 1995)

Winter, J.M. and Robert, Jean-Louis (eds), *Capital Cities at War. Paris, London, Berlin 1914–1919* (Cambridge, 1997)

Wood, Roy C., *The Sociology of the Meal* (Edinburgh, 1995)

Wrangham, Richard, *Catching Fire: How Cooking Made Us Human* (London, 2009)

Wright, Lawrence, *Home Fires Burning. The History of Domestic Heating and Cooking* (London, 1964)

Young, Michael, *Army Service Corps 1902–1918* (Barnsley, 2000)

Young, Michael, *Waggoner's Way. Royal Corps of Transport 1891–1991* (London, 1993)

Zweiniger-Bargielowska, Ina, 'Building a British Superman: Physical Culture in Interwar Britain', *Journal of Contemporary History*, 41:4 (2006), pp. 595–610

Zweiniger-Bargielowska, Ina, '"The Culture of the Abdomen": Obesity and Reducing in Britain, circa 1900–1939', *Journal of British Studies*, 44:2 (2005), pp. 239–273

Index

Index

Index

Williamson, Henry, 179
Willison, Denis, 71
Winter, Denis, 6
Winter, J. M., 36, 42–3, 46,
World Health Organisation, 231

Wrangham, Richard, 10
Wyndham, Horace, 28, 34, 86

Young, Michael, 38
YMCA, 219–20